ZODIAC
AN EXPLORATION
INTO THE LANGUAGE OF
FORM, GESTURE AND COLOUR

Edited

by

Gertraud Goodwin

TEMPLE LODGE

Temple Lodge Publishing Ltd.
Hillside House, The Square
Forest Row, RH18 5ES

www.templelodge.com

First published in 2019

A CIP catalogue record for this book is available from the British Library

ISBN 978 1 912230 39 6

Designed and typeset by yellowfish.design
Printed and bound by Gutenberg Press Ltd., Malta

CONTENTS

FOREWORD
WHAT RIPENS IN THE MUTE OF SILENCE

In the Egyptian Hathor temple of Dendera, not far from the Valley of the Kings, the Zodiac is for the first time to be seen in its entirety – carved in stone, in a small chapel on the roof of the temple. What has been handed down from olden times are only single pictures. Only in 50 BC - when the Egyptian, and even the following vast Greek time was over - the Zodiac emerges. Why so late? Why were the old cultures so silent about it?

In order to get a sense for this question, I sometimes give a talk in seminars. One should close one's eyes and imagine the countenance of one's own mother - how difficult this is! We are so closely united with our mother, as if the umbilical cord was never completely severed, so that to posit her outside of ourselves does not result in our being able to distil in ourselves an image of her. Maybe this was comparable to the Zodiac in the old cultures.

The formative power and emerging from this cosmic round was experienced and felt so strongly that one could not bring it to a finished picture. Only when this language of the stars was largely extinguished was it possible to draw these twelve cosmic forces from Aries to Pisces.

As Rudolf Steiner describes for the birth of Christ, that he entered the world just when a last remnant of spirituality was still able to recognise him, so it is with the Zodiac as well. Almost at the same time this cosmic twelvefold will was hewn in stone, when a last sensing still existed for this peripheral grand force.

An interesting phenomenon in this respect is the calculation of the calendar. The Jewish calendar begins 3761 BC, the Chinese calendar 2636 BC, the Egyptian calendar around 4200 BC, in each case more than a thousand years before these cultures came into existence. These early cultures have backdated the beginning of their time calculating. They backdated it to a time in which the umbilical cord to the cosmos disconnected itself, as the writing of the stars became earthly writing. It is interesting, that the arrangements of the zodiac of Dendera, according to the archaeologist/ astronomer Guiseppe Maria Seti in his book, *The Mystery of the Sky – History and Mythology of the Starsigns* – also mirrors the date 4000 BC. The Spring Equinox seems to be in Gemini in this sandstone relief of Dendera. Following this perception then, the Zodiac has manifested quite late, at the same time pointing to an early time before physical writing, when the scriptures of the stars could still be read.

Today we stand again at a threshold. The language of stars has long since faded away, but a new door has begun to open. It is a door which Rudolf Steiner formulated in verse in the following words:

The stars once spoke to man. It is world-destiny that they are silent now.
To be aware of this silence can become pain for earthly man.
But in the deepening silence there grows and ripens what man speaks to the stars.
To be aware of the speaking can become strength for spirit-man.

In this silence and out of it, man begins to turn to the stars. This can be seen impressively in the cornucopia of artistic reflections of the Zodiac, which Gertraud Goodwin has brought together in this book for the first time, framed by Rudolf Steiner's Twelve Moods on the Zodiac, the eurythmy gestures, and the capitals of the small domed space of the First Goetheanum in Dornach, Switzerland.

With pencil, charcoal, in watercolour or oil colour on paper, or free sculpture, then carved in wood, cast in plaster or metal as relief for free sculpture, we find a unique abundance of this new speaking to the Zodiac. It is a speaking which is also always a listening, which even brings into a picture how we can build new sense organs to understand the cosmos.

To the fact that the world of the stars speaks again means that for us all the same stars arch above us, and yet every human being has their own zenith, their very own star radiating above themself. In this sense may this beautiful collection of a cosmic sensing and searching by the artist Gertraud Goodwin stimulate us to develop our own very personal language of the stars. Then, that which Rudolf Steiner put at the beginning of his "Leading thoughts" may fulfil itself; that the cosmic in man unites itself with the cosmic in the universe.

Wolfgang Held, May 2019
translated by Gertraud Goodwin

The stars once spoke to man.
It is world-destiny
That they are silent now.
To be aware of this silence
Can become pain for earthly man.
But in the deepening silence
There grows and ripens
What man speaks to the stars.
To be aware of the speaking
Can become strength for spirit-man

Rudolf Steiner
Given to Marie Steiner 1922

INTRODUCTION
Gertraud Goodwin

That the stars of the Zodiac were the origin in the creation of our physical body was a stable knowledge in old cultures, from the Middle Ages and before. This knowledge has been re-enlivened and given new meaning through Rudolf Steiner's Anthroposophy. It is also re-emerging in various strands through the New Age movement over the last 60 years.

Once one starts to research into the Zodiac and its influence onto the earth and man, a wealth of written material can be discovered, all complementing each other and giving different aspects to how the zodiacal creative forces are working on earth. Rudolf Steiner gave specific indications to the eurythmists, twelve individual gestures and colours depicting the forces of the twelve zodiacal areas. These relate to the consonants and the twelve musical minor and major keys. In the small cupola of the First Goetheanum, two-times-six columns form a circular space, related to the Zodiac. In its centre stood the wooden sculpture of the Representative of Man. These two-times-six wooden columns had carved capitals relating to the Zodiac – a lesser known and little researched fact. In this collation of artistic research, more of the zodiacal form language of these capitals will be explored.

I was made aware of the zodiacal forces as a language of form through my sculpture teacher Reimar von Bonin (1930 – 1996) in his teaching and his own sculptural work. To his carved reliefs an individual chapter is dedicated. A small group of people met in Grindelwald over Christmastime in 1990/91 with Reimar von Bonin, the eurythmist Diotima Engelbrecht, and a few interested artists, to explore the forces of the Zodiac during the Twelve Holy Nights. This gathering has inspired me in my sculptural and graphic work over my whole artistic career. I have worked with the Zodiac as a sculptural and graphic subject a number of times. During the Twelve Holy Nights, where the zodiacal forces have a specific microcosmic influence, I felt stimulated and rewarded to work artistically with it, which gave me a growing new dimension to this time of the year. This has become an inner need to get in touch with and celebrate these forces, which give this time of the year a special meaning, grace and inwardness hard to find elsewhere. This will be addressed in an individual chapter.

The tremendous amount of written material on the zodiacal forces has as a basis the realisation that there are these twelve realms of particular constellations of fixed stars in the sky, which emanate specific forces. These forces interact and are brought to life and movement by the forces of the planets to create and form all living beings on the earth. This means that the actual initiator and origin of life and form lies not in the matter of the single cell itself, but is brought about/realised through cosmic forces. For science, this is a hard but necessary threshold to overcome, a change of paradigm which would free the self-inflicted material assumptions and limitations of centuries (since the abolition of the

spirit by the church convened council in 869).

Once one begins to acknowledge and to think that spiritual forces are the basis for all life on earth, new and awesome vistas open up. For the artist this cosmic dimension can become a lifeline to her/his creativity and research, which brings a new sense, depth and new meaning to her/his work and enables the expression of a felt sense. For me, everything began to fall into place: a vast and ever expanding field of sculptural and graphic research opened up, each completed piece of work beckoning me to take the next step. In this way, the quest for the Zodiac and its emerging language of form together with Metamorphosis, and its developmental, rhythmic transformational qualities, became the two legs I stand and rely on in all my artistic work over the last 30 years. (See my book *Metamorphosis – Journeys through Transformation of Form*.)

Working artistically on both themes, Metamorphosis and the Zodiac, brought me to the realisation that both are present in every form: the form language of the Zodiac gives the particular form element, or gesture, while Metamorphosis develops, enlivens and rhythmicises all becoming of form. The source material of my background studies came in equal measure from three different sources: Medieval/Rosicrucian literature, New Age literature and Rudolf Steiner's Anthroposophy; (from the Greek – *anthropos* = man and Sophia = wisdom, hence anthroposophy means the wisdom of man). I found that these three fields did indeed build upon one another and complemented each other. In myself I found readiness, joy and answers to my greatest questions: where does form come from, what are its sources? And is there a higher order and logic to it? I found answers in a way realising, that I had begun to tap into a realm which will take centuries to explore.

Looking back over my various sculptural and graphic expressions of the last 30 years I can see a progression, a change of parameters in the direction of a simplification and purification which comes close to a metamorphic transformation in itself. One's instrument, my own body, its life forces and my inner development bring their own possibilities and limitations of expression into play, so each rendering of the same theme becomes a stepping stone for the next one. All twelve formative forces of the Zodiac as well as Metamorphosis have an omnipresence on earth and work together creatively on every living being. However, specific form-impulses have particular areas in which they express themselves as the main force. This is always achieved in the greatest harmony with all the other forces working completely interdependently. From the many relationships to other qualities, like the consonants, virtues, areas of the human body, colours, eurythmy gestures, elements (earth, water, air, fire), musical keys and many more, in which the zodiacal forces express themselves as if through different instruments, a harmony begins to emerge, which informs me of an ever rounder picture of one particular force of the Zodiac. As a sculptor I am looking for gesture, for a particular ensouled form in space. I realised, that the twelve zodiacal forces form a language of form not unlike the way the alphabet in its consonants forms the basis of language, and like the alphabet the Zodiac forms words and concepts. I felt I began to "read" form as such, natural forms as well as artistic creations, and to develop an understanding of what they were saying, through the exploration of the Zodiac in sculpture.

This discovery was for me like an epiphany, a reassurance in my inner sensing and hope for how all things are interconnected. I dedicated a number of sculptural and graphic explorations to the exploration of this language of form. The awe and wonder for every living being in nature, crowned by the human form, increased manifold in my feeling and thinking. New, unfathomable worlds began to open up, there was so much to learn and to discover! What would come about, when two or even three forces of the Zodiac would work together? There were sculptural tasks for a number of lifetimes! It felt as if I was becoming more conscious of elements of form which I had been using all along, which would order and group themselves into clearer and more one-sided gestures, speaking of a particular mood and quality, which I felt were originating from the individual regions of the Zodiac. The various artists presenting their own work on the zodiacal forces give a tremendously rich tableau of authentic, individual approaches, giving us insight into this vast realm of creative forces, visible all around us – and acknowledging, where these forces come from. There are many different aspects to the zodiac on many different levels and a vast number of books have been written on these. They are all important, complementing each other and slowly build a more comprehensive picture of this mighty, all-encompassing cosmic script – the Harmony of the Spheres.

Many of the publications are in German. But I will list the ones I became familiar with in the list for 'Further Reading'. In this publication, I am concentrating on artistic work carried out of the work with the zodiac, particularly sculpture, graphic work and painting. However, some artists who have worked with the zodiac have published their own publications. I will list them here below as far as they are known to me.

1. Margot Rössler – Band I und II (only in German)
2. Hilde Raske, *Farbenstudien nach den Zwölf Stimmungen von Rudolf Steiner* ISBN 3-85636-143-X
3. Hilde Raske, *The Language of Color in the First Goetheanum. A Study of Rudolf Steiner's Art*, Walter Keller Verlag, Dornach, Switzerland
4. *Anthroposophischer Kalender Im Jahre 1966 nach des ICH Geburt zu beziehen: Förderkreis des Kalender-Impulses Rudolf Steiner*, Postal address: Rudolf Steiner Bau A-5026 Salzburg, Friedrich – Inhauserstr. 27

THE TWELVE MOODS/INTRODUCTION TO RUDOLF STEINER'S VERSES

Gertraud Goodwin

Drawings by Aurel Mothes. 1993. A3 in Charcoal.

A number of artists whose work is seen in this book have had Rudolf Steiner's meditative verses of the Zodiac as a background to their work. These verses built a mysterious but stable centre for my explorations: even though I only grasped the meaning of a line here and there, I felt drawn to these verses again and again, as if they were encompassing a hidden essence of the Zodiac which would reveal itself only over time and through my own artistic work.

Rudolf Steiner gave the meditative verses "Twelve Moods", to the early group of eurythmists on 29th August 1915, after they had accomplished their fundamental training. Each of the twelve verses consists of seven lines, always in the same sequence given by the seven planets as follows:

☉	**Sun**	*Arise, oh shining light,*
♀	**Venus**	*Take hold of growth and becoming,*
☿	**Mercury**	*Lay hold of the weaving of forces,*
♂	**Mars**	*Yourself ray forth, life-wakening.*
♃	**Jupiter**	*In face of resistance, gain;*
♄	**Saturn**	*In stream of time, disperse;*
☽	**Moon**	*Oh shine of light, abide!*

On the occasion of its first presentation on stage Rudolf Steiner gave an address after the eurythmy presentation. This address and an introduction by Ruth Pusch together with all the twelve verses are published by Mercury Press as *Twelve Moods*.

From the address by Rudolf Steiner:

"... Without doubt there is an intense longing in our time to gain the connection between the material life and the spiritual life... very few Europeans today have a clear feeling of seeking the essential nature of the other worlds connected with and lying at the basis of our world. If you consider teachings that are offered today about poetry, about art, you will frequently notice how everything artistic leads back to something higher, and yet how difficult it is for people today really to sense the connection with this higher element."

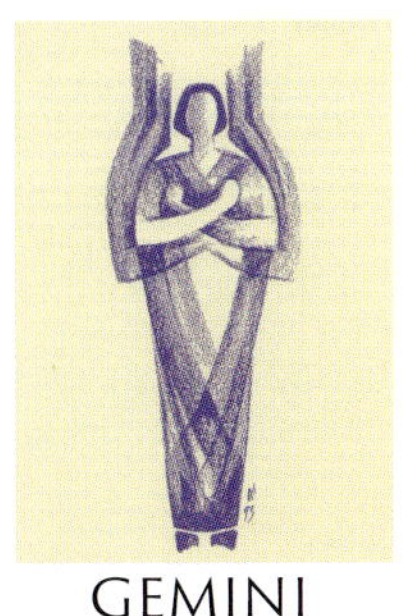

GEMINI

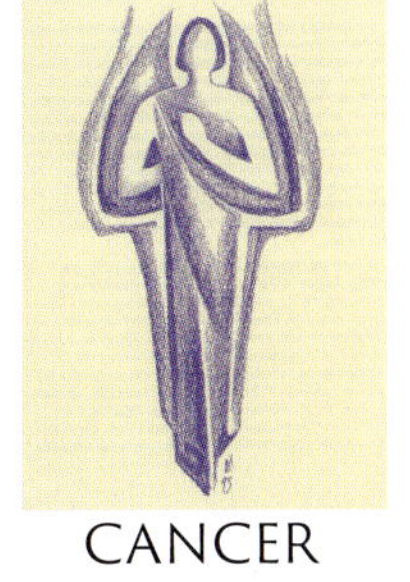

CANCER

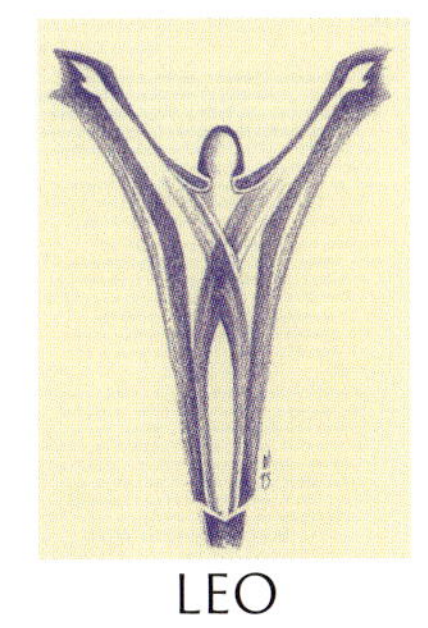

LEO

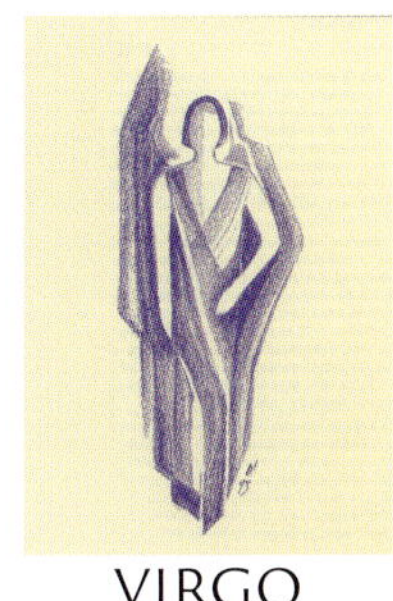

VIRGO

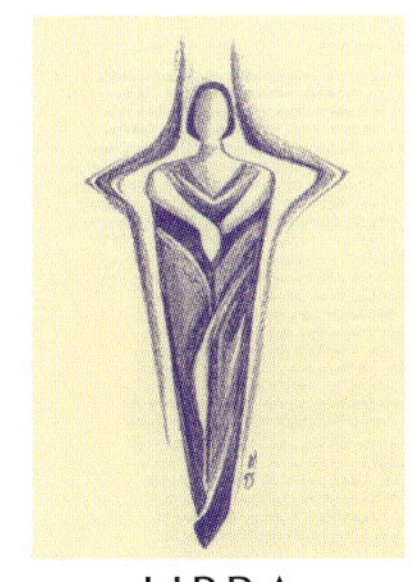

LIBRA

SCORPIO

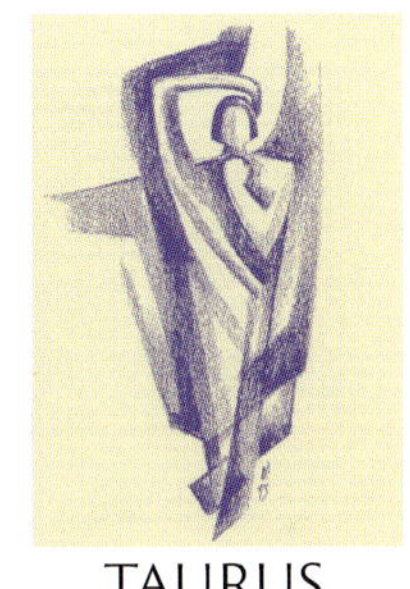

TAURUS

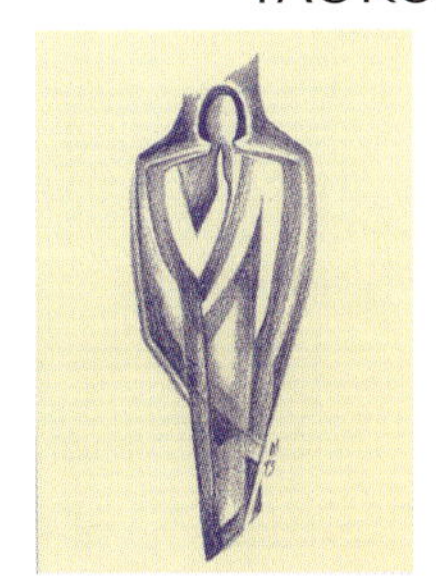

ARIES

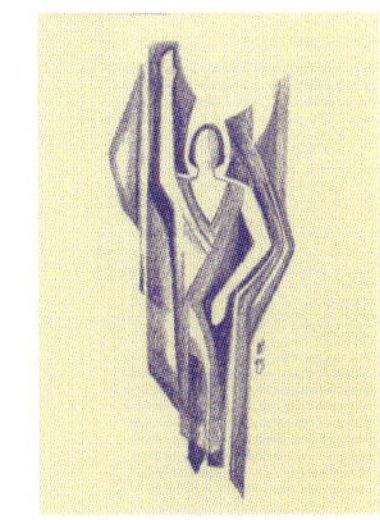

PISCES

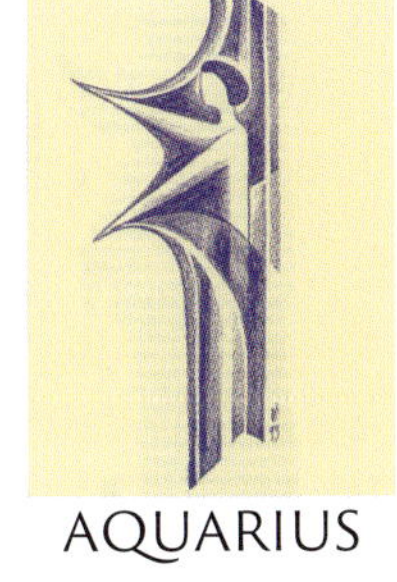

AQUARIUS

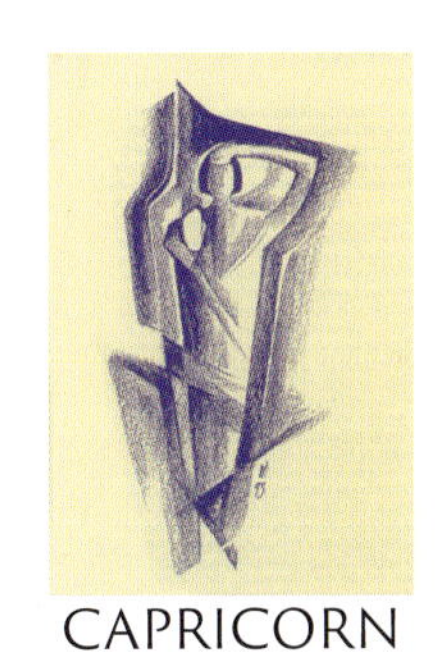

CAPRICORN

SAGITTARIUS

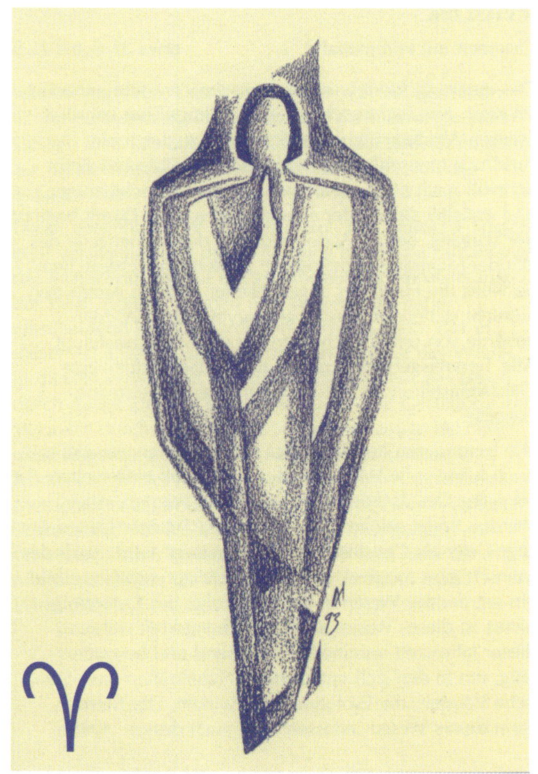

ARIES

☉ Arise, oh shining light,
♀ Take hold of growth and becoming,
☿ Lay hold of the weaving of forces,
♂ Yourself ray forth, life-wakening.
♃ In face of resistance, gain;
♄ In stream of time, disperse;
☽ Oh shine of light, abide!

☉ Erstehe, o Lichtesschein,
♀ Erfasse das Werdewesen,
☿ Ergreife das Kräfteweben,
♂ Erstrahle dich Sein-erweckend.
♃ Am Widerstand gewinne,
♄ Im Zeitenstrom zerinne.
☽ O Lichtesschein, verbleibe!

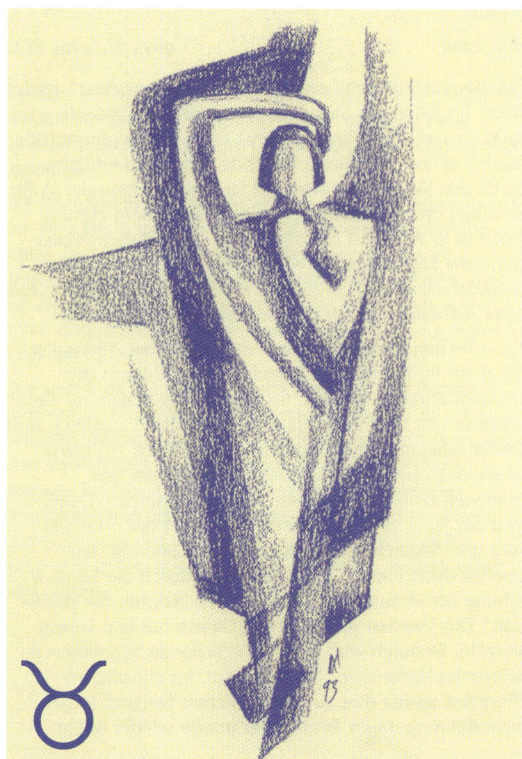

TAURUS

☉ Brighten, oh glory of being,
♀ Reach into the power of becoming,
☿ And weave the thread of life
♂ Through worlds imbued with being,
♃ In mindful revelation,
♄ Into radiant life-awareness.
☽ Oh glory of being, appear!

☉ Erhelle dich, Wesensglanz,
♀ Erfühle die Werdekraft,
☿ Verwebe den Lebensfaden
♂ In wesendes Weltensein,
♃ In sinniges Offenbaren,
♄ In leuchtendes Seins-Gewahren.
☽ O Wesensglanz, erscheine!

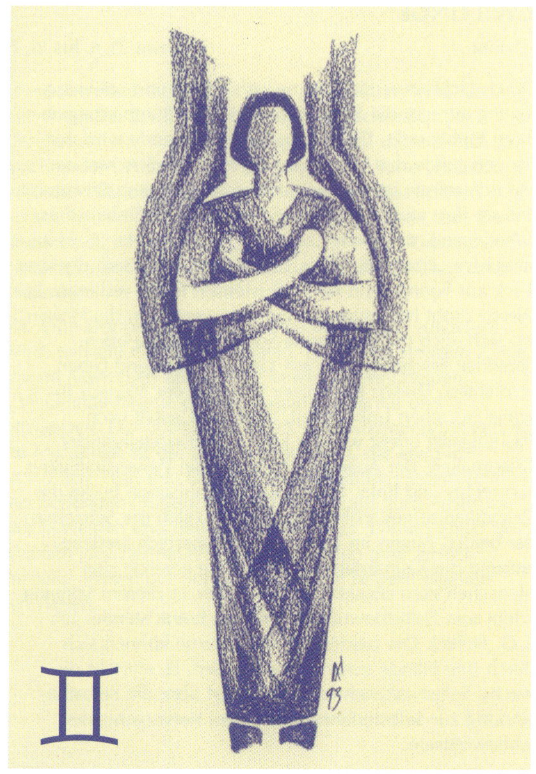

GEMINI

☉ Reveal yourself, life of sun,
♀ Stir up what tends to rest,
☿ Embrace what desires to strive
♂ Towards a mighty prevailing of life,
♃ Towards a blessed knowing of worlds,
♄ Towards a fruitful maturing of growth.
☽ Oh life of sun, endure!

☉ Erschliesse dich, Sonnesein,
♀ Bewege den Ruhetrieb,
☿ Umschliesse die Strebelust
♂ Zu mächtigem Lebewalten,
♃ Zu seligem Weltbegreifen,
♄ Zu fruchtendem Werdereifen.
☽ O Sonnesein, verharre!

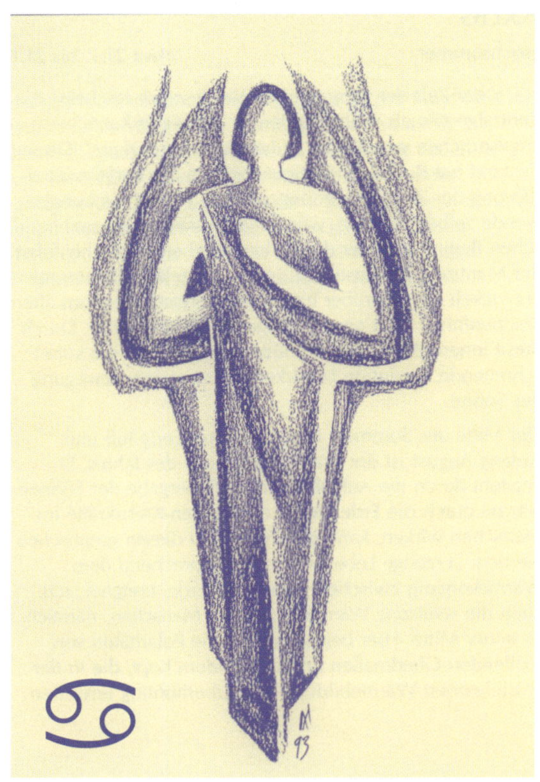

CANCER

☉	You resting, luminous glow,
♀	Engender warmth of life,
☿	Enwarm the life of soul
♂	To meet with vigour each test
♃	And permeate itself with spirit
♄	In quiet, light-outstreaming.
☽	You luminous glow, gain strength!

☉	Du ruhender Leuchteglanz,
♀	Erzeuge Lebenswärme,
☿	Erwärme Seelenleben
♂	Zu kräftigem Sich-Bewähren,
♃	Zu geistigem Sich-Durchdringen,
♄	In ruhigem Lichterbringen.
☽	Du Leuchteglanz, erstarke!

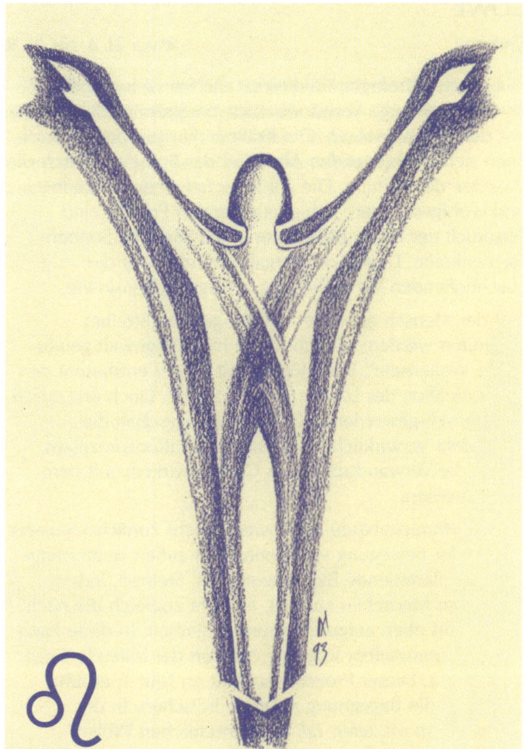

LEO

☉	Invigorate with senses' might
♀	Matured existence of all worlds,
☿	Perceptive element of beings,
♂	Toward the firm resolve 'to be'.
♃	In the surging shine of life,
♄	In the prevailing pains of growth,
☽	With senses' might, arise!

☉	Durchströme mit Sinngewalt
♀	Gewordenes Weltensein,
☿	Erfühlende Wesenschaft
♂	Zu wollendem Seinentschluss.
♃	In strömendem Lebensschein,
♄	In waltender Werdepein,
☽	Mit Sinngewalt erstehe!

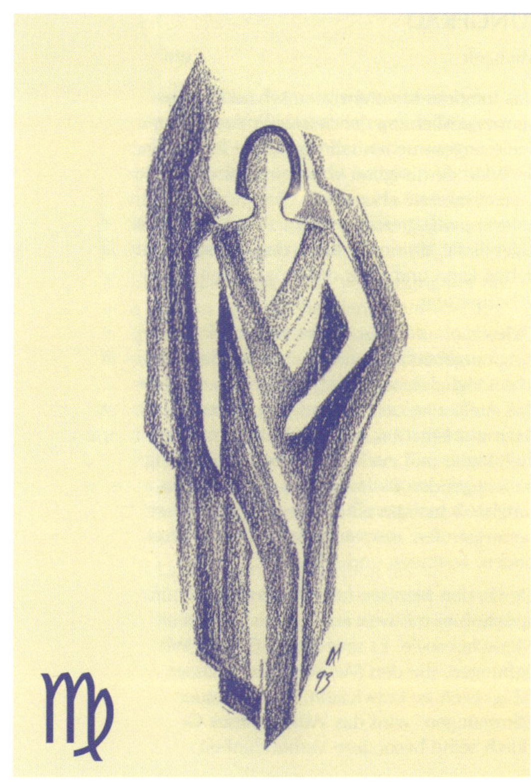

VIRGO

☉	Behold the worlds, oh soul!
♀	Let the soul take hold of worlds,
☿	Let the spirit lay hold of being,
♂	Work out of powers of life,
♃	Upon will-experience, build,
♄	In blossoming worlds, put trust.
☽	Oh soul, comprehend the beings!

☉	Die Welten erschaue, Seele!
♀	Die Seele ergreife Welten,
☿	Der Geist erfasse Wesen,
♂	Aus Lebensgewalten wirke,
♃	Im Willenserleben baue,
♄	Dem Weltenerblüh'n vertraue.
☽	O Seele, erkenne die Wesen!

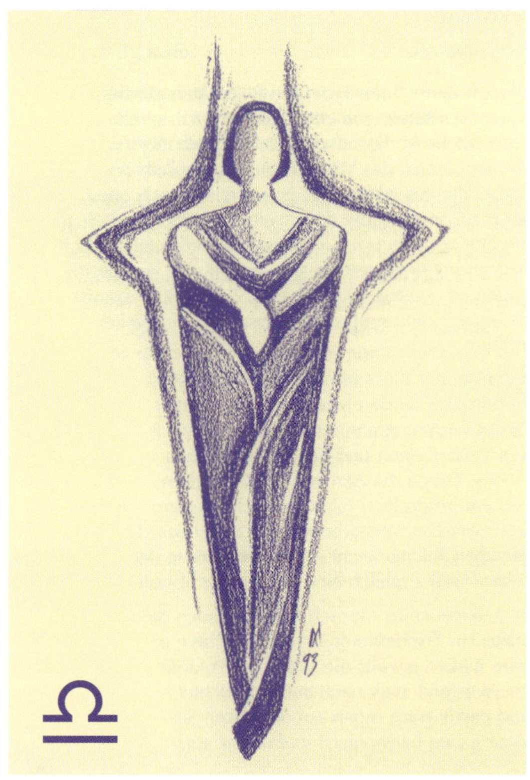

LIBRA

☉	The worlds are sustaining worlds,
♀	And being perceives itself within being,
☿	Existence bounds itself with existence.
♂	And being stirs and causes being
♃	To pour out deeds that unfold,
♄	To rest in world-enjoyment.
☽	Oh worlds, uphold the worlds!

☉	Die Welten erhalten Welten,
♀	Im Wesen erlebt sich Wesen,
☿	Im Sein umschliesst sich Sein.
♂	Und Wesen erwirket Wesen
♃	Zu werdendem Tatergiessen,
♄	In ruhendem Weltgeniessen.
☽	O Welten, traget Welten!

SCORPIO

☉	Existence consumes the being,
♀	Yet in being, existence is held.
☿	In activity, growth disappears,
♂	In becoming activity pauses.
♃	In worlds that prevail and punish,
♄	In the chastening that shapes and forms,
☽	All-being sustains the beings.

☉	Das Sein, es verzehrt das Wesen,
♀	Im Wesen doch hält sich Sein.
☿	Im Wirken entschwindet Werden,
♂	Im Werden verharret Wirken.
♃	In strafendem Weltenwalten,
♄	Im ahndenden Sich-Gestalten
☽	Das Wesen erhält die Wesen.

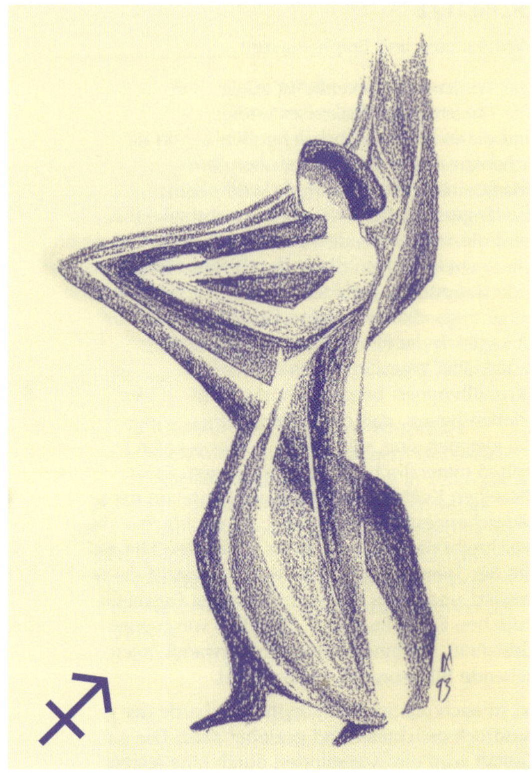

SAGITTARIUS

☉	Becoming achieves the power 'to be',
♀	Into what is, the might of becoming dies.
☿	Achievement resolves the desire to strive
♂	Into prevailing will-force of life.
♃	In dying, there ripens prevailing of worlds,
♄	Forms disappear within forms.
☽	What has come to be, may it feel what is!

☉	Das Werden erreicht die Seinsgewalt,
♀	Im Seienden erstirbt die Werdemacht.
☿	Erreichtes beschliesst die Strebelust
♂	In waltender Lebenswillenskraft.
♃	Im Sterben erreift das Weitenwalten,
♄	Gestalten verschwinden in Gestalten.
☽	Das Seiende fühle das Seiende!

CAPRICORN

⊙ May what is coming, rest on what has been.
♀ May what has been, surmise what is to come,
☿ For a vigorous present existence.
♂ Through inward life-withstanding
♃ May world-beings' guard grow strong,
♄ May life's working blossom forth,
☽ May what has been endure what is to come!

⊙ Das Künftige ruhe auf Vergangenem.
♀ Vergangenes erfühle Künftiges
☿ Zu kräftigem Gegenwartsein.
♂ Im inneren Lebenswiderstand
♃ Erstarke die Weltenwesenwacht,
♄ Erblühe die Lebenswirkensmacht.
☽ Vergangenes ertrage Künftiges!

AQUARIUS

⊙ May what is bounded yield to the boundless.
♀ What feels the lack of bounds, may it create
☿ Bounds for itself in its depths;
♂ May it raise itself in the current,
♃ As wave, flowing forth, sustaining itself,
♄ In becoming, shaping itself to existence.
☽ Set yourself bounds, oh boundless!

⊙ Begrenztes sich opfere Grenzenlosem.
♀ Was Grenzen vermisst, es gründe
☿ In Tiefen sich selber Grenzen;
♂ Es hebe im Strome sich,
♃ Als Welle verfliessend sich haltend,
♄ Im Werden zum Sein sich gestaltend.
☽ Begrenze dich, o Grenzenloses.

PISCES

⊙ In what is lost, may the loss find itself,
♀ In what is gained, may the gain lose itself,
☿ In what is comprehended, may comprehending seek itself
♂ And sustain itself by sustaining.
♃ Through becoming, uplifted to existence,
♄ Through existing, interwoven with the becoming.
☽ May the loss be gain in itself!

⊙ Im Verlorenen finde sich Verlust,
♀ Im Gewinn verliere sich Gewinn,
☿ Im Begriffenen suche sich das Greifen
♂ Und erhalte sich im Erhalten.
♃ Durch Werden zum Sein erhoben,
♄ Durch Sein zu dem Werden verwoben,
☽ Der Verlust sei Gewinn für sich!

RELATIONS - CONNECTIONS - CORRELATIONS
Gertraud Goodwin

When researching the Zodiac it becomes quickly apparent, that our forebears all over the world had a deep knowledge and recognition of all the various influences of the zodiacal forces on all walks of life. Man lived in the past in a deep connection with the celestial harmonies of the spheres, this was his homeland and everything on earth was related to it. In fact there was nothing, which was not connected to the Zodiac. This sense of being held and embedded in a cosmic harmony has been lost by modern man, replaced by materialistic securities, which leave an inner void and sense of spiritual homelessness in many. Artists often bring with themselves a longing for a deeper connection to our true origin, often coupled with a capacity to tap into realms of a spiritual nature through imagination and creativity. Human imagination and creativity may be closest to how the zodiacal forces themselves are working into all spheres of life. And maybe we can find a new gateway to re-connect with the Zodiac through art inspired directly by it.

The artists sharing their work in this collation have all their very individual approach to the subject, finding inspiration from various sources and relationships. I found inspiration from a number of often different connections for each one of the zodiacal moods, starting from what spoke to me most clearly.

There is a tremendous wealth of literature on many relationships from many different directions. On the internet now too are many interesting web pages of serious research to be found. A similar chart as the one printed here fell into my hands many years before I engaged myself actively with the Zodiac. I remember being doubtful and unbelieving about all I read there, but kept it all the same.

This chart became like an entrance, a starting point for me from where I began my research. There were a few other subjects on the original chart which I chose not to include here as they did not help me personally in my quest. Instead I added a few others which I found helpful. The original chart was also in black and white only.

What at first may only be concepts and words, feeling strange and far fetched, slowly builds substance and a felt sense for each of the zodiacal moods. Some relationships may stay a riddle for a long time, whereas others are immediately obvious. This is completely different for each person. It has to do with our own individual instrument of perception, our bodily upbuild, our capacities, gifts and limitations, which show themselves so beautifully in each artists individual approach and expression.

It is fascinating how very individually we are tuned and therefore can tune into a very particular set of information which resounds in ourselves like a memory of the Harmony of the Spheres! And only all of human beings together can resonate like a microcosmic orchestra what this macro-cosmic, all creative foundation and origin of all being, is sounding forth, sustaining all of life. The contributions of the artists here is then like a first tuning of their instruments, practising the scales.

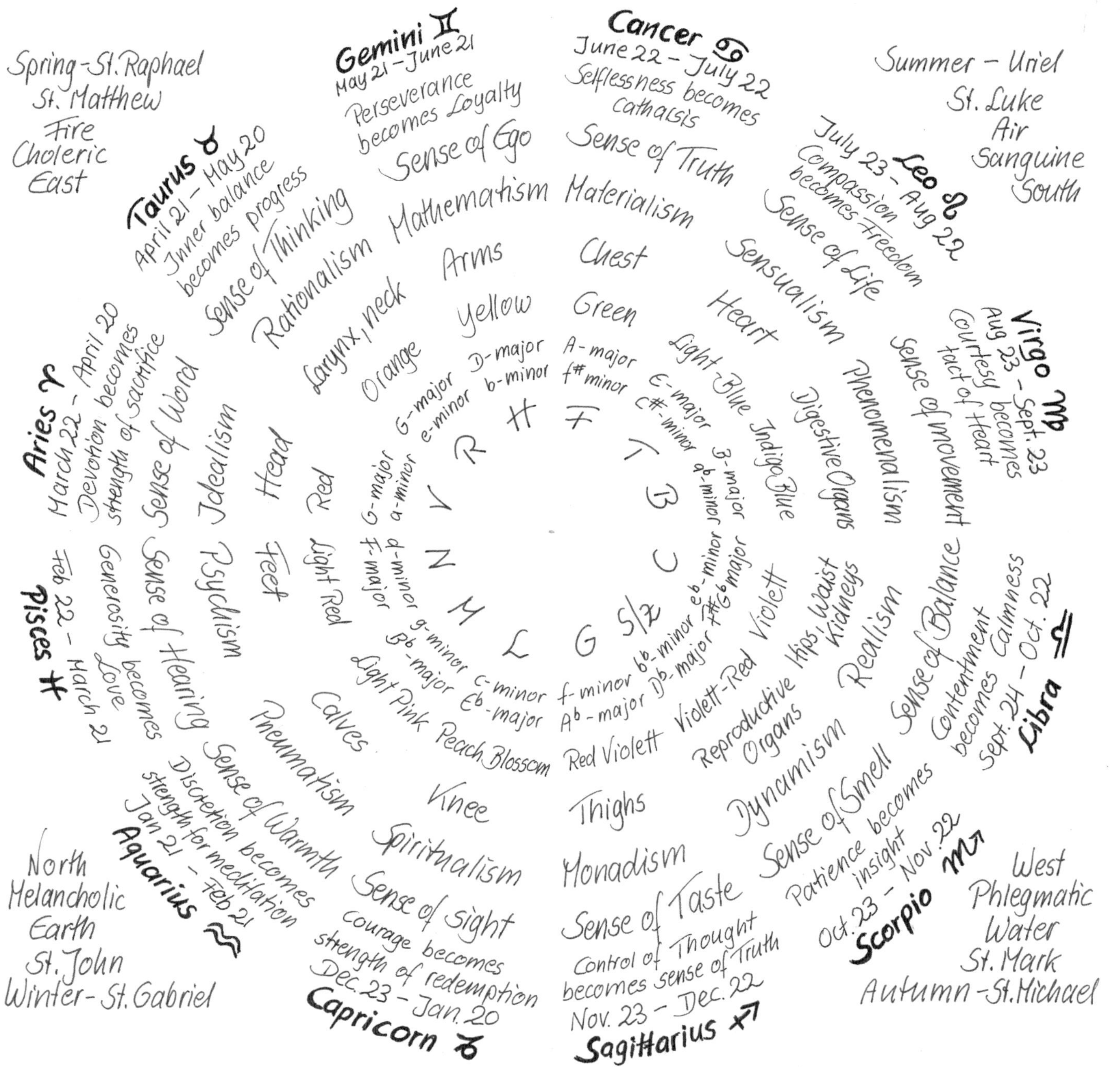

Spring - St. Raphael
St. Matthew
Fire
Choleric
East
Gemini ♊ May 21 - June 21
Perseverance becomes Loyalty
Sense of Ego
Cancer ♋ June 22 - July 22
Selflessness becomes catharsis
Sense of Truth
Summer - Uriel
St. Luke
Air
Sanguine
South
Taurus ♉ April 21 - May 20
Inner balance becomes progress
Sense of Thinking
Leo ♌ July 23 - Aug 22
Compassion becomes Freedom
Sense of Life
Rationalism   Mathematism   Materialism
Virgo ♍ Aug 23 - Sept. 23
Courtesy becomes tact of Heart
Sense of movement
Arms   Chest
Larynx, neck   Sensualism
Aries ♈ March 22 - April 20
Devotion becomes strength of sacrifice
Sense of Word
Heart   Phenomenalism
Orange   Yellow   Green
Digestive Organs
Idealism
Light Blue   Indigo Blue
Head   Red   Green
A-major   D-major
G-major   b-minor
e-minor   f#-minor
G-major   E-major
a-minor   C#-minor   B-major   D-major
f-major   d-minor   c#-minor   d-minor
Light Blue   Indigo Blue
Pisces ♓ Feb 22 - March 21
Generosity becomes Love
Sense of Hearing
Psychism
Feet   Light Red
F-major
V R H F
V N T B
N M L G S/Z U
Realism
Aquarius ♒ Jan 21 - Feb 21
Discretion becomes strength for meditation
Sense of Warmth
North
Melancholic
Earth
St. John
Winter - St. Gabriel
Calves   Light Pink   Peach Blossom
b-minor   eb-minor   f#-minor
c-minor   Ab-major   Db-major
Bb-major   Eb-major
Red Violett   Violett-Red   Violett
Reproductive Organs   Hips Waist Kidneys
Sense of Balance
Libra ♎ Sept. 24 - Oct. 22
Contentment becomes Calmness
Pneumatism   Spiritualism
Knee   Thighs
Dynamism
Sense of Smell
Scorpio ♏ Oct. 23 - Nov. 22
Patience becomes insight
Capricorn ♑ Dec. 23 - Jan. 20
Courage becomes strength of redemption
Sense of Sight
Monadism   Sense of Taste
Sagittarius ♐ Nov. 23 - Dec. 22
Control of Thought becomes sense of Truth
West
Phlegmatic
Water
St. Mark
Autumn - St. Michael

RUDOLF STEINER'S VERSES FOR THE TWELVE MOODS OF THE ZODIAC

Summarised translated text out of:"Der Tierkreis". Studienmaterial der Freien Hochschule fuer Geisteswissenschaft. Von Michael Aschenbrenner. 1969. Translated by Gertraud Goodwin.

♈ ARIES

☉ *Arise, oh shining light,*
♀ *Take hold of growth and becoming,*
☿ *Lay hold of the weaving of forces,*
♂ *Yourself ray forth, life-wakening.*
♃ *In face of resistance, gain;*
♄ *In stream of time, disperse;*
☽ *Oh shine of light, abide!*

The "shining light" in the sun-line becomes the "glory of being" in the verse for Taurus then "being, or life of the sun" in Gemini. This enhancement penetrates from outside to the inside, to the essential. The efficacy of the light to bring the beings of the world into visibility in space, is waking up strongly at the time of Aries, and unfolds ever stronger and more victorious towards summer. The first four lines tell us about the deeds of the light of the sun. "Arise", "Take hold", "Lay hold of" - the beginnings of the first three lines, are all words of deed, encouraging and demanding. It gives the mood of pressing and urging for awakening and departure which goes through all of the Aries verse. "Growth and becoming" Sun-line, and "weaving of forces" Venus-line, are strongly indicative of the burgeoning life of spring. In the Mars-line, direction, goal and stability are given to this life.

Mars-line: "life awakening" - Aries has to learn to take hold of himself in the present moment, in being, with consciousness - and not always to press forward. Jupiter-line: often, Aries breaks down due to his own resistance, and more often than not it is his own stubbornness which he has to learn to overcome! (See virtue.) Saturn-line: it is important that solidification into form is transcended, so that something new can come into being. It is the "dying and becoming". Moon-line: In order to have light in the balance of the soul it is always necessary to be aware of the spirit-light.

During embryological development, the Aries-forces are working into the undifferentiated brain, and the foundation for the 12 nerve-pairs is laid as the basis for our life of the senses. It is an image for the 12 streams of the Zodiac, and thus Aries is the "overture" in the world concert of the creation of man. The motive of Aries is the breakthrough from the darkness to the light. In the symbol for Aries, ♈ we find the form of the fountain, and also the ram's horns. It shows the strong impulsiveness of the Aries nature, which is more directed towards physical substance. A metamorphosis can be experienced to the Iamb, which is a new phase of development for the Ram. Then the forces of cognition will come from inside! Thus the readiness for active self-sacrifice stands opposite to the denial of sacrifice, the egocentric stubbornness:

3 Firesigns:　　♈ **Aries :** *Cold fire of the head*　　　♌ **Leo :** *Hot fire of the heart*　　　♐ **Sagittarius :** *Fire of the limbs*

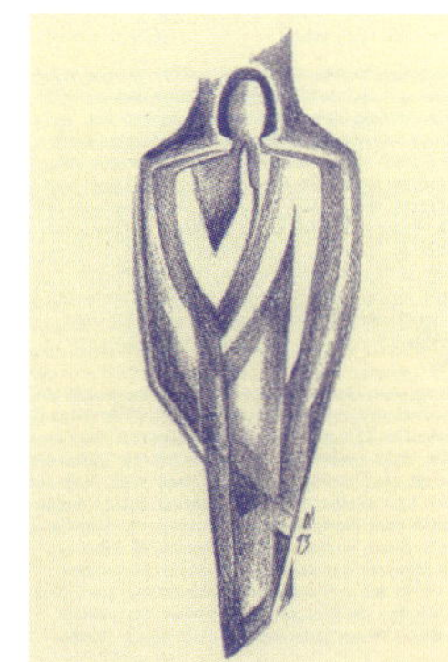

EURYTHMY "W"
THE EVENT

The head is the centre of the whole human being. The head is the metamorphosis of the whole body of the last life: in it, the whole zodiac is gathered. Aries' element is fire, which always means sacrifice. The warmth on Saturn during the development of the Earth was a sacrifice of the Thrones. In the impulsive nature of Aries, this virtue of the sacrifice takes on the form of enthusiasm. In Idealism, the real world would be without sense and meaning, if not all the Ideals would be present in the world processes. The idealist takes his forces of enthusiasm again and again out of the sacrificial fire of Aries.

Ill-making forces of Aries only come into existence through man's egotism on earth. Then we encounter haste and over-eagerness, impatience and inconsideration running against the resistance of karma and destiny. Aries has a lot of positivity, forces of zeal and energy, he is moving and organising - himself as well as others. He is able to see the goal constantly far ahead, the potential in people and things - and goes for it. A born leader, he can initiate and see projects and events through to the end.

Out of the star sign of the Ram come these building forces which work on the round head: its form a complete image of the universe. The spherically formed head is born out of the universe. This birth is "The Event". In old historic pictures we often see the Ram looking back - and this is like a looking back of Man on to himself, to that from where he came: out of the universe. When a child is born with deformities of the head, or when it can't find its uprightness; then the sculptural head-forces can be stimulated through the sound "W". If it is a question of a deformity of the physical body, then we have to take consonants to work on it. But when the force of uprightness has to be taken hold of from the Ego, from within, then exercises using vocals like "A", "U" or "I" are needed.

♉ TAURUS

☉ *Brighten, oh glory of being,*
♀ *Reach into the power of becoming,*
☿ *And weave the thread of life*
♂ *Through worlds imbued with being,*
♃ *In mindful revelation,*
♄ *Into radiant life-awareness.*
☽ *Oh glory of being, appear!*

After Aries, the breakthrough to the light, the light now spreads itself in thriving and streaming fullness — how we experience it in nature during the month of May.

Sun Line: After "Arise" in the Aries verse we now hear: "Brighten" ... which is like a calling to the light to reveal more of its inner being. Every expression of nature is a manifestation of the creative world spirit of the logos of the word: this logos "speaks", its speech is the created nature. (Relationship to the organ of speech - larynx!). In this sense, both the inner glory of being is meant, this overflowing source of creative forces during that time, as well as the outer light, which grows in strength.

Venus Line: The sun manifests its mightiest life-giving forces, bringing about sprouting growth in never ending abundance. And it is the longing of the spirit of nature to be taken in consciously by a feeling human being.

Mercury and Mars Lines: It is not a beginning any more like with Aries, it is already active, "reaching into" and "weaving the thread of life", and all plant-beings reveal themselves fully. All this activity has its goal in the "mindful revelation": the spirit forces reveal themselves ever more. Taurus' mighty forces of life have to be guided and fulfilled spiritually - that is their goal.

Saturn Line: The more the growth reveals itself, the more it goes also towards its destination and its origin: the seed and also death.

Moon Line: Spirit/form has to be master of substance, of matter. It is again substantiated in this line, how all the sprouting growing life in man and nature, is a revelation of the living spirit.

Astrology: Taurus qualities are strongly dedicated to the Earth, to everything physical, also in a way to the superficial in it. As a consequence of the strong materialisation one can encounter a selfish love, toughness and persistence, when Taurus forces are too deeply connected with the earth. One also meets a strong sensuality: the larynx will become the organ of fructification in the next stage of the Earth's development. But also Taurus born people put their full forces into tasks which come towards them, and are untiring in their efforts to reach their goal. They usually have an abundance of life-forces, and can be a bit dull in their thinking. Actually they are only really happy, when they can load themselves with heavy weights, because they are longing to become finally properly tired.

In the Ram, man is looking back into the cosmos. Now those forces are beginning to move, which bring man to a deed, to an answer to the cosmos. The larynx and all the organs in the neck region have been built out of the star forces of the Taurus sign: the inner mobility expresses itself in human speech. The formation of the whole human being is orientated towards the building of sound and speech. Again, deformities of this region of the body can be helped by practising the sound "R".

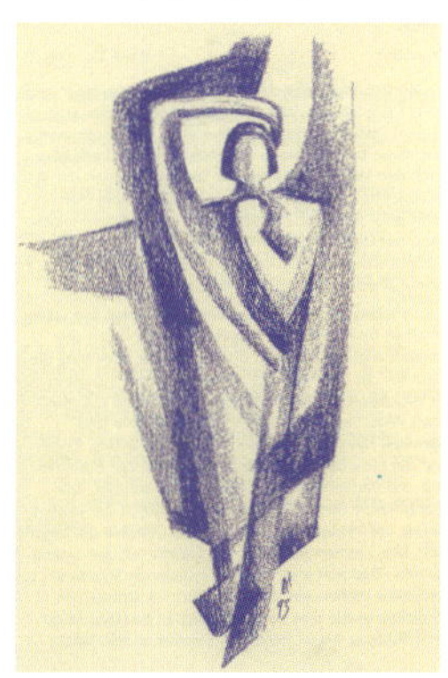

EURYTHMY "R"
WILL, DEED

♊ GEMINI

☉ *Reveal yourself, life of sun,*
♀ *Stir up what tends to rest,*
☿ *Embrace what desires to strive*
♂ *Towards a mighty prevailing of life,*
♃ *Towards a blessed knowing of worlds,*
♄ *Towards a fruitful maturing of growth.*
☽ *Oh life of sun, endure!*

In the course of the year, the sun reaches its highest point, it is the victory of the light over the darkness.

Sun Line: This time of the greatest possibilities of unfolding in nature, has to be used.
Venus Line: Nothing is stagnant, everything moves in constant transformation - but not without a definite goal.
Mercury Line: This desire to strive endlessly, must be held in bounds, in form, so that everything finds its destination. It also is the time of fructification, where birds, insects and wind bring about the process towards the building of the fruit and seed. The Mars Line tells us about the mighty life of a plant-being, which is now visible fully in its most perfect and complete image. This is also expressed in the firm standing of the feel in the Eurythmy-gesture for Gemini. These highly tense and sublime faculties of the height of the year must not be wasted by spilling and squirting them all over the place, but they have to be held and put in the service of life. Three times we hear the admonition "towards" what the forces must be orientated towards. It also is a threefold calling to stay truthful to the Earth in the Mars, Jupiter and Saturn lines. In the Jupiter Line we hear that to understand the world truly, we have to learn to accept our destiny, to become, what we have decided to become. This knowledge, to understand the world, we can only gain on the earth. (Again: Gemini-gesture, eurythmy.) Saturn Line: In order to proceed in one's development, to ripen, man has been placed onto the Earth, because only on Earth can he come to freedom and independence. Moon Line: To be able to achieve this loyalty to the Earth we need the continuing forces of the Sun - but also of the spiritual Sun : ... "endure"! The spirit Sun is necessary to balance the polarities of good and evil again.

☉ Breakthrough to the Light
♀ Pressing flooding of the Light
☿ Full streaming, pouring out of the Light fully revealing itself
♂ Man stands in the world.
♃ Life and Death forces stand opposite each other.
♄ Polarity of· Light and Darkness or:
☽ extinguishing of consciousness and awake consciousness.

Astrology: The Gemini nature is always two fold. It has to do with symmetry, with right and left, male and female in oneself. With the arms and hands, man can take hold of the world - and of himself. Through the sense of Ego, man recognises another human being's individuality. This duality brings the quality of fluctuation and inconsistency as potential problems into this sign: not to be here nor there, and not concentrated on the here and now. There can be spiritual clarity - but also ecstasy; then unclarity, and absent-mindedness - but also great intellectuality and subtlety. Lucifer tries to lead man astray and away from his path on Earth by showing him the spiritual light and his origin in the spirit and light of the universe. In earthly intellectuality, Ahriman tries to fetter man to the Earth.

Thus the Gemini nature always has to develop perseverance, and seek for the balance between light and dark, between the physical and the spiritual breath. He can be an excellent actor, changing his character quickly with mercurial vivacity.

Through the sign of Gemini, man gains his bilateral symmetric order. The right and the left side of man are welded together through the forces of Gemini. Thus man becomes "capable for deed, for activity": what could we do on Earth if we would not have both our arms, hands and legs! Up to the two halves of the brain this symmetry is going, giving us the possibility for our conscious action through the crossing over of all the nerves from the brain. With children who can not grasp their body and incarnate properly and therefore can't come into the doing, we practise to hold their right ear with their left arm, or to touch the left toe with the right hand.

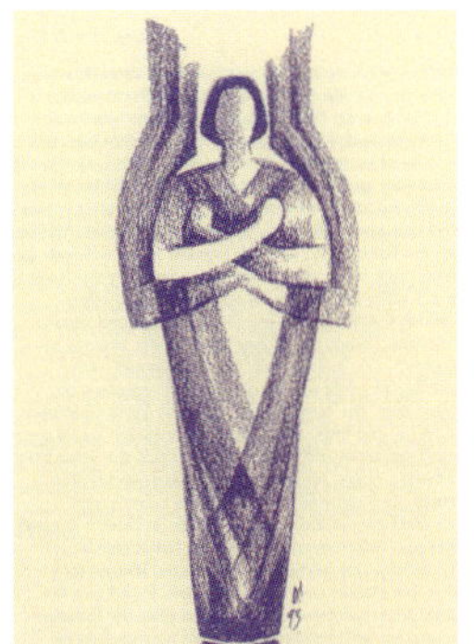

EURYTHMY "**H**"
CAPACITY FOR
THE DEED

Two souls alas! reside within my breast,
And each withdraws from and repels its brother.
One to the world is bound in clinging lust,
The other soars, all earthly ties unheeded,
To join ancestral gods, far from this dust,
In fields where nought mundane is needed.

J. W. von Goethe, *Faust* I, Scene 2

 CANCER

- ☉ *You resting, luminous glow,*
- ♀ *Engender warmth of life,*
- ☿ *Enwarm the life of soul*
- ♂ *To meet with vigour each test*
- ♃ *And permeate itself with spirit*
- ♄ *In quiet, light-outstreaming.*
- ☽ *You luminous glow, gain strength!*

Out of the demands of "arise" ♈ , "shine forth" ♉ and "reveal yourself" ♓ something has become which one can look at. It has come to rest, like in the full growth and maturity of the plants. By that time, all plants have been fructified and are now working inwardly on a ripening process of the seed.

Sun Line: Out of the "shining light" ♈ , "glory of being" ♉ , "life of the sun" ♓ has become, the "luminous glow" of Cancer: everything has been intensified, contracted and made inward. Warmth is more dense and inward than light. Warmth builds the transition from the etheric forces to the beingness of the substances. The heat during July has often the most intense heat of the year. This Cancer warmth we meet in the Venus and Mercury Line. But it must not burn, or die through the heat, and therefore it has to be ensouled, "to meet with vigour each test" - Mars Line. It is the turning point of the year, the Earth has exhaled its breath to the utmost and now comes the great verification: the building of the fruit and seed - and also the preparation for the building of the new bud for the next year! In the Jupiter Line we hear that only if the interpenetration with the spirit has been achieved properly, the seeds will be fruitful themselves. Then, "in quiet light bearing", Jupiter Line, one can go towards the dark side of the year: Cancer stands polar-opposite to Capricorn, the Christmas time. Now those forces have to be gathered which have to be made inward in the dark side of the year, therefore: "you luminous glow, gain strength!" is resounding in the Moon Line.

After the St. John's day, begins already the great dying in nature. The soul of the Earth is totally exhaled when the Sun reaches Cancer. It has then fully surrendered itself to the cosmos, in order to take in the spirit and seeds from the stars. It is a spiritual interpenetration. In Capricorn, these forces are then carried down into the depth of matter, when outwardly the Earth is rigid and rests in itself. But only then the Earth can give forth new strength for growth.

In the chemical ether lies the secret of transformation of the substances: it imitates differentiation, separation and brings substances together again - a threefold process.

There is a <u>longing</u> (Moon) for that which lies hidden (Cancer - a crustacean). Cancer wants to <u>feel</u> that, which lies hidden in the shell. In the sign for Cancer ♋ , we see two spirals which do <u>not</u> touch each other: this is an indication that one development comes to an end - and a new step of development indicates itself. <u>In between</u> lies the jump of metamorphosis: Past and future, the movement down and up and that, which lies <u>in between</u>, the third element, is the fruit and purpose of the whole development. The shell is not built for its own purpose, but to harbour and contain something!

Astrology: Cancer personalities tend to close themselves off from the outside, to ripen and bear their fruit within. They have great capacities to mother and tend caringly to others and love to build houses and have families. The Cancer type tries to look for a careful solution to problems and avoids risks and dangers. He cares and prepares extremely well for the future. A difficult point is his self-consciousness, as he always relies on the judgement of those around him. He wants to make the world serve him - but he doesn't want to penetrate into it himself. So he lives between cautiousness, anxiousness and comfort. He looks for a firm footing in lower regions and strives to condense the lofty regions in such a way that they, too, can grant him as much support as the material world. This is due to the descending movement of the Sun at this time of year. What could - and should - be a path <u>through</u> the depth thus becomes a way <u>into</u> the depth: the love for the material world and the sense perceptions becomes a prison. Materialism.

More and more, the formation of the physical body goes from outside towards the inside. The gesture of Gemini leads us up to our own skin, where we feel ourselves: In Cancer, we begin to loosen ourselves from the outer cosmos. The gesture shows an enclosing of the chest from left and right, from front and back. This gesture separates an inside from an outside and encloses it. The chest-region builds itself, to enclose and protect the heart and lungs. Thus a motif for an action can ripen within and can come from within.

Ita Wegmann: In his breast organisation, man takes in the air from outside and breathes it out again. In this process he experiences like in a material picture what happens in respect to his higher sheaths in waking and sleeping and in birth and death. Sleeping is a breathing out of consciousness, of the astral body. Death is a breathing out of life, of the etheric body. This building principle of Involution and Evolution comes from the starry region of Cancer .

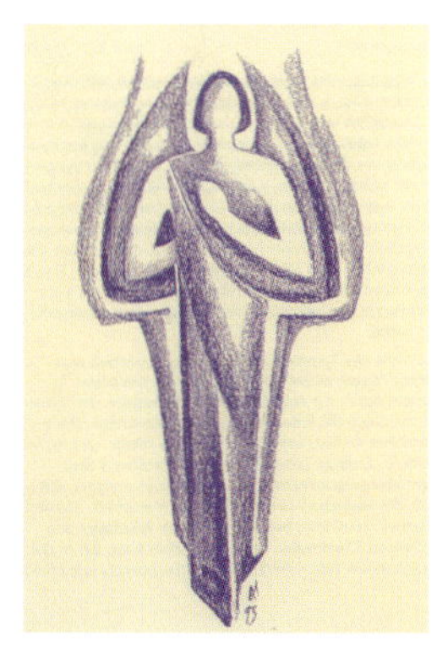

EURYTHMY "F" "V"
IMPULSE,
(MOTIVE) FOR
ACTION

♌ LEO

☉	*Invigorate with senses' might*
♀	*Matured existence of all worlds,*
☿	*Perceptive element of beings,*
♂	*Toward the firm resolve 'to be'.*
♃	*In the surging shine of life,*
♄	*In the prevailing pains of growth,*
☽	*With senses' might, arise!*

After the turning point which occurred in Cancer, after this quieting down, the holding, we meet a different mood in Leo. The light-forces of the Sun have started to diminish, the days become already shorter - but its mighty nature comes out only now, enhanced to its full strength: under its scorching heat, fruit and seeds ripen. This transition from the strongest radiation of light to the most intensive efficacy of warmth means a further intensification, which has already started in Cancer.

Sun-Line: "Senses' might" can have two meanings, from the word of sense as meaning, and meaningful, as well as the word of the sense as an organ. Sensualism, Leo's worldview, orientates itself solely through the sense organs. And when it can penetrate through sense perception to the spirit which is hidden within the things, then the true meaning is found. Venus-Line: "Matured existence of all worlds" shows us what has become, the physical, which has gelled through the forming-forces of the light. And this physical outcome has to be invigorated with senses' might, with spiritual meaning. The Sun can express itself most purely in the sign of Leo. It is called the heart of the world (Sun) because it harmonises the outer and inner planets like the human heart, which mediates between the regions above and below in the human organism. In the middle between above, the past: the "matured existence of all worlds", and below, the future: "the firm resolve 'to be'", live the lion-forces of the heart in: "Perceptive element of beings" - Mercury-Line. In the Venus, Mercury and Mars Lines we can see the threefold human being in thinking, feeling and willing in the past, present and future. Because through feeling alone we can never get to a true shaping of life... But the ripening is never possible without painful experiences. Saturn-Line: "In the prevailing pains of growth". The colour of Leo, of the flaming enthusiasm, is not red as we would expect it - but blue: the colour of the consciousness pole. This serious mood stands behind the Saturn-Line.

The sound "T" has a definite and ordering principle in many languages: this principle is necessary, to let the fruit ripen in the human being. TAO - in the old Hebrew wisdom "T" had the occult meaning of the "I". In the sound "T" we can experience a gesture towards a point, the centre. This is the experience of the "I" in its firmness and strength. The ego has to gain strength out of the Leo-forces, becoming, shaping itself, completing itself - which is the meaning of the Moon-Line: "With senses' might arise!".

The movement downwards and inwards is continued further in Leo. The heart is man's central organ, with it and in it we feel the origin of our feelings. Rudolf Steiner ... "*If we look for something in man similar to what is found in the Lion, it is the human breast where the rhythms meet, the rhythms of circulation and respiration ...*" (out of the lecture circle: "*Man as a symphony of the creative world*".) When our blood is perfused with warmth, and this warmth penetrates the feeling of the soul, this gives man the virtue of courage and magnanimity. Outer peacefulness has settled in; Leo belongs to the so-called "signs of rest" together with Taurus, Scorpio and Waterman. Between Leo and Waterman we have the strongest contrasts between sublimity of the heights and the depths of the grave of the earth.

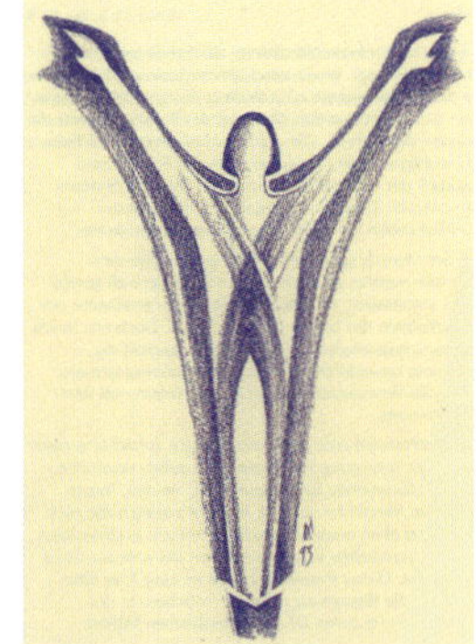

EURYTHMY "D" "T"

FLAMING

ENTHUSIASM

Astrology: In the power of the senses shows itself the faculty to enjoy everything, that brings joy to the senses, what is luminous in a kingly way, what is sun-like - but also a clinging to pomp and luxury. Through the blood as the carrier of the Ego, Man began to feel himself as an individual, as a personal being. Blood is also the carrier of heredity, emotion and karma and all that is connected with the lower part of our personality: with our passions and carnal lust. The hardening in the blood-ties leads to egoism and self-love.

There are three aspect of the sun-forces: **To give light -** *Helios*   **To carry life -** *Dionysos*   **To give love -** *Apollo*

Parsival can only become the King of the Grail when he is able to ask the question out of compassion. A King carries the karma of his people in his heart. The Leo-impulse : To seek the unity of Kings and shepherds - in the sense of ... "*At the turning point of time*". Kings and shepherds cross each other's paths at the birth of the Jesus-child. *Foundation Stone Mediation*

Now we come to that which fulfils us inwardly, in which our being has its inner centre. Heart and blood circulation come into being; they build in us a whole human being everywhere there are blood vessels, everywhere there is the streaming of the blood. What there is physically as the organ of the heart and the blood vessels absolutely belongs to the building of the whole of man as it follows out of the twelve-foldness of the zodiac. Rudolf Steiner, June 7th 1912, "*When we for instance put opposite to the limbs, which we have looked at already, the blood circulation, then we have something which lives merely in the inside, it is an inner separation.*" We have arrived at the zodiac sign of Leo, which can be understood as an animal of the heart. The gesture for Leo leads us out of the centre of the heart in flaming enthusiasm out into the width of space, in order to receive from there the fructification in the "T" or "D".

VIRGO

☉ *Behold the worlds, oh soul!*
♀ *Let the soul take hold of worlds,*
☿ *Let the spirit lay hold of being,*
♂ *Work out of powers of life,*
♃ *Upon will-experience, build,*
♄ *In blossoming worlds, put trust.*
☽ *Oh soul, comprehend the beings!*

When the Sun moves into Virgo, the turning towards within is even more decisive. In nature, we already see the wilting forces of Autumn beginning to work. The sign of Virgo often is a virgin with a ripe ear of corn in her hand. Its biggest star is named "Spica" - ear of corn. The strong turning towards within is given expression in the Virgo-verse through the first and only call to the soul - whereas in all other verses the signs themselves are called upon. All seven lines of the verse address themselves to the human soul.

This enveloping harbouring gesture we meet in many languages through the sound "B" : boat, beach, boot, beaker, hebrew: "beth" = house, both, binding, building, belonging, befriending, betoken, etc. also with the sound "P". In both sounds, the direction is not only towards inside, but also towards outside: in embracing something, it is protected and separated from the outer world, a skin is being built. The direction towards the surface, much stronger still in the "P" than in the "B" is strongly visible in the Eurythmy gesture. It also gives us a hint for understanding Virgo's worldview, Phenomenalism, which looks at the outer phenomena of the world, at the surface of things. That from one point of view the sense of sight is also connected with this sign, helps us to understand the Sun-Line of the Virgo-verse: "Behold the worlds, O Soul!". The motif of "taking hold" we know now from the "B" and "P" gesture, and meet it now in the Venus and Mercury Lines. "Belly, bottom, bower, pregnancy, power ...

etc. all words where the sound "B" and "P" are expressing their swelling, expanding qualities of life, the fullnesses of ripening forms and fruit, the abundance of harvesting. Fruitful = *uber* in latin, life - *bios* in Greek. Thus we understand the Mars-Line: "Work out of powers of life". The wilful character of "B" and "P", which we can meet in many words like *battre* (french: beat, defeat), boxing, *buttare* (italian - fling, throw) etc. comes out in the Jupiter-Line: "Upon will-experience, build". Out of this positive, strong "standing on the Earth with both feet" mood of Virgo, with its bottom line of "reasonable disillusion" and with the security of this nourishing shelter we can grow trust into the further process of the world. This announces to us the Saturn-Line: "In blossoming worlds, put trust". Inner firmness and building on one's own ground are particular characteristics of Virgo. The sound and healthy feeling of one's self can go astray in two directions: into the over increased feeling for the self in presumption pride and arrogance, in boasting - and to the other side into a hardening, separating oneself off by putting a hard armour around one's heart.

For both "illnesses" we find the healing in the first two lines: to look out into the worlds, to behold! And in the spirit lay hold of being - which we do through thinking. Both activities - perceiving and thinking - are necessary to grasp the full reality of things in freedom (Rudolf Steiner's *Philosophy of Spiritual Activity*). The forces of thinking shine over to Virgo from the Fishes which are opposite, and with which she has to unite herself to come to true cognition. This is called for in the demand of the Moon-Line: "O soul, comprehend the beings!". Forces of thinking and forces of growth have the same origin, they are two expressions of the same etheric life-forces. So it is not surprising that both forces are united in Virgo, and are part of the etheric cross in the whole Zodiac.

All the forces of the second quadrant, ♋ ♌ ♍ have to do with the secrets of nourishment, the secrets of the transformation of substances. The image for Virgo is the Virgin with the ripe ear of corn. It is a strongly "etheric" sign: it transforms the astral forces in the food - bringing it into the growing plants and releasing it again in the intestines. The virgin transforms the astral heavenly forces into etheric life-forces. Leo-forces transform the etheric forces received from Virgo into those forces which build up the physical body.

♋ **Cancer :** *transformation of the physical*   ♌ **Leo :** *transformation of the etheric*   ♍ **Virgo :** *transformation of the astral*

They all have in common the direction towards within, the intensification of the sun-forces into love, light and life. Mercurial processes penetrate the substances, analysing them, dissecting and separating them, which is the vital process for our nourishment so that they can be built into our organism. The constant movement "peristaltic" in the intestines supports this process. The same forces stimulate our thought processes as well. In the star sign of Virgo the eternally-spiritual virginal forces are united: Demeter, Ceres, Erigone, Asträa, Dike, Fortuna, Isis, Maria, Sophia, Eva (the cosmic eternally feminine). The inward process of the Virgo-forces leads to a deepening in consciousness, through which man can learn to recognise that he carries the world within himself. If this path is not taken far enough, then man stays attached to the small and insignificant, he will become pedantic and a bureaucrat. As a sign of ripeness, Virgo-forces also lead to the dissolving of form. In the moral field of the soul, this can be seen as a tendency to violate formalities or transgress customs : courtesy doesn't come easy.

Astrology: Seed-Ripening/maturing, ordering, collecting; to have a sober sense for the useful. But also curiosity, pedantic and brooding. To digest spiritually, to understand - but also to be persistent in a pedantic way.

In the region of the Virgo-forces we meet an inner organ world which doesn't open itself any more to the outside: Spleen, Liver, Gallbladder, etc. with the solar plexus, the "brain" of the intestines - "We have here a part of the human being, which we can call the actual inside in respect to the physical organisation - and it is important here, that there is no direct relationship any more to the outside". (Leo - heart/lungs.) In this region of the body, which is built out of the cosmic forces of the Virgo, man's soul can ripen in inner seclusion. Virgo often is depicted with an ear of corn - a sign of ripeness. "Flaming enthusiasm" the Leo gesture which is totally turned to the cosmos, is followed by "reasonable disillusion", the zodiac gesture of Virgo. In Curative Eurythmy, the sounds "B" and "P" have a harmonising and quieting effect on the whole region of the solar plexus.

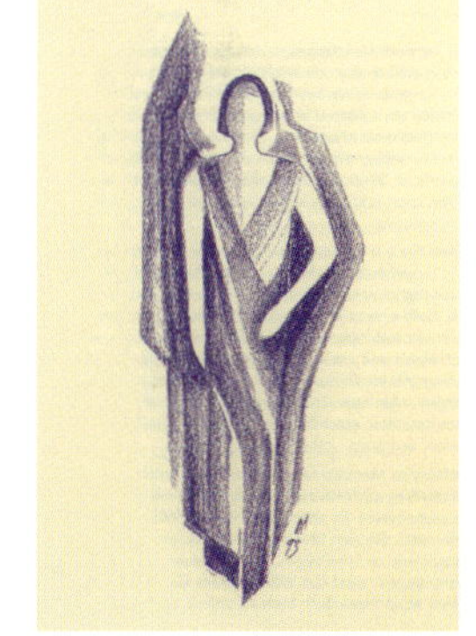

EURYTHMY "B" "P"
WILL, DEED

♎ LIBRA

Now we are coming to a time when Light and Darkness are holding the balance between each other. In Aries, the Sun began to strive upwards, in Libra, the Sun goes down towards the darkness of Winter; it is a mood of the horizontal, the quietness of Autumn.

The theme of equilibrium resounds in the Sun Line in an all encompassing way - and is modified in each of the lines in a characteristic mood: in the Venus Line we can feel a devotional, loving and understanding equilibrium between being and being. In the Mercury Line we hear, how one existence doesn't close itself off from another but lives in the equilibrium of being for itself and being together with the other. And thus, a sameness creates another sameness in the Mars Line.

In the Autumn, Man is called on to contrast the dying in nature with cognition of the spirit and to penetrate it with his will forces. This spirit knowledge should make Man enthusiastic for social deeds - which we hear in the Jupiter Line. But this activity towards outside has to be in balance with calling to mind an inner, quiet world enjoyment - thus resounds in the Saturn Line.

The sound, which mirrors the being of Libra, is given by Rudolf Steiner as the "C". It is very similar to the sound "Z", but is much finer and more light and is used only for light and fleeting movements for Libra. (The sharp "Z" is the sound for Scorpio.) This lightness of being in levity is the important characteristic of every scale: the lightest touch can bring it out of balance into a swing from right and left, totally immersed into the play of gravity and levity. The polarity of light and darkness is the domain of the celestial Libra.

"Libra's worldview is realism: it is founded on the observation of the reality of the sense world." (Aries: Idealism!)

Eurythmy mood for Libra: "The careful pondering of the supposition for Thinking". This is Libra's characteristic attitude: the quiet weighing, the attitude of "*fine ita et studio*" (lat. for : No day without study).

The physical scales has its point of gravity in the centre. The image of the celestial Libra is calling Man to find his centre and to act out of it, out of his "I" to seek the balance between the forces which try to pull Man upwards and the forces which try to pull Man down. St. Michael, who starts his rulership in the year in Libra, is Man's guide on this decisive path for Man and the evolution of

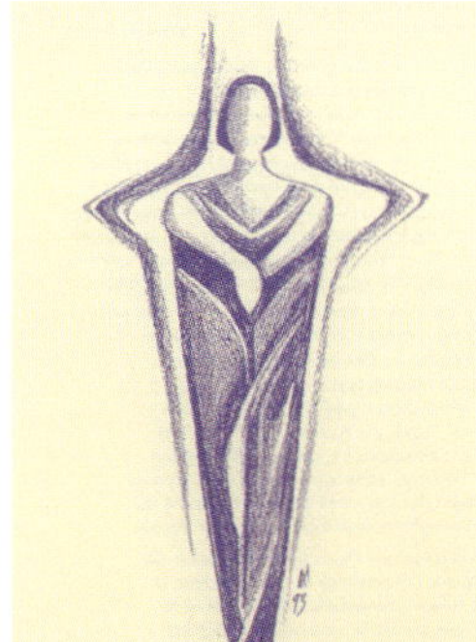

the world. We often see him depicted with the scales in his hand! The uprightness in us we can only find and hold with the help of Aries - and only through that can we hold the scales. Thus the motive of the cross arises! He is not demanding - only showing the way. In the verse for Libra, we hear no demands except in the last line: O worlds, uphold the worlds! This can only happen out of equilibrium. Thus we see the stars of Libra in the sky like a majestic cosmic image/memorial, which stands for the balance between the lighter signs above and the darker signs below, between the light of the Spirit and the gravity of Earth.

Astrology: It is a sign of aesthetic development, with a strong love for beauty and harmony. Libra is deft in dealing with others, has a highly developed knowledge of the art of getting along, and can often get what it wants from another by apparently giving in. It is the sign of the sweet and beautiful goddess Venus - also a cardinal, positive sign! Libra excels at taking the initiative in such a way that others do not realise the initiative has been taken. It is the sign of the simplest relationship, the one-to-one, and Libra has difficulties in thinking of other modes of relationship. The self is developed only in connection with another self: it needs the dialogue. Libra is an air sign, and in all its encounters with the world, both in art and relationship, it has the usual air sign difficulty in dealing with intense feeling.

After taking hold of the inside in Virgo, the gesture for Libra guides us towards a seeking for balance between inside and outside. In this region, the hips are being built, whereby we find our posture for balance. Man begins to integrate himself from inside into the earth forces through his limbs. The gesture of the stretched-out arms with the hands upon each other we could not build without our hips. It is a gesture which only the upright, standing man can do in a variable process of finding and holding his equilibrium. This standing upright in this gesture enables man to carefully ponder the supposition of thinking.

♏ SCORPIO

With Scorpio, the sequence of signs under the night star signs begins. These correspond also to man's lower organisation, the pole of the Will. Thus are the worldviews of the lower star signs impulsated by the Will element. In the most explicit way this is the case with Scorpio's worldview, Dynamism, which sees the world as onesidedly dominated by the forces of the will. Of the strongest will nature is also Scorpio's sound, "S", "Sch": Through this sound one can influence man and animal strongly with one's will - in a stirring, provoking way as well as in a quieting and soothing way, depending on its intonation. Language uses the "S" to indicate the taking hold of matter and penetrating into matter: to saw, serrate, secant, secede, secession, seclude, section; latin: *secare* - to cut, *sancire* - to wound, *sagitta* - the arrow, *serra* - the saw, etc. But not only the separating qualities are present, also those of uniting, lat. *simul* - together, *socius* - the friend, *suere* - to sow; the greek syllable - *syn* - with, appears in many words with the meaning of "together": synchronise, synthetise, synopsis; synphonie. In old Hebrew wisdom, the occult meaning of the sound "S" was that of the human body. Scorpio's gesture points downwards - this direction also goes with the "S" in eurythmy. This motif appears in : sinking, sole, lat: *sub* - under, *sulcus* - farrow, *solum* - ground, Tibetan : *sa* - earth, Russian : *semlja* - earth. Thus we see the rigid and hard quality of "S". The downward gesture also has the meaning of thinking, highlighting the forming quality of thinking, of bringing something to a point.

All or most of these qualities are pointing towards the outer, outward, physical being of things. The sharpness of thinking, the certainty in being, taking hold of the physical, the relationship to rigidity and fixation. But the creation of outer existence is at the expense of the inner, the being. This is then what we hear in the Sun-Line. This happens always, when a being comes into outer existence! In the growing of the plant, its spiritual being disappears more and more whereas the physical comes ever more into existence. In the physically smallest seed, its spirit-being reaches its highest degree, all future possibilities are in it. In the Venus-Line we hear an opening, a being ready for a new existence. In the physically smallest seed, its spirit–being reaches its highest degree, all future possibilities are in it. In the Venus-Line we hear an opening, a being ready for a new appearance into the world of forms. In the next two lines we meet another polarity of inside and outside: the polarity of becoming and producing. The production goes into the world, and the more there is, the less are the possibilities of becoming. This is something the artist knows very well! This we hear in the Mercury-Line, speaking of movement, activity and striving towards a goal. But greater dynamic and tension lives in the stage of becoming, of the not-yet-born, where the production is held hack. This we hear in the will-mood of the Mars-Line. The next two lines move in a moral sphere. In the wise quality of the Jupiter-Line lives the punishing, balancing justice of the world! And what is this guilt which is connected with Scorpio? In the beginning of the Fall was the separation from the Spirit World. Death and destruction, hatred and darkness are all at home in this sign. It is the star sign of Ahriman. But the experience of guilt and sin is a necessary step on the path to independence and freedom of man. So we hear in the Saturn-Line: thanks to the Saturn forces we are in an organically closed system in this life as well as in another and in the whole of earth's evolution. If man was exposed only to Saturn forces, he would harden in himself completely and would rigidify under Scorpio. If not, the Moon, the opponent to Saturn, would work against it. In the positive mood of the Moon-Line we hear a therapeutic element, which is, and has to be, present in every one of the "twelve moods." This is the deepest aspect of the forces of Scorpio, who will again lift himself out of the depths of death, hatred and darkness into the light heights of the Spirit, metamorphosing into the eagle - to that sign of the heavens, from which it once fell.

Man's sex organs, through his sexual drive, can pull him down furthest towards animal nature, if only carnal lust is expressed. Sublimated, they enable man to reach the highest creative deeds. Taurus life forces—Scorpio death forces. From Scorpio come the attacks towards a darkening of Man's consciousness. The Ego of Libra stands between the light-forces of Virgo and the darkness of Scorpio in the middle. With the metamorphosis of the physical body, death is overcome: Christ has taken the sting of death.

♎ **Libra** : *physical union in marriage*　　♏ **Scorpio** : *Union with another being in the etheric*

In reproduction a union takes place with another being who wants to come down from the spirit to the earth. Also through death a union takes place of the dead being's soul with the sublunar sphere of Kamaloka. The union of Mars' forces and water create enormous tensions - steam! The soldiers of the Roman legions of the Caesars had the symbol of Scorpio on the buttons of their uniform - showing the daemonic part of Mars in Scorpio. (The lighter part of Mars shows itself in Aries.)

In the Scales we seek for the incorporation into the outer world - in Scorpio, we take into ourselves this outer world, in nourishment as well as in sense-perceptions. Everything, that we take in, that penetrates us from outside, is, in a sense, a kind of poison, "a kind of poisoned sting". We have to analyse it, we have to defend ourselves. And while man defends himself against the outside, the inside is forming itself. In the lower man, the sexual organs and the metabolic organs come into being; in the higher man, the front lobe of the brain, in how we transform our perceptions into thoughts. Therefore, this sign is represented by Scorpio with its poisonous sting as well as by the Eagle, an image for the forces of thinking.

EURYTHMY "S" "Z"
REASON

♐ SAGITTARIUS

- ☉ *Becoming achieves the power 'to be',*
- ♀ *Into what is, the might of becoming dies.*
- ☿ *Achievement resolves the desire to strive*
- ♂ *Into prevailing will-force of life.*
- ♃ *In dying, there ripens prevailing of worlds,*
- ♄ *Forms disappear within forms.*
- ☽ *What has come to be, may it feel what is!*

Form is strongly related to creation: it brings into form that which has not yet become, not yet born. But in the moment of being born into form, it solidifies and loses the capability of changing. This is the meaning of the Sun and Venus Lines.

This joy of creativity has reached its goal in the Mercury Line: it has become form. Thus it belongs already to the past. Only in the Mars Line we meet an activity, a new will-element, which also belongs to Sagittarius. But this activity does not go outwards, it has more the character of resting in itself, of holding back. Thus the will-element in this sign is more turned in on itself in order to consolidate and become firm, to define the being itself inwardly. It is a collected force which prepares itself for future activity. In one of the verses (right) of the Soul Calendar for this time, we can find this mood expressed very well.

To waken up to the future's task through the treasur'd past is then the main theme of the first line of Capricorn: "May what is coming, rest on what has been". We are in the time of the darkest winter, a time when death is nearest in nature. But just towards this force of death, Sagittarius becomes victorious: the sting of death in Scorpio is overcome; death here is not an end but a gateway to a new enhanced life. And so we hear in the Jupiter Line of Sagittarius the wisdom which lies in death. We can think of Christ's sacrificial death through which unending grace and salvation has come to the world. The sense of death prevents form existing forever - untransformed. Forms have to go - so that new forms can come into being. This we hear in the Saturn Line. But the forms don't disappear into nothingness, they live on in the new forms.

Sagittarius' worldview is Monadism, which directs its glance towards the existence of the single being. This they call "the monad". But this single being must not insist upon itself, its own ego only, closing itself off. Therefore the Moon Line encourages it to open itself, to feel itself related to the same world with its "what has come to be" (past) to "may it feel what is" (the present).

Again we feel a strong will-element in Sagittarius, expressed strongly in its sounds of "G" and "K". But their activity is of a different nature than that of the "S" in Scorpio: it is not magically penetrating - but has strength, fighting stamina, overcomes resistance victoriously. We meet those sounds frequently in words which express these qualities, and which are related to light and fire: glance, glow, glisten, lat: *ignis* = fire, greek: *candere* = to glow, *kaiein* = to burn, *keleos* - flaming, Japanese: *kaiy* = fire, *akari* = light, Egyptian: *kek* = light etc.

EURYTHMY "**G**" "**K**"
THE DECISION

Sagittarius is awake and has a sharp eye. The "decision" (eurythmy gesture) needs the clarity of thinking. We often see Sagittarius depicted as a centaur. This means that it doesn't only fight against forces from outside, but also against that which pulls Man down into gravity and into his lower drives, against the animal in him. This also needs the light of consciousness! This finds expression in many words: go, get, keen, keep, kick, kindle, king, knight, know, etc. Activity needs resistance, in order to become active. We can feel through both sounds the firmness and physicality of things. The eurythmy gesture shows a pushing away from oneself.

In the darkness of Sagittarius, religion has its origin with its gift of faith and prophesy. Trust is the main quality of Sagittarius, a basis for community building. The danger of religion lies in those darkening forces which obscure the everyday consciousness. "The light shone into the darkness, and the darkness did not understand it". Not understanding the spirit light which still shines in this depth of darkness, leads to the rigid dogma in science and to the stiff fanaticism in religious beliefs and in general. This is an ever present danger for Sagittarius. There, clarity of thinking and light in consciousness are necessary to overcome these tendencies. Again - we see the image of the centaur in front of us, and call to mind the art of archery, which until today is a great art; in Zen Buddhism archery belongs to the highly spiritual education of Man. It says: "the arrow has to loosen itself from the bow as the snow falls off the bamboo leaf".

In the gesture of Sagittarius we see the emphasis of the upper arm and the thigh. The formation goes ever more from inside towards the outside - from the "Thought" (Scorpio) to the "decision". Organically, this means that the limbs are being built adequate for a life on Earth. This gesture with the sound "G" or "K" following, can be used successfully in Curative Eurythmy with people who are cramped in the lower part of their body.

♑ CAPRICORN

May what is coming, rest on what has been.
May what has been, surmise what is to come,
For a vigorous present existence.
Through inward life-withstanding
May world-beings' guard grow strong,
May life's working blossom forth,
May what has been endure what is to come!

Nothing of earthly gravity and darkness of winter is in these lines. There is an inner light radiating outward, pointing towards the future. There is a similar mood in the Soul Calendar verse (right) of this time:

In the sign itself, we can see an inner rising - through to something new, like the animal Capricorn having this capability to jump up high from the position of rest. This carries the courage and impulse of will, which are guided by thinking:

Mood for this time towards within: *Courage for waking*
Mood for this time towards outside: *Courage to dare*

It is a primeval swing upwards, the time of the birth of Christ, the change from the old to the new year and the Baptism in Jordan. The Sun has reached its lowest point during the 12 Holy Nights: the astral and etheric body of the Earth penetrate each other totally. This is the time of the spirit birth into the most mineralised Earth. But it is the time of the change in the year - and for the world, which is expressed in the Janus head, looking back and forward towards the future. The stiffness of the mineral world is one of the outer traits of Capricorn, a clinging to the past, not being able to bear the future, holding on to everything, which is old, antiquated and dogmatic. And in the darkest depths lies the primal substance of the Thrones, pointing towards the high spirituality of the birth of the spirit.

♋ **Cancer** : *Fruitfulness in the physical*   ♑ **Capricorn** : *Fruitfulness in the spirit*

People born in this sign can show a tendency towards exclusion; they can be insisting, and have a capability to look forwards and backwards in life. They usually are very successful in their material achievements, are loyal and keep things and people together. They cling to the past and can have a great gift of reverence.

Out of the spheres of the Capricorn of the Zodiac, the forms of the knee are being built. In its anatomy it shows great drama: the crossing over tendons and the kneecap, which is not in connection with any other bone, give the knee a great freedom of movement. In the knee-joint, a balance of movement has to be found between the forces of gravity, rising through the foot and lower leg - and the forces coming down from the upper leg. Thus the knee can appear to us as coming into existence out of a whirl of forces.

In the Eurythmy gesture for Capricorn lives a strong tension between the left hand, which touches the forefront, and the right arm, which is stretched out. In between, the sound ″L″ arises : it holds itself in itself and overcomes gravity. This sound has the capability to unite, to balance between past and future, between Ahriman and Lucifer. In between stands the Representative of Man: a deeply Christian image. The balance comes about through the rhythm in the ″L″. It is the sound of life as such, of all life. All life is a creative process: it arises out of the interpenetration of substance with Form.

EURYTHMY ″**L**″

THE DISCUSSION
OF THE THOUGHT
WITH THE WORLD

♒ AQUARIUS

⊙ *May what is bounded yield to the boundless.*
♀ *What feels the lack of bounds, may it create*
☿ *Bounds for itself in its depths;*
♂ *May it raise itself in the current,*
♃ *As wave, flowing forth, sustaining itself,*
♄ *In becoming, shaping itself to existence.*
☽ *Set yourself bounds, oh boundless!*

We hear the motif of the borderline six times! The sound "M" is the most inward, soul embued sound: the inner presupposes an outside, towards which it wants to border. The being of the "M" wants to overcome this border. In the line of the Sun we are called upon to overcome our own Ego in order to devote ourselves to the spirit which has no borders. The "M" is the main representative of the swelling, voluminous sounds: much, most, mass, massive, etc. In the striving to widen ourselves, to disperse ourselves also lies the danger to lose ourselves. It becomes a task to seek for the balance between the boundless and the holding oneself in the boundaries of one's own "I", which is a calling we hear in the Venus and Mercury Line. In the Mars Line we have the quality of the will and courage, which we meet in words like mighty, majesty, majestic, mysterious, etc.

In the Jupiter Line we can sense the wisdom of the forming power which we need to counterbalance the formless qualities in the "M", like in: muddy, murky, mellow, mist, mud, stammer, muddle. Then, out of a fruitful chaos, it can shape itself in becoming Saturn Line. Also in the sound "M" lies the strength of memory: Our life would flow away like a wave without memory and thinking. It has the strength to unite itself with things and has therefore a deep connection with man's physical body.

The sun goes towards the light: one can have hope again towards the future. The opposite of Aquarius, where we have the coldness of the grave is the Lion, where we have the greatest heat in the year. Aquarius rises to the greatest harmony in man. It is together with Gemini (clarity of cognition) and Libra (justice and spiritual strength for Love) in the triangle of the AIR and the LIGHT ETHER. The Aquarius, those qualities unite themselves with hope and inner joy and serenity. Three light-signs: Faith, Love and Hope.

Astrological qualities of Aquarius have hope, joy, exuberance, and serenity, boundlessly pressing outwards, seeking the new community of man in a revolutionary way. Their sense for freedom is great. They cannot tolerate narrowness and borders, always striving for harmony and friendship - but they can also feel themselves to be superior.

Out of the zodiacal sphere of Aquarius the lower arm and lower legs are formed. In the Eurythmy-gesture, which is the only one which moves, we see the seeking for the balance in the movement streaming from below up and down again continuously. Looking at the two bones which form the forearm we can see, that the joint of the elbow is totally formed by the ulna, which tapers towards the hand, ending there in a small plane to build the joint. The radius bone begins broad, with a large plane at the joint for the hand and then tapers towards the elbow. Very clearly one can see in these two bones the streaming from above, downwards and upwards again.

The same is true for the shinbone, but for the capacity to stand upright, both joints, the knee and the ankle, have their strong unity with the shinbone, whereas the fibula has become a sidebone.

Out of the sphere of Aquarius works that force on man, through which he got the inner movability of the seven planets. Only through these man got his true human form. Through the 7 planets, the 12-fold animal body is coined as the human form. Man's etheric body carries the movability of the 7 planetary forces out of the region of Aquarius.

The sign of Aquarius ♒ was the sign of the closed lips in the old Mysteries: it was the highest secret, to know how man develops from the animal to the human. This secret was told silently - with pressed-together lips.

EURYTHMY "M"

MAN IN THE BALANCE
OF HIS THREE FORCES
OF THINKING, FEELING
AND WILLING

♓ PISCES

☉ *In what is lost, may the loss find itself,*
♀ *In what is gained, may the gain lose itself,*
☿ *In what is comprehended, may comprehending seek itself*
♂ *And sustain itself by sustaining.*
♃ *Through becoming, uplifted to existence,*
♄ *Through existing, interwoven with the becoming.*
☽ *May the loss be gain in itself!*

The theme of the verse resounds as gain - and loss; as the changing relationships of becoming and being, also of accepting and denying. The first two lines show us the positive side, the acceptance of the loss: the downfall of present, existing things gives us the possibility and is the precondition of the new beginning of becoming. But we have to be inwardly ready for the loss in order to be open for continuous new changes: this sounds to us through the Mercury Line.

Our time today is the time of Pisces: 1413 - 3573. It is the age of the fall of old forms of consciousness, of old ties - a time of loneliness and the standing in front of the nothing, the void. It is the time of change also, of new contents and new possibilities.

R. Steiner: *"In pure thinking you will find the Self, which can hold itself"* 1907. If we are able to take hold of ourselves through thinking which is conscious of the I, then we are able to gain new inner stability.

See the Mercury/Mars Line. Jupiter and Saturn Lines: they show us the motif of destiny which passes over from being to becoming continuously. The becoming in one life will be the being of the next life.

The sound "N" is a nasal sound and therefore has a strong relationship to man's inner life. "M" is directed more to the outside. In speaking the "N" we feel the weight more in the direction towards within, the movement rolls back after only a short touch towards the outside. The separation is stronger that the unity, and with it the negation. But "N" is capable for both - to separate and to unite, according to the pronunciation. "N" sounds more conscious and clear, and speaks more to man's thinking qualities, the consciousness: no, never, number, nerve, narrow, number, notice, notion, name, norm, note, etc. Whereas "M" is more connected to man's feeling and his heart. "N" is the sound of destiny: it carries the motif of singling-out, of individualism, of the fleeting movement. It has an inner dynamic and intensity of sensation in words with strong inner emotion.

In our speech it is able to encompass the most opposite poles: from nothing, never - to new, beginning - it is like a phoenix out of the ashes, a sound of resurrection.

There is a deep connection of Pisces to the Christ being. In Christ the polarity of Death and Life is suspended. "In Christ, Life becomes Death" - resounding strongly in the Moon Line. In today's age of Pisces, the Christ-Sun unites itself with the etheric of the Earth. In the Christ Being, the duality of the Macrocosmos and Microcosmos is Harmonised.

I CH TH Y S (*Ichthys* = greek for fish)   Jesus CHrist *Theon HYios Soter*   Jesus Christ God's Son Saviour

WATER - TRIGON : heavy destiny, loss, suffering, serving, others, dependency, hostility, restricted, freedom, chaos, negligence, blurring

Birth   Death   Karma

For the fifth time in world-evolution we experience the time of Pisces in our present world epoch: 1413 - 3573. Again man is loading guilt upon himself, the white race experience the Karma of materialisation. Now is the time to take hold of the spirit of Life to bring about the change, the crossing of the threshold to the Spiritual World.

Out of the zodiacal realm of Pisces the feet of man are built. Man's whole physical body is now complete, and he stands freely between the forces from above and the forces from below. The gesture indicated that man's feet are adequately made to stand firmly on the ground - but now they enable us to lift ourselves off the ground. In walking, we just briefly touch the earth and lift ourselves off from it. With our feet we move across the Earth, seeking for our destiny.

In a magnificent, moveable flexibility the feet have the greatest adaptability to the earth. There is the firm heel; the sensitive toes to feel gently, where we are going, the ball of the foot which rolls with soft malleability in every step, and the miraculous building of the arch which enables us to dive into gravity and rise again out of it. In the foot we see again the three-foldedness of the whole of man

EURYTHMY "N"
THE EVENT HAS
BECOME DESTINY

WORKING WITH THE ZODIAC DURING THE 12 HOLY NIGHTS

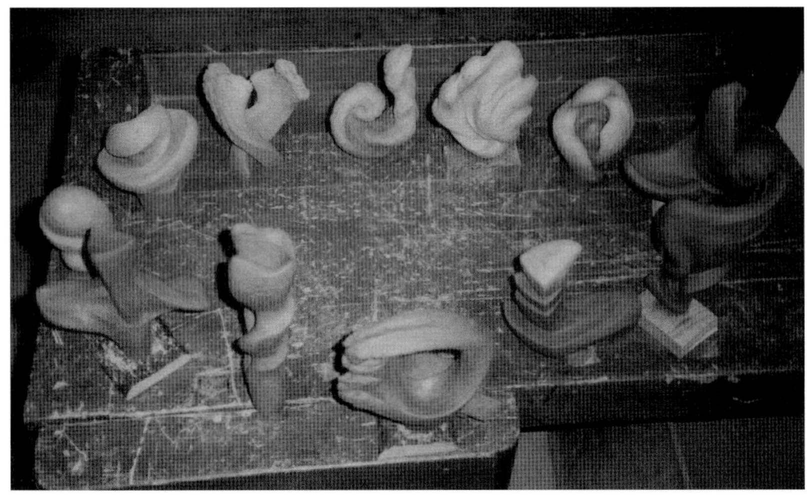

Stimulated by my experience in 1990/91 in Grindelwald, I wanted to create a similar possibility in my studio for this special time of the 12 Holy Nights. This took place three times over the years with a group of interested friends and students. The idea was to meet every day of the 12 days for the whole morning to work artistically. After an introduction, each person modelled, drew or painted out of the zodiacal mood for this particular day. At the end of each morning we showed each other what we had created and shared our experiences. The afternoons and evenings could be spent in nature, in a quiet, contemplative mood, reading, writing – or following one's social engagements. At this time of year it is particularly difficult to extricate oneself from family and friends, so this decision to work with the Zodiac has to be announced early enough to find the necessary space and understanding.

The nature and quality of these 12 Holy Nights and days is like a microcosmic condensation. Different movements interpenetrate: the old year comes to an end and one has the desire to bring things to a conclusion so that the new year can begin unburdened. One can sense true chances for a new beginning. After the winter solstice on 21st December, the sun begins slowly to rise again: the birth of the Christ Child on the 24th December occurs into this beginning rising of the sun and the 12 Holy Days and Nights are imbued and enlivened with this outer and inner happening. The 12 Holy Nights end with Epiphany on the 6th of January, which is the Three Kings' Festival. It is also the day of the baptism of Jesus in the river Jordan, when the cosmic Christ Being united himself with the body of Jesus. One could then say that the space of time of the 12 Holy Nights embraces the transformation of the Jesus child born in the manger, who brought the impulse of wisdom into the world, to the birth of the Christ Being, who brought the impulse of Love into the world. Rudolf Steiner formulates this in the following way:

"The 'wisdom of the outer world' becomes inner wisdom in man from the stage onward of the earth evolution. And when it is intensified in man, wisdom becomes the seed of love. Wisdom is the precondition for love; love is the result of wisdom reborn in the I of man."

From *Occult Science*, GA 13

To spend this time like in a retreat for oneself, creatively contemplating and actively dedicating oneself to the actual forces at work, can throw a new light on the unfolding of one's next year, imbuing it with an inner spiritual strength which can open up other and new dimensions for one's life. Even if it was only possible a few times to celebrate this special time with a group of likeminded people, it always was my desire to spend at least an hour or so on my own every year during the 12 Holy Nights with a particular artistic emphasis. This can happen in many different ways: in small plasticine models, drawing sketches, or painting sketches, contemplating the 12 virtues or the 12 worldviews, or the 12 meditative verses which Rudolf Steiner gave to the eurythmists. Every aspect of the Zodiac can give a concentrating, internalising and inwardly strengthening quality to each day as a counterbalance to an often hectic social schedule.

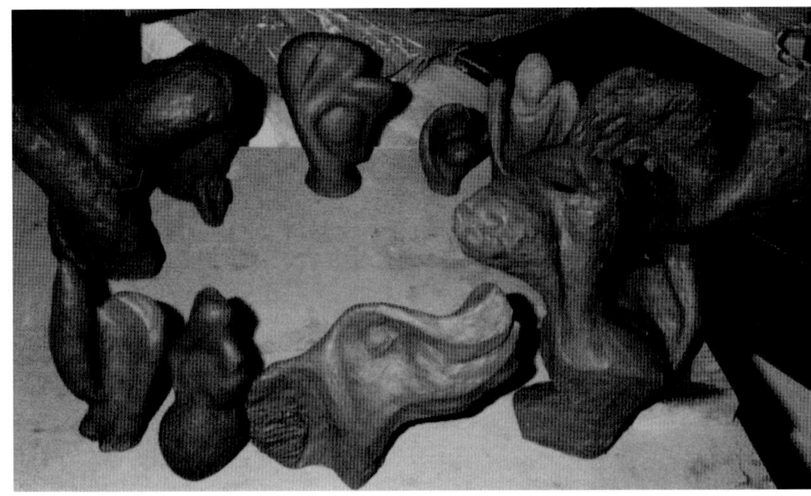

There are three different approaches I know of, regarding the order and sequence of the Zodiac. Starting with Aries on the evening of the 24th December, Taurus on the evening of the 25th December and so on. Esoterically, the 24-hour day begins at 6pm on the previous evening. It is the opportunity for a conscious tuning in with reading a particular text pertaining to the day, in preparation for the following night with its cosmic influences. This was the order Reimar von Bonin introduced me to and with which I have worked. Another order is to begin on the 24th December with Pisces and go backwards to Aquarius, then Capricorn, etc. This will give a different insight into the workings of the macrocosm into the microcosm. Yet another starting point can be to begin with Capricorn on the 24th December, the month in which the 12 Holy Nights take place. Then one could go forward to Aquarius, then Pisces, Aries, etc., or backwards, depending on the emphasis one is looking for. There may be other approaches.

The sun goes through all the 12 Zodiac constellations and has a different force in each one. In this sense one can shed a particular light from each one to the others.

Sergei O. Prokofieff describes in his book, *The Twelve Holy Nights and the Spiritual Hierarchies* how a contemporary spiritual insight into living with the Zodiac during the 12 Holy Nights can be found through Anthroposophy. There he begins with Pisces and ends with Aries. Contemplating these different starting points is a subject leading into important further depths.

Further Reading for the 12 Holy Nights:
Isabel Anderson, *Die Zwölf Heiligen Nächte*, Ogham Bücherei, ISBN 3-7235-1098-1
Cordelia Böttcher, *Das Buch der 12 Heiligen Nächte. Inspirationen für das neue Jahr*, Clavis, ISBN 3-934839-01-0

WORKING WITH COLOUR DURING THE HOLY NIGHTS OF 2017–18
Gertraud Goodwin

Using colour for the first time during my work on the Zodiac during the Holy Nights 2017/18 spurred my interest in the pure Zodiac colours and their expression. I wanted to create an experience as if the formative forces of that particular day would leave a trace on the paper. For a while each day I tried to tune in and listen to what those forces express through colour: a moment of recognition, wonder and surprise. I decided to paint with the oil-crayons I had used since I was a small child. As a background colour I used the colour Rudolf Steiner gave to the eurythmy gestures of the Zodiac. Then I used the three colours for each consonant, which derive from the particular Zodiac realm, also given by Rudolf Steiner to the eurythmists. Each of the three colours has a particular aspect, expressed in gesture, the dress of the eurythmist; feeling, which would be the colour of the veil of the eurythmist; and character, an emphasis of the sound expressed in consciousness and muscle tension in particular areas in the body.

These four colours together were my starting point, different each day.

I deployed the colours boldly. Then I covered the whole card with a dense layer of black. With a sharp letter-opener, I then began to scratch fine lines into the black layer, gradually revealing the colours underneath, slowly finding a mood and a composition. The uncovered colour has changed: it is no longer the pure, sweet colour of Paradise, but has gained a mysterious depth and new dimension. It has had the experience of being extinguished, and is now as if washed and tinged through the tragedy and experience of life: from darkness towards the light. It has become richer, more profound and liminal through this process, as if matured. This process intrigued and interested me.

Black as a colour has now a great presence in the picture. In his *Theory of Colour*, Goethe describes the relationship of the active warm, and passive cool colours to black in the following way:

No. 830. The colours of the active side placed next to black gain in energy, those of the passive side lose. The active colours conjoined with white and brightness lose in strength, the passive gain in cheerfulness.

Wolfgang von Goethe, *Theory of Colour*, Part IV Effect of Colour with Reference to Moral Associations.

It is as if the colours shine through the darkness, the stark contrast giving them an immediate and spontaneous appearance. A sense of the colour's eternal but obscured presence made itself felt, which we perceive only there where we take the darkness actively away: this message shed its coloured light towards my coming year.

From my drawing and sculpture experience, gesture and form were always my main concern. Now the demand was quite different, as the colour itself has its own language in which it wants to express itself. To look for the right balance between just an open field of a colour mood and a gesture for a particular Zodiac quality was my quest.

As quite inexperienced with colour, I felt it was a challenge as well as a gift – but foremost a joy! Colour opened up for me a more intimate inward, and soul imbued realm of tenderness, immateriality and liminality. These seem to be qualities I am becoming more able to appreciate and now am looking for in my late sixties. At the same time, my sculptural work also seeks a more fragile, transparent and open quality.

Every single colour resonated in me, opening up particular qualities:

> **Aries**/*red* made a triumphant, joyous overture into verticality.
> **Taurus**/*orange* moves around a centre spreading with powerful life, vigour, energy
> **Gemini**/*yellow* radiates abundantly into the periphery, not losing itself through binding crossing.
> **Cancer**/*green* drawing inwards, building an inner space of warmth.
> **Leo**/*light blue* spreads itself mightily into the periphery, from where it brings back the forces to its centre, rhythmically.

The first five colours lead one through the "day rainbow", their natural quality can be inwardly followed and experienced directly.

The following seven colours, going from indigo through purples and rose-coloured nuances, offer a more inward, winter experience.

> **Virgo**/*indigo*: Eternally circling/spiralling to internalise and build in.
> **Libra**/*purple*: A serious, centred pondering, sensing the balance of right and left, top and bottom.
> **Scorpio**/*violet*: From the greatest expanse to the strongest contraction.
> **Sagittarius**/*reddish violet*: A circular holding/containing the dynamic diagonal.
> **Capricorn**/*peach blossom*: A decisive vertical centre creates a presence through the horizontal flow.
> **Aquarius**/*pink*: A continuous flow up and down, in and out, giving and receiving.
> **Pisces**/*reddish pink*: The ensouled cross.

The motifs from the designs of the "night rainbow" pictures came to me much more from a previous experience with those particular Zodiac moods, rather than out of the colours themselves. I also tried to keep to the particular "key" regarding mood and gesture with which this sequence was started.

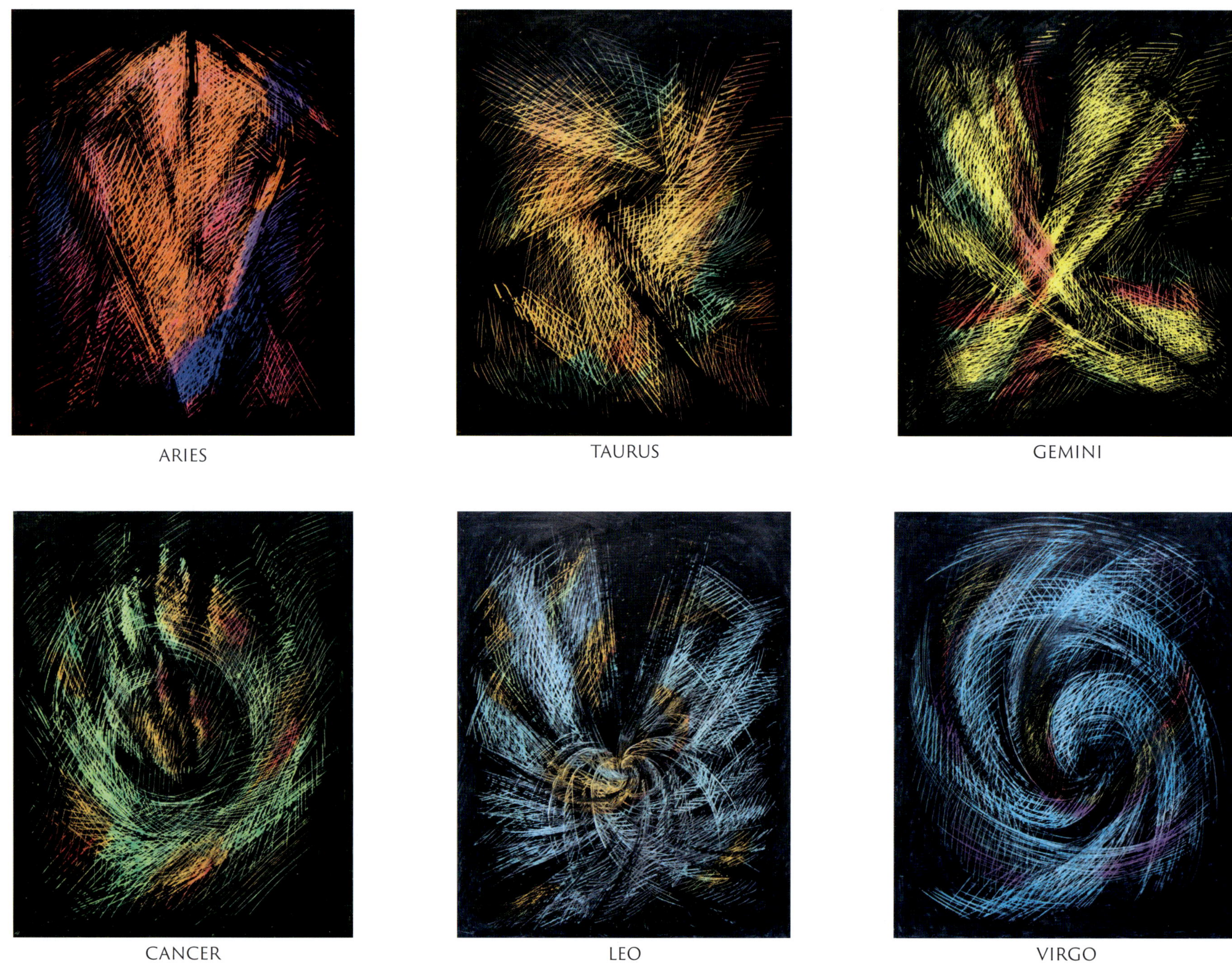

ARIES

TAURUS

GEMINI

CANCER

LEO

VIRGO

LIBRA

SCORPIO

SAGITTARIUS

CAPRICORN

AQUARIUS

PISCES

WORKING WITH COLOUR DURING THE HOLY NIGHTS OF 2018-19
Marije Rowling

2018. 21 x 21 cm. Tissue Paper.

During 2018 I followed each Zodiac sign and made many different drawings of all the changing gestures (see ZODIAC Marije Rowling). Then during Advent I thought about how to give more meaning to the Christmas time. The beautiful translucent colours of tissue paper transparencies have always inspired me in various ways. Then I had the idea to create a small transparency for each of the Holy Nights, based on the Zodiac sequence.

I pinned up all the chosen drawings in the right order as reference, and selected many different hues of tissue paper. My light box was the work surface.

From Christmas Eve onward I again read Prokofieff's corresponding part of *The Twelve Holy Nights and the Spiritual Hierarchies*, referring to each sign for each day. During the next morning, I created the gesture of the corresponding Zodiac sign. So during that time I created the whole series once more.

These spontaneous transparencies could not have been made without all the preparatory work during that year and were a real joy to create.

GEMINI
CANCER
LEO
TAURUS
VIRGO
ARIES
LIBRA
PISCES
SCORPIO
AQUARIUS
CAPRICORN
SAGITTARIUS

ARIES

TAURUS

GEMINI

CANCER

LEO

VIRGO

LIBRA
SCORPIO
SAGITTARIUS
CAPRICORN
AQUARIUS
PISCES

THE FORMATIVE FORCES OF THE ZODIAC
Edwin Boeck

1985. 90/120 cm. Cement and Lime.

In this body of work the idea that the forces of the Zodiac are a true language of form came to me for the very first time. This sequence was created within 9 months in 1985.

First it was sculpted in clay in its original size between 90cm and 120cm, then cast in a mixture of cement and lime in a lost mould process, then worked through to texture and finalise the surface. Each sculpture was worked at with its complementing opposite Zodiac sign – Leo, Aquarius, etc. Through these sculptures, one particular mood of the Zodiac is addressed.

The qualities of the Zodiac can be perceived in their purest form in the formation of man. Rudolf Steiner gave us 12 meditative verses (see also introductions), which give insight into the moods of each sign through the seven lines showing their relationship to the seven planets. There are numerous other relationships, for instance in the 12 worldviews, the seasons and festivals of the year and many others, in which we can find these formative forces of the Zodiac. So the original quest was to make visible these formative forces through the means I had to make them accessible to the onlooker.

As representative examples I will guide through four Zodiac signs, which stand at decisive places in the course of the year, revealing light and darkness – Cancer and Capricorn, and Aries and Libra, which explain the orientation and movement in space.

In Aries, the first sign in the course of the year – the newly arising forces of spring show a bundled, energised formation, rising from below upwards and a gesture from within outward, a tense and fulfilled fiery dedication energising the form into its very surface.

Libra opposite Aries is for half of the year a formation between the light and dark. Movements from right and left are seeking to balance each other in an airy dance. Concave planes show forces, which are directed from without towards inside.

Cancer is the sign for warmth in the height of summer. Man feels himself embedded in a nature fulfilled and slowly dissolving. The sculptural gesture has an inner strength resting in itself. Like the sun, which comes to a moment of rest in its highest point during its course through the year, the sculpture too comes to rest in itself, in its planes. Its movement rests as if in a dreaming sleep. What has been achieved is being enclosed and protected.

Opposite Cancer stands Capricorn, striving towards the light, wakeful and upright. Crystalline planes emerge. The sun is at its lowest point, rising nevertheless. And so the form rises, overcoming the past. Inner form-forces, which have struggled upwards towards freedom, have taken themselves back. Forces from outside have become so strong, that a breakthrough is appearing.

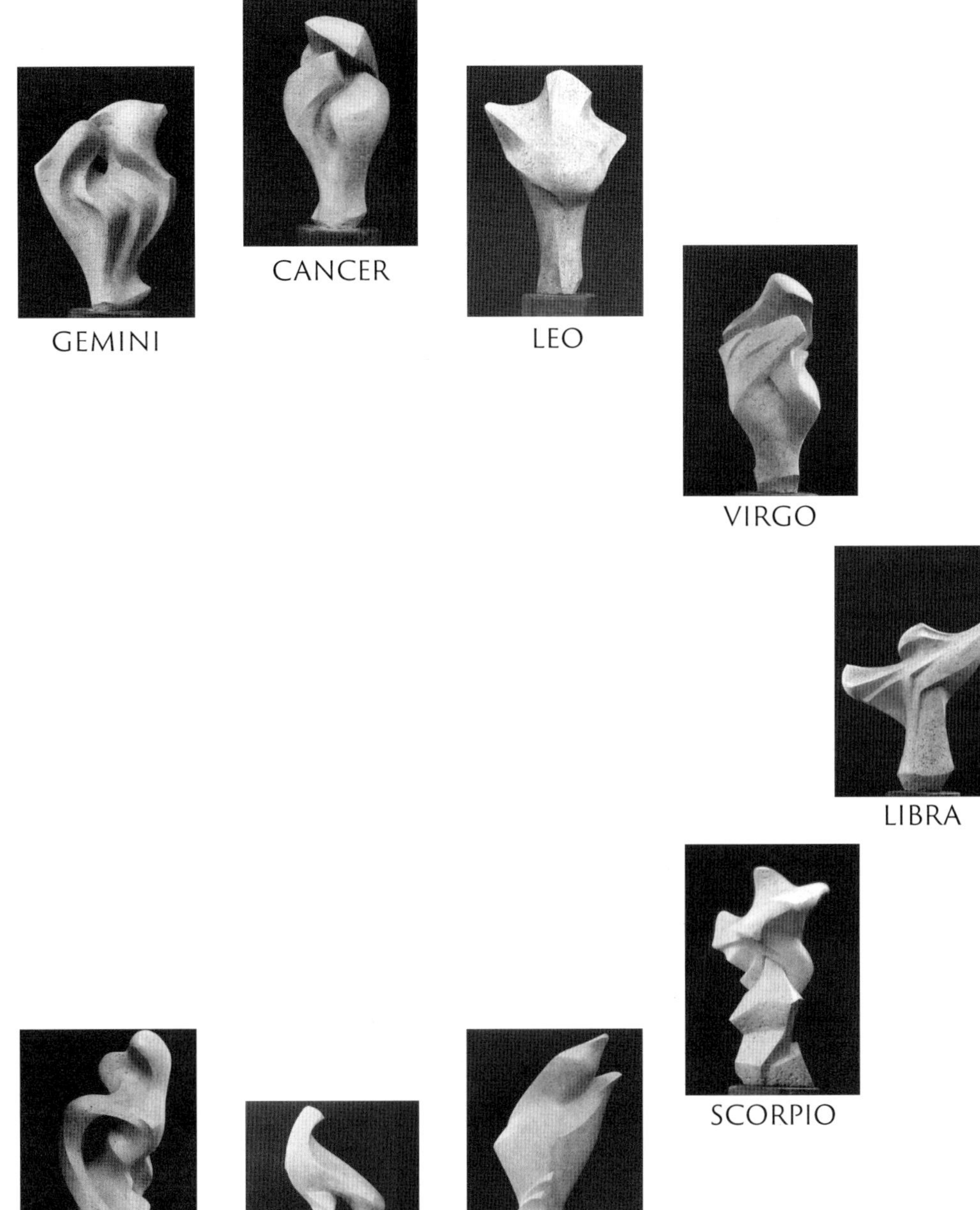

CANCER

GEMINI

LEO

TAURUS

VIRGO

ARIES

LIBRA

PISCES

SCORPIO

AQUARIUS

SAGITTARIUS

CAPRICORN

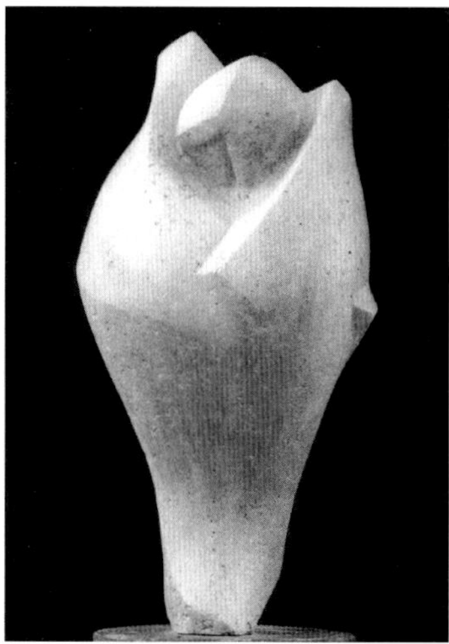

ARIES
Concentrated seed force.
Making its way from below towards above.
Invigorating, awaking by the light.

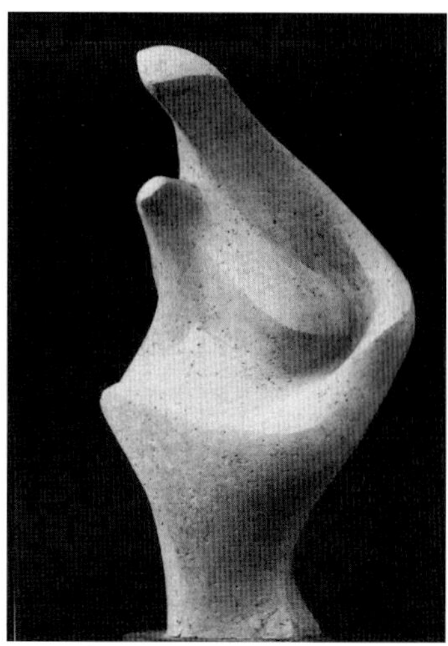

TAURUS
Rooted strongly, stretching.
Feeling the periphery.
Resting in itself. Fruitfully sleepy.

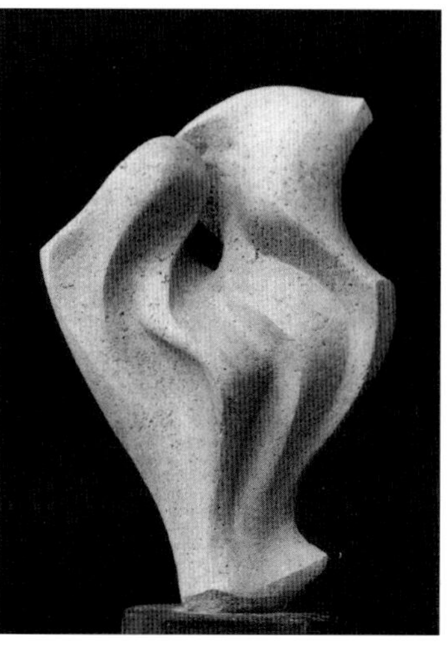

GEMINI
Winged levity.
Dividing itself out of a wholeness and
yet not separating itself.

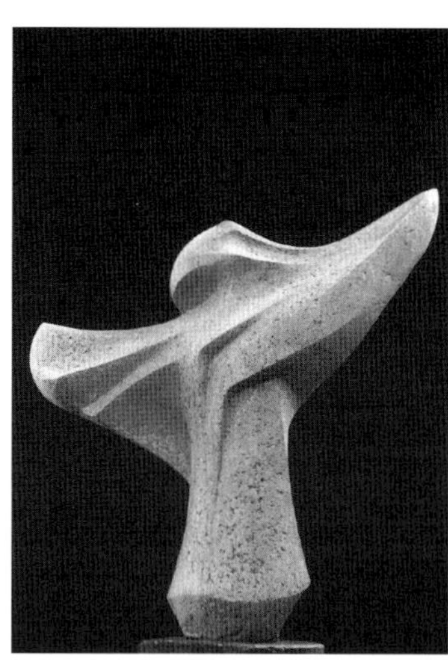

LIBRA
Airy considerate bearing.
Weighing itself in the horizontal
and showing uprightness.

SCORPIO
The below is conquered by the above.
Inner strife as expression of
a seemingly endless battle.

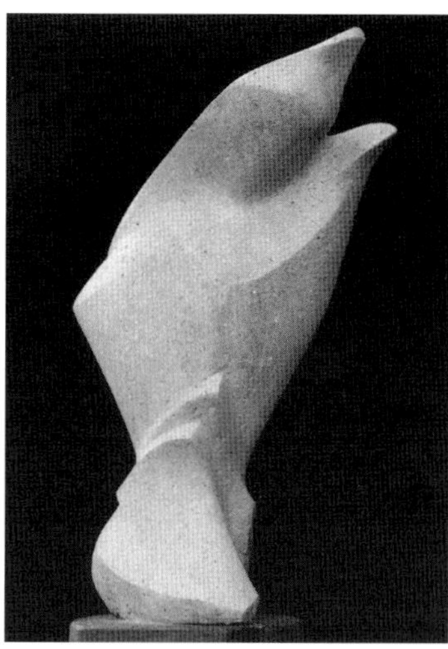

SAGITTARIUS
Aimful willing.
Everything united towards one goal.

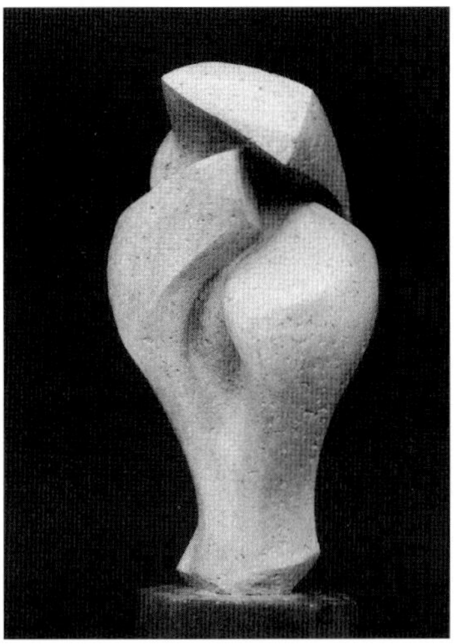

CANCER
Glowingly reaching its height.
Movement filled with warmth.
Preserving something inside.

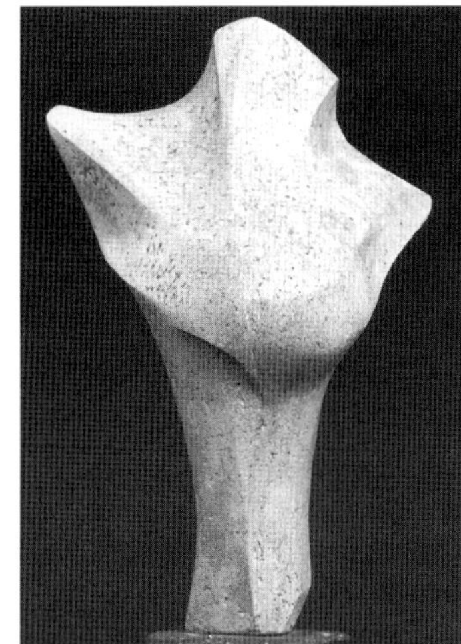

LEO
Glowing radiation of the centre.
Grasping space and experiencing oneself,
losing oneself.

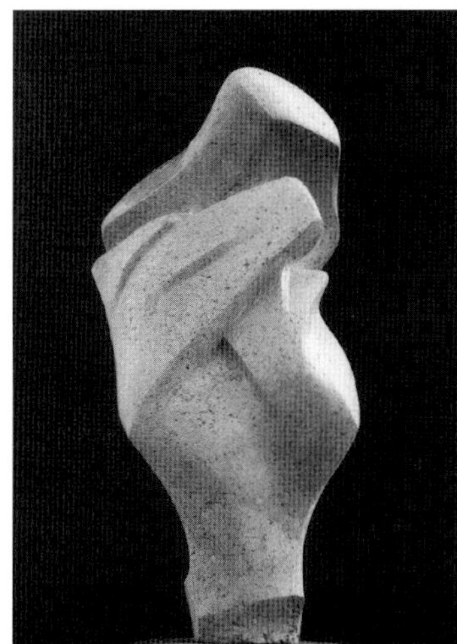

VIRGO
Cooling maturity,
carried towards within and yet
turned towards the world fully awake

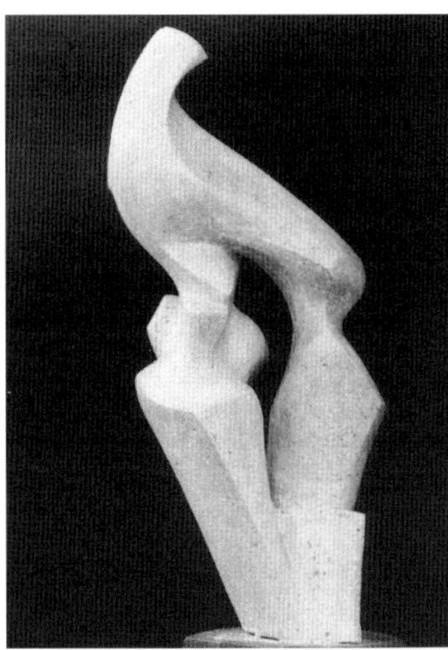

CAPRICORN
Ascending towards height.
The old and hardened is left behind and substance
reduced – which brings clarity and light.

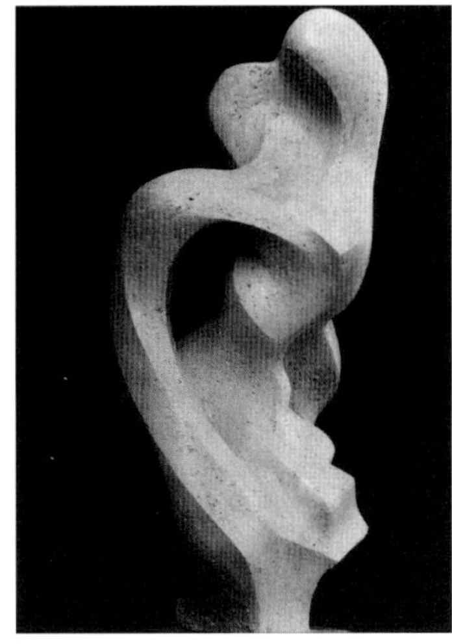

AQUARIUS
Dissolving yet held.
In an arch freeing itself towards levity.

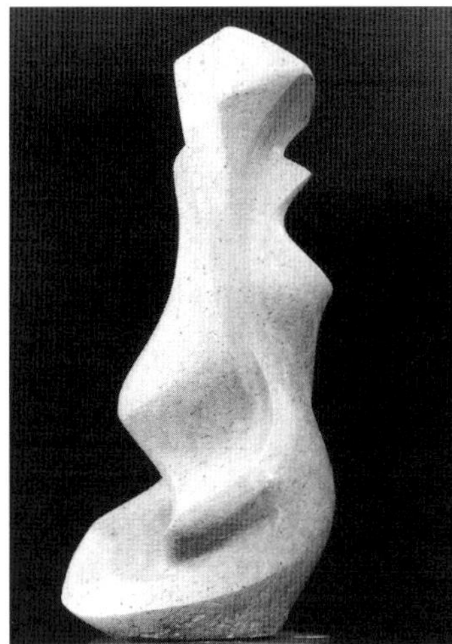

PISCES
Streaming downwards and losing itself,
at the same time ascending with strength
up to the light.

EXPLORATION OF THE SCULPTURAL AND GRAPHIC LANGUAGE OF THE ZODIAC
Dorothea Kuth

2015-2016. 25/40 cm. Patinated Fired Clay.

This work is the dissertation at the end of a three year sculpture - and graphic training at the Hoathly Hill Sculpture Studio from September 2015 to July 2016.

An extensive study of the zodiac from medieval, Rosicrucian and anthroposophic material built the background of this work, out of which that was filtered out, which spoke most strongly. Working on the sculptural gesture first, then drawing it, completing one constellation before starting the next one. This exploration became more and more a research in which all the steps were documented graphically and in writing. The text here is only a very small part of what I originally wrote. The aspects and relationships of the zodiac are very rich and deep, and my first encounter only opened up this vast subject of the Harmonies of the Spheres.

Every one of the zodiacal gestures stands on its own, in its very own quality and individuality, making a whole with the others - so there is no metamorphosis between them. However, during the work on the last three drawings there came to me suddenly with an inner certainty a sense of a true metamorphosis: a movement which goes from Capricorn, uniting past and future, towards Aquarius, uniting man and angel in limitless boundaries to Pisces, where agreement into destiny and karma occurs, so that in Aries the idea of a new beginning can take place.

After ten months of sculptural and graphic work I felt deep satisfaction, greatest trust and gratitude to be bound into this wise cosmic circle as a human being. We all carry a part of each zodiac sign in ourselves, trying to recognise positive and negative qualities which we can learn to understand, to control and to enable in order to develop ourselves further and rise up towards our true humanity.

One can get the impression that this unfathomable wisdom of the zodiac poured itself from the whole cosmos into all of nature's kingdoms. As human beings we can feel ourselves like bound in and guided when we sense these forces of the zodiac in our life and begin to acknowledge and understand them. How much I learned in this year, through the creation of the sculptures and drawings, about nature, my fellow human beings and about myself, is too much to write down here! I am filled with gratitude for this new beginning understanding of the dimensions of man and world which reveal themselves through the zodiac.

Drawings: The compositions of the drawings, always done after the sculpture, lean on the sculptural composition. But through the qualities of light and dark and the possibility to include the surrounding, new aspects opened up which often enhanced and widened the subject for me.

CANCER

GEMINI

LEO

TAURUS

VIRGO

ARIES

LIBRA

PISCES

AQUARIUS

CAPRICORN

SAGITTARIUS

SCORPIO

ARIES

Sculpturally, I wanted to express a dynamic verticality, which finds its forces out of an unrolling convex, three-dimensional spiral. This gesture can be felt like a breakthrough to the light with the fiery forces of Mars. In nature, the growing buds in springtime, exemplify these forces. In man, these forces carry through and accomplish thoughts and deeds in the world.

TAURUS

The forces of Taurus are nourished by the element earth and the planet Venus. They imbue the sculpture with strong life-forces which express themselves through steady, powerful, voluminous and differentiated convex gestures.

The powerful forces of transformation are expressive in nature through expanding form and substance. In man they show themselves in great vitality, and a will to work with endurance and stamina.

GEMINI

The element of air and the planet Mercury coin this sign.

Its sculptural gesture expresses levity, symmetry/duality and movability, held together through a crossing over of the two sides.

In nature, these forces bring the plant life to its full expansion, always balancing out the growth of the whole plant.

In man, these forces express themselves through versatility, playfulness, a disobliging and little endurance. Sanguinity.

CANCER

This sign is dominated by the element of water and the planet Moon. Through a double spiral shaped holding gesture, the inner space created has a watery flow from one side to the other. A reaching out and receiving gesture in between and an opening towards the bottom are the sole communication with the outside.

The process of fructification in the blossoms shows the strength of this sign.

In man, material, homely and comfortable feelings characterise the care and love for family.

LEO

The element of fire and the planet Sun rule this sign. A vortex-like movement goes through the whole form: receiving and open to the periphery, the movement is intensified, swinging from the front to the back and from right to left, thereby creating two open spaces like in a heart.

These forces enable man to have strong self confidence, pride and centre stage, leader capacities. These are coupled with a sense of dignity, courage and a necessity for freedom.

VIRGO

The element of earth and the planet Venus rule this sign. In the sculptural gesture, inner and outer space interpenetrate each other in a gesture which receives and embraces at the same time. The sculpture stands firmly on the ground, expressing trust and inner stability.

In nature this holding gesture enables a quiet and steady ripening of the seeds.

In man, qualities of silence, a sense of duty, patience and modesty are great strengths.

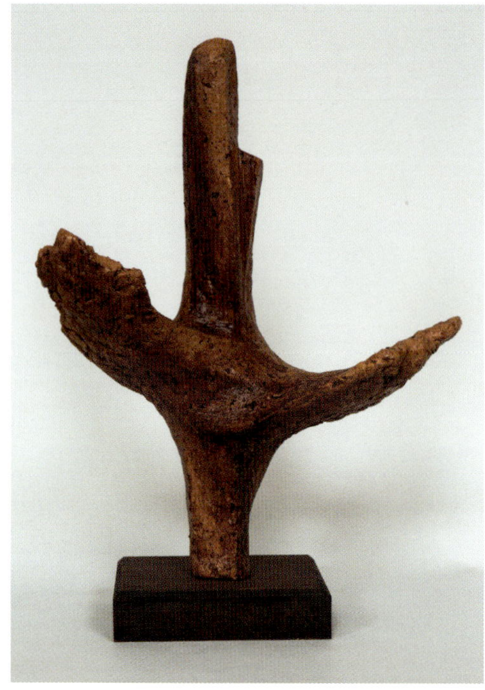

LIBRA

The element of air and the planet Venus give this sign its character.

The sculptural theme is a seeking of an overall balance between verticality/uprightness and horizontality/spreading itself, between centre and periphery, in a moving gesture.

The second half of the zodiac, from Libra to Pisces, shows its forces in nature in more inward capacities rather then outer visible phenomena. This capacity to seek a balance in all circumstances is inherent in all of nature's processes.

In man, Libra gives a sense of harmony and beauty and a capacity for justice, proportion and a balance between intellectual forces and forces of the heart.

SCORPIO

This sign is ruled by the element of water and the planet Mars.

In the sculptural gesture I wanted to express a polarisation between below and above, between a dark and sharp, crystalline bottom and a freeing, light and widely spreading top. Ultimately, this is a question of separation and a healing of this separation. This double nature shows itself in nature in death and disintegration on the one hand, the capacity to concentrate creative energies into the new seed.

In man, a tendency to isolate, contract and destroy can manifest, paired with great intelligence, technical skill, strength of concentration and great ideas, grasping what holds the world together.

SAGITTARIUS

The element of fire and the planet Jupiter are at home in this sign.

The sculptural gesture seeks to express the diagonal: a clear, goal orientated gesture is being held with a counterforce and balanced with verticality.

This tension can result in shooting beyond the goal, in man it can be sharp and insulting, but also creative to the last. A free spirit, interested in the world and wanting to connect all things wisely, man dominated by Sagittarius can also be unreliable, lonely and religious, measuring all on his own goal and vision. The centaur, the animal in man can also fight against his own base nature.

CAPRICORN

AQUARIUS

PISCES

In this sign, the element of earth and the planet Saturn are the creative energies.

In the sculpture, I wanted to express a quality of the present as a connection between the past and the future. It is the time of the end of the old year, and the beginning of the new year.

Characteristics of the animal Capricorn can give insights into the qualities of this sign in man. With a great urge towards freedom and the capacity to jump high and far, the connection to the earth is never lost. Striving to high spiritual ideas, with overview and a hunger for always more, is paired with taking risks, ambition and calm.

The element of air and the planet Saturn rule this sign.

As a fundamental archetype for the sculptural mood, the double curved plane in a three-fold composition felt to me the appropriate choice. Levity in a wing-like, dynamic standing wave, balancing a duality with joy and clarity was to be achieved.
It is a tall order to unite a more human element of boundaries with an angelic, boundless quality with a resting security within.

In Aquarius, all the other signs of the Zodiac are like drawn together to create the perfect human being. Aquarius is more at home in the spiritual world than on earth, but has a longing to be part of all that is on the earth, wanting to help and support altruistically with deep feelings, and a sense of truth.

The qualities of water together with the planet Jupiter rule this sign.

As a sculptural composition, the crossing or cross felt to me expressive of the more earthly flow of water through a horizontal movement interpenetrated by a more cosmic aspect in the vertical, a quality of the threshold to the spiritual.

The motif of gain and loss builds the transition between becoming (Aries) and dissolving (Aquarius).

People born in this sign have an openness for the spirit, a sensitivity for their fellow human beings, expressing itself in empathy, selfless-ness, great adaptability and generosity.

DRAWINGS

2016. First group: 110 x 90 cm. Conté, Graphite and Charcoal. Second group: A6. Pencil.

The drawings were always made after the sculpture. In a large format, they were executed with HB, B and 2B conté crayons and charcoal. From a number of small sketches, I slowly found the appropriate gesture in the large format. During this year of engaging with the Zodiac, much has happened: the drawings developed one by one technically, became freer and more secure in their execution as my own style developed more and more.

Through the mutual effect of light and darkness, this particular kind of drawing enables the unexpressed, the spiritual, the gesture and law beyond the visible to be expressed, by renouncing the sensation of colour and depict these qualities in modest humility. Thus the hours spent with drawing can become like real intervals of meditation – particularly when various techniques of hatching are being used. I would like to say that it is similar to the process of creating a sculpture in clay in that a space opens on the paper into which intuitive elements can quietly stream in. The art is to perceive these "gifts", to enhance them selflessly and not to draw over them inattentively.

Having the quality of beingness of each of the Zodiac moods in my consciousness, the composition and characteristic gesture for each one developed during the process of drawing it. This process was accompanied by considerations regarding the circumference, if it was flooded through by light or confined by darkness, how rigidity of symmetry could be avoided, how movements are carried through and the relationship between light and darkness are expressive of the particular Zodiac mood? Further perceptions then show me, if the whole composition would need quieting down with a layer of lighter or darker hatching. In what kind of relationship is the main motif with its surrounding? Does the motif express the qualities of a particular Zodiac gesture?

Drawing with great openness and with the confidence of intuitive help, well knowing how powerful the influence of the zodiacal forces are on man and the earth, I asked myself: why did I manage to bring the drawing for Libra to such a spontaneous, harmonious conclusion, and why was the drawing for Leo such an insurmountable challenge? How and in which way the cosmic forces intervene and take hold of my being and my doing, asking for self-recognition and my will to develop? Through the drawings I was able to come specially close to these questions: they have fascinated me and will engage me for a long time to come, way beyond the mere skill and technique of light and darkness shaded drawing.

In the middle of my sculptural and graphic work on the Zodiac was Christmas. During the 12 Holy Nights I tried to draw every day one of the Zodiac moods in a small format, starting with Aries on 25th December and going forward to Taurus on the 26th etc. I ordered them in such a way that the polar opposites always stand opposite to each other: I was fascinated how they complement each other in their polarity with great wisdom, and how they mirror the sun's course, our seasons and the development of the plants. The parallel to our human characteristics is likewise overwhelming. What does Aries need from Libra, and vice versa, in order that they may find the right elements to balance and harmonise themselves? Cancer for example is seeking protection with his shell in his own inner space, while Sagittarius always protects himself by climbing and leaping ever higher up with great risk. I could sense how this mysterious and all-embracing wisdom of the Zodiac is poured out over the whole world, the cosmos and all penetrated realms of nature.

As human beings we may feel ourselves guided, bound in and anchored, when we experience and understand these forces of the Zodiac in our life.

CANCER

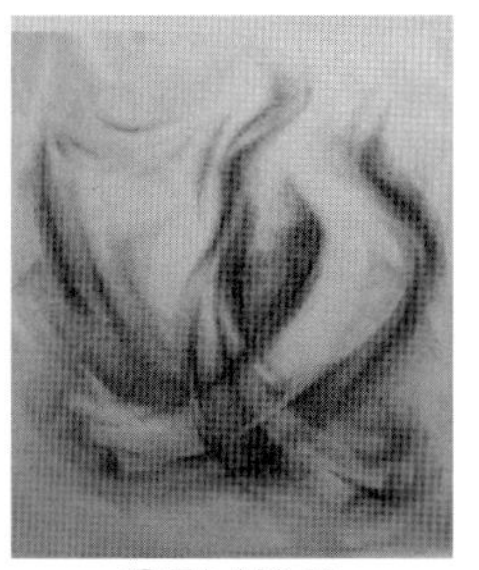

GEMINI

LEO

VIRGO

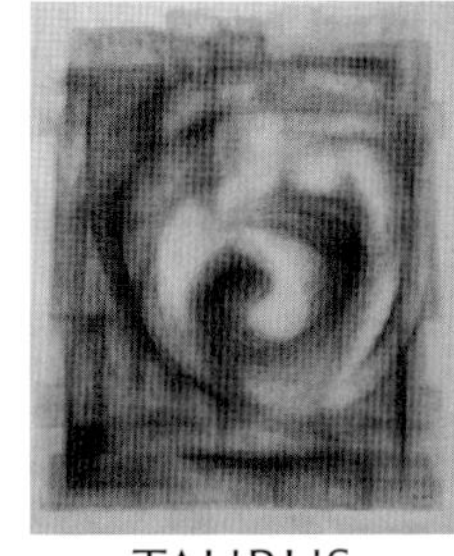

TAURUS

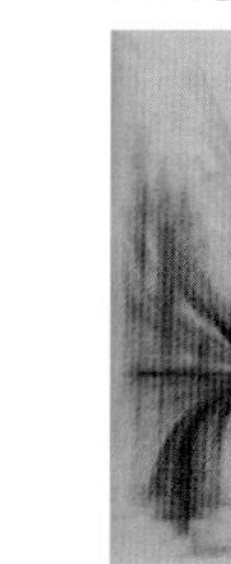

LIBRA

ARIES

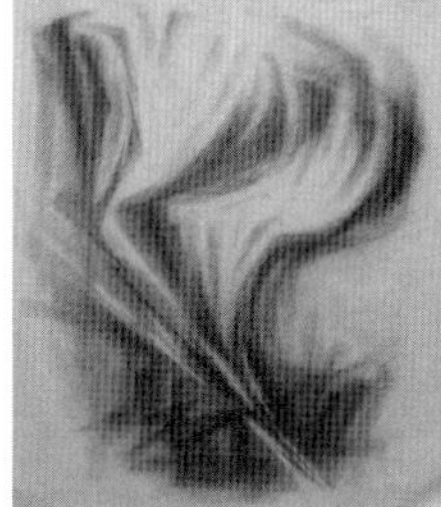

SCORPIO

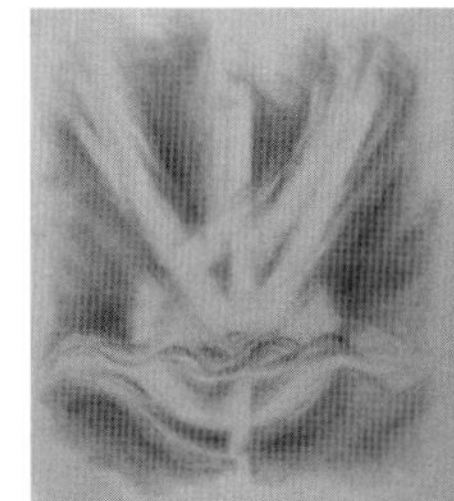

PISCES

AQUARIUS

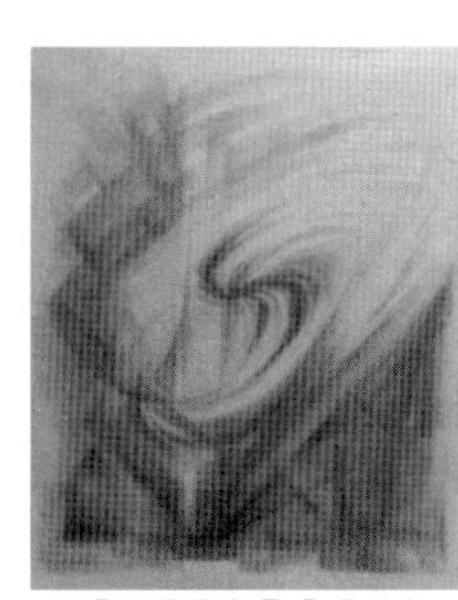

CAPRICORN

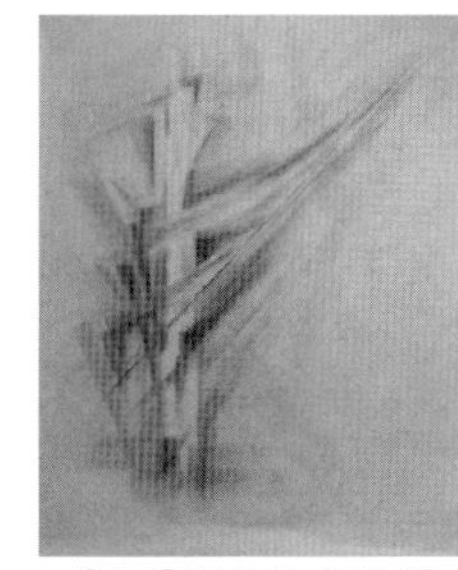

SAGITTARIUS

ARIES

TAURUS

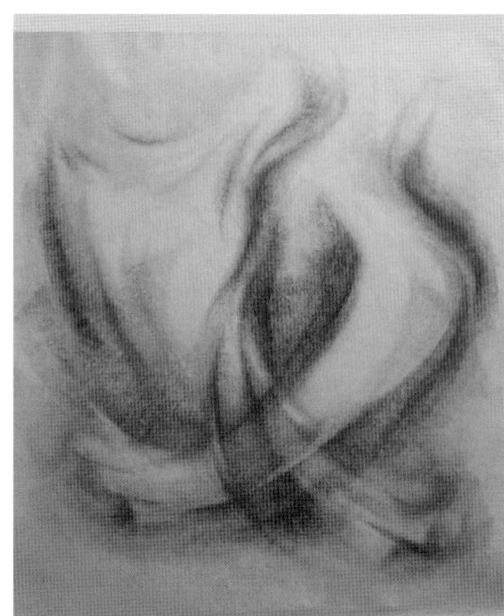

GEMINI

CANCER

LEO

VIRGO

LIBRA

SCORPIO

SAGITTARIUS

CAPRICORN

AQUARIUS

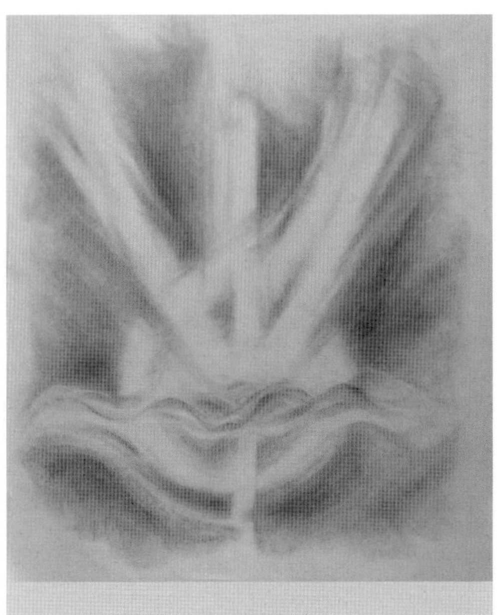

PISCES

ARIES

TAURUS

GEMINI

CANCER

LEO

VIRGO

LIBRA

SCORPIO

SAGITTARIUS

CAPRICORN

AQUARIUS

PISCES

ZODIAC
Manning Goodwin

1994-95. 35 x 45 cm. Patinated Plaster.

A summary of notes put together by Gertraud Goodwin out of various resources as a starting point to study each Zodiac constellation were the basis on which I drew for the sculpture forms here displayed. The reader will see that many of the forms derive in the first instance from the sign that designates the particular constellation being sculpted. While I was still working at the Hoathly Hill Studios there was a group of sculptors and sculpture students who met twice a month for two consecutive days working together on the appropriate mood of the month, sharing ideas and exchanging experiences. Out of this, it became clear to me that there is a wealth of cosmic wisdom which I wanted to explore further. I set to work dedicating all my sculptural time at the Studios to working through each constellation again in a much larger scale, developing the form idea further and eventually casting each form in plaster, patinating each in the appropriate planetary colour. This gave me a reverence for the cosmic forces at work.

CANCER

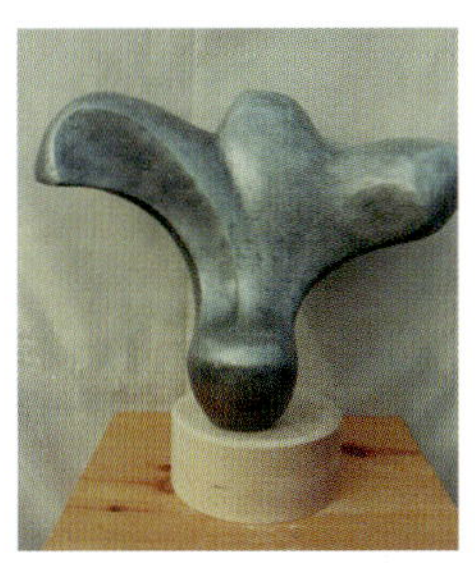

GEMINI

LEO

VIRGO

TAURUS

LIBRA

ARIES

PISCES

AQUARIUS

CAPRICORN

SAGITTARIUS

SCORPIO

ARIES

This is a confident vertical sculpture forked into two directions with a head-like form moving in one direction and the tail-like more passive branch helping to stabilise the movement. It feels as though the movement is flying, leading or even ramming. The form has a sun-like clarity and a Mars-like thrust. One can imagine it as having a glory of bearing and a self-assertion in the light.

TAURUS

The sculpture is reminiscent of the zodiacal sign, like a figure of eight with an open top. It branches above into two powerful movements right and left. It seems in the many burgeoning forms below the two branches to represent a surfeit of bullish strength almost as though it seeks tiredness, laden as it is with weight. But the organ represented by Taurus being the larynx, we can imagine these forms seeking also to express themselves, and in the case of the two forms between the branches, one quickly moving and the other bell-like, that two intonations of the larynx are suggested.

GEMINI

There is a bilateral symmetrical order to this sculpture. The organ for Gemini is the arms, but here they take wing, suggestive of Taurus as the Sign of Lucifer. There is, nevertheless, a centre forward-moving activity reflective of a strong Ego.

CANCER

LEO

VIRGO

The sign for Cancer shows two interlocking forms. The sculpture above shows the two forms in communication and comprehension of each other, each selfless yet prepared to meet each test with vigour. Below, the forms remain separate but formative with an expectancy that now in July the fruit and the seed are beginning to form. Things are made inward, the sun provides warmth as well as the light and through the luminous glow, strength is gained.

The overall shape suggests the chest and heart, having also an inner chamber. The surface is in movement, rippling and throbbing, like a "surging shine of life". The overall form is assertive, standing its ground with courage and magnanimity in a kingly fashion. The sun of August has made further movement from light to heat, ripening the seeds and the fruit. Leo and its form has a sense of life.

Virgo stands on the earth with both feet and an inner firmness. She must take hold of the forces of thinking and cognition: "O soul, Comprehend the beings!" The etheric is strong, supportive of movement, growth and thinking. There is also a turning within into the central verticality – representative of her help within the human 'I', her sense of movement and her 'eyes' remind us that she represents the sense of sight. Virgo is surrounded by dancing movement of forces which help her in enclosing and enveloping herself in a quieting turn within.

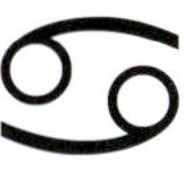

LIBRA

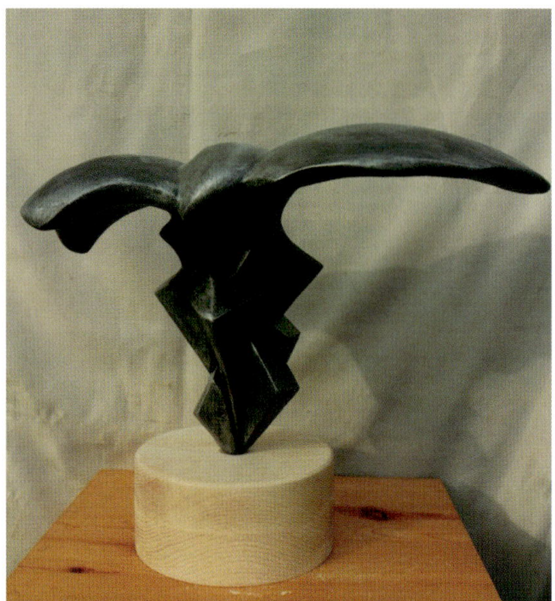

SCORPIO

SAGITTARIUS

The sculptural form derives from the sign for the constellation of Libra with its horizontality and its fulcrum. Libra shows her sense of balance in the two wings, which also indicate her Element as air/light ether. Lightness of being is the characteristic of any scale, and the wings must be of equal weight, completely balanced between levity and gravity. This aids when it comes to balancing out social initiatives, which Libra does well physically but also metaphorically – her world view is Realism, in contrast to the Idealism of Aries. Words suggesting Libra's mood are, contentment, calmness and equilibrium – "O worlds, uphold the worlds!" and symmetry suggestive of aesthetic beauty and harmony, thus bringing to mind Venus, the planet with which Libra is associated.

With Scorpio, begins the sequence of signs relating to man's lower organisation, corresponding to the pole of the will, and in Scorpio's case with the worldview of Dynamism, which sees the world determined by forces of the will. In the sculpture the energetic triangulation beneath the 'eagle' wings, as though from a rocky perch, can also be seen as active will forces sent below, as in a Scorpio's sting.

What human beings take in from outside in their upper being – as in sense perceptions – results in a kind of poisoned sting, which as downward gesture brings inside a forming quality of thinking, like bringing something to a point -- the Eagle is an image for thinking, and Scorpio's virtue is 'patience becomes insight'. On the other hand, in the lower man, the metabolic will and sexual organs come into being and are a forming better represented by Scorpio.

In Sagittarius we are in darkest winter – death is our nearest in nature. But Sagittarius will be victorious, overcoming the sting of Scorpio; death is not an end, but a gateway to new enhanced life. Sagittarius pertains to the will realm. First, the creative capacity is its gift. The sculpture has a definitiveness of three form elements: a central flight or swish upwards, a "trigger" form at the back moving upwards, and rock elements below arresting the movement making the sculpture locked or cocked. Second, the will element turns in on itself, consolidating and becoming firm, a collected force preparing itself for future activity – cocked, the central arrow form ready for flight. The sculpture has strength and its associated organ, the thigh, has strength. The virtue of the sign is 'control of thought becomes sense for truth'– the arrow aims towards the centre. This will-strength aims to a truth based on trust, helping community building.

CAPRICORN

AQUARIUS

PISCES

Out of the grounded cradle form of confidence in the present and secure retention of the benefits of the past, arises a perky, two-folded form, recollecting the past as crystalline in its tail, but moving courageously forward to the future. The sign for Capricorn/Goat bears in its inner rising a capacity to jump up high from a position of rest.

The organ in the body in which Capricorn has its expression is the knee – a place of freedom of movement balanced between the forces of gravity below and the impulses from above.

Although Capricorn's influence is at the darkest time of the year during the Holy Nights, there is in the form a sense of new light arising out of the darkness.

The Aquarius sculpture has a restless seeking quality, moving upwards, but trying different directions, as though striving to be free, but also wanting to find a border for its restless, boundless spirit. By its nature Aquarius is unable to abide boundaries. Does that sound like water? We'll come back to that question later. Spirit has no boundaries. And in quest of spirit we must overcome our own ego, so as to devote ourselves to the spirit. Aquarius has a sense for freedom and can not tolerate narrowness and borders, while always striving for harmony and friendship.

Man's thinking must become completely alive and fluid, like a watery substance, and finally etheric. When this is attained, man is then in a position to understand the impulses of Angelic beings in his etheric thinking. Baptism by water evoked in the baptised a partial separation of their etheric body from the physical, admitting of a direct experience of their Guardian Angel.

In the sculpture we can see a two-sided swish upwards with a contrasting and enabling bulbousness downward feet-on-the-ground settledness below. It is at once a wave-leaping and a plunging form like a fish! Recall the sign: two-sided semi-circles connected in the middle by a horizontal line making an upper and a lower region. There are polarities also in Steiner's verse describing Pisces: gain and loss, accepting and denying, comprehending and thereby self-understanding, existing and becoming.

Our time today in the Pisces Age stands before the void, but has the prospect of new possibilities in thinking and consciousness.

THE TWELVE CONSTELLATIONS (ZYKLUS)
Philip Nelson

2003. 24 x 18cm. Oil, gold, silver, copper, sand, gouache, precious and semi-precious stones, watercolour on canvas.

During the year 1992, I begin to imagine while painting other abstract motifs, that it would be possible to create artistically the twelve constellations of the Zodiac in a completely abstract composition. This would be similar to a mandala; the difference being that it would be a totally Christian esoteric archetypical formation. This realisation that came to me was a force that lived in me through the coming years and accompanied me through hundreds of other motifs. For over ten years, I let it live in me and never made a single sketch or put down a brush stroke on paper, but knew that the right moment would eventually arrive when I could bring forth what was living in my soul.

Finally in the spring of 2003 an art publisher visited me, and after touring my studio asked at the end of the conversation if I would be interested in doing a calendar for his firm for the following year. I responded positively and began immediately that evening to bring forth into the world what had been silently blossoming within me. The starting point for these paintings was a deep engagement with a text by Rudolf Steiner on the twelve moods of the Zodiac. Coupled with the twelve atmospheric colours that Rudolf Steiner had given to stage eurythmists and related colour studies that came from Ilona Schubert and Elena Zuccoli that were lent to me, what had been alive in me all this time was now very rapidly completed in one month. They were photographed, printed and then hung together in a large exhibition in the autumn of 2003.

These twelve constellations were the first of three transformations that I have completed. The other two being the twelve motifs printed in *Metamorphosis – Journeys through Transformation of Form* edited by Gertraud Goodwin, and the *Seven Cultural Epochs* to be printed in 2019.

*

On the occasion of a visit to his studio, Michaela Spaar a journalist, said the following:

"I immersed myself in these twelve paintings. I have the impression as if the luminosity and the power of the colours makes these works glow beyond their discreet grey iron frame. One can only imagine the layers of colour and substances underneath the velvety, shimmering, granular / gritty and partially relief-like surface. Nelson tells me which substances he mainly uses: oil colour, water colour, gouache and pastels, together with different quartz sands from Lanzarote, Africa, Japan and the USA. He grinds precious stones such as opals, azurite and pieces of copper, bronze, silver and gold. The gold shines out of the centre of every one of those paintings. An intensive, inner, almost magical radiance emerges out of these paintings: the transformed abundance of the colours and materials seems to take on a characteristic beingness all of its own.

"In his studio the various materials stood all tidily arranged: here coloured pigments and tubes of colours; there quartz sands from all over the world in containers, on a shelf minerals, precious and semi-precious stones. In another room were special kinds of wood and rusted pieces of metal. Since childhood, Nelson had been collecting things from nature as well as objects which had become unusable. He developed a particular love for the substances of the earth. It is his innermost concern and desire to bring these substances, which are mostly hidden in the earth, into the light; to transform them artistically, to ennoble and spiritualize them. For this reason he also calls these pictures 'alchemical pictures'. The task of man, of the artist is, according to Nelson 'to transform everything; the earth has to become as transparent as a crystal.' The kind of transformation that the individual, dead substances have undergone, can only be surmised. The paintings radiate an incredible strength and intensity. It seems as if they develop out of each other and nevertheless stand completely on their own. The vertical element dominates almost all twelve paintings, the horizontal element is only added with some; a connection of both elements to a cross-like formation with only a few. The cycle as a whole facilitates, alongside a dynamic and harmony an upright strength through which the onlooker/observer finds his own centre." [1]

1. From the article "Die Erde muss wie ein Kristal werden" Nr. H1, 12 october 2003. 82 Jahrgang Das Goetheanum, Dornach, Switzerland.

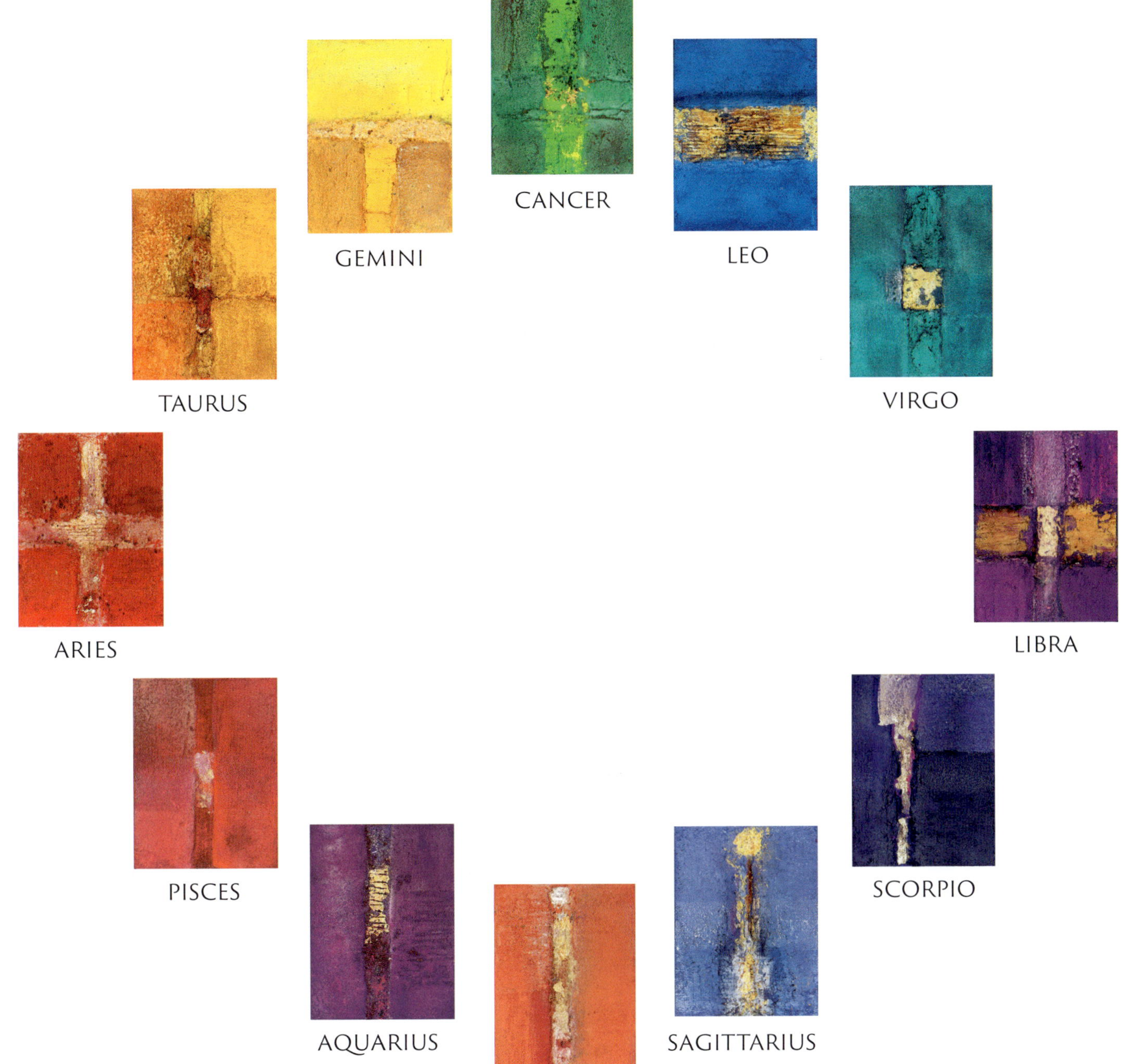

GEMINI
CANCER
LEO
TAURUS
VIRGO
ARIES
LIBRA
PISCES
SCORPIO
AQUARIUS
CAPRICORN
SAGITTARIUS

ARIES
TAURUS
GEMINI
CANCER
LEO
VIRGO

LIBRA	SCORPIO	SAGITTARIUS
CAPRICORN	AQUARIUS	PISCES

TWELVE COLOURED EXERCISES ON THE VIRTUES
Stephan Krauch

2002. 20 x 20 cm. Watercolour and Wax Crayon.

We hope you enjoy the pictures. And if we speak of enjoyment – where do you actually experience joy? In the pictures, or in yourself? Aren't the pictures purely and simply a reflection of the impulses that we carry in ourselves all the time, but which we often do not notice until they are reawakened by the contemplation of a picture that interests us?

In the light of the paradigm change currently taking place in medical research in connection with the wellness concept, questions about joy and inner contentment have acquired a new order of significance. What is at issue is the mobilisation of inner forces through activity on the part of the individual. In these times, marked as they are by unhealthy patterns, uncertainties and anxieties, we need to pay all the more attention to the abilities that lie within us, and the possibilities we have of developing them. One of Rudolf Steiner's many suggestions in this connection was that we should consider those powers of transformation that have been known to humanity since ages back – the virtues.

Stephan Krauch's pictures for twelve months, painted so as to reflect the moods of the twelve virtues, are intended to stimulate an inner dialogue with the person who contemplates them.

As an entry point to this dialogue, each picture is accompanied by a little exercise. This invites you to enter a state of inner stillness. In this self-created inward space of the soul, the qualities of the twelve virtues may be discovered. These are to be found in every human being, as are also the vices. In this way the virtues may be experienced as powers which rise from within us, and not as something that approaches us from without, as is the case with commandments and prohibitions. They are brought to life through our act of attention. This is what spiritual practice with the help of the pictures is designed to achieve.

The exercises were created on the basis of experiences derived from a series of seminars in adult education.

The layout of the exercises results on one level from the virtues themselves. They can be divided into three sets of four.

The first four exercises are designed to stimulate a new way of looking, through the virtues of courage, discretion, generosity and devotion.

The second group of four focuses on the area of relationship. Through inner balance, persistence, selflessness and compassion, my relation to myself, and thus to my environment, will change. The last four exercises, based on courtesy, contentment, patience and mental discipline, bring to light, through the discovery of a new attitude of mind, the way in which I am in harmony with the world.

Claudia Grah-Wittich

JANUARY

DECEMBER

FEBRUARY

MARCH

NOVEMBER

APRIL

OCTOBER

MAY

SEPTEMBER

AUGUST

JULY

JUNE

JANUARY
Courage becomes redeeming power

Every new perception, every change, every development in our lives takes courage. We leave the safe ground of the familiar to embark on unknown and unforeseeable experiences. The courage to commit ourselves to such a course lies within us. If we discover it, a power grows in us which frees us from old patterns.

Perception exercise

Look at the picture. What stands out?
Am I attentive to my first perception?
Whatever I observe, I go with the experience.
The courage to take seriously what I experience in
the process of perception reveals to me
the meaning of the picture.

FEBRUARY
Discretion becomes meditative power

When we can restrain the unasked voice in ourselves and make it fall silent, so that we become quite still, we create a space in which something different is revealed to us. In this way we become aware of the power through which we create our inner images, and observe them. By limiting ourselves in relation to the outside world, we can extend ourselves within.

Perception exercise

Gaze on the picture without intent. Remain a while in this
state. Keep quiet. Shut your eyes, and let the picture come up
before your inward eye. Try to hold onto it.
Become aware of the inner power by means of which the
picture is produced.

MARCH
Generosity becomes love

Just to allow other ways of seeing from that which we are used to, we often have to overcome something in ourselves. Fears and uncertainties may arise. We feel as if we are losing what is our own. By making constantly renewed efforts, we find that openness, interest and understanding come into being. In this process of letting go, generosity can develop; it becomes love.

Perception exercise

Shut your eyes and think of a lovely summer day. It is warm,
and everything around you communicates joy and excitement.
Now look at the picture, and describe it. Then create a mood
of scepticism in yourself. In this critical state of mind,
look at the picture again. Has it changed at all?
In which mood is attention drawn more to the colour, and
when is it drawn more to the form? The mood I am in brings
out different aspects of the picture.
What is the picture really like?

APRIL

Devotion becomes sacrificial power

The whole consists of the individual parts. An idea lies at the bottom of everything. These connections often escape us. Reverence grows through our putting up with apparent imperfection in the light of perfection.

Perception exercise

Let the picture work on you as a whole. What impression
does it leave you with?
Now cover up parts of the picture in succession. Describe
your impressions once more. Take note of the significance of
the individual parts for the whole.

MAY

Inner balance becomes progress

In my interaction with the world, I experience a constant struggle to achieve inner balance. In what relation do I stand to the world? Everything that I perceive requires of me the creative act of participating in the accomplishment of change, requires that I progress rather than stand still.

Perception exercise

Contemplate the picture for a while. Then observe yourself.
How do you stand in relation to the picture, what physical
posture do you adopt, what is your breathing like?
Pay attention to the picture again, and then to yourself.
When are you relaxed, where do you feel constriction?
Where do stillness and movement arise? Switching the focus
of attention between the inner and the outer changes the
quality of your attention and so also your impression
of the picture.

JUNE

Persistence becomes loyalty

Once I have finally reached a state I aspire to, it is soon gone again. Through constant repetition, examination and adjustment of my habits, I repeatedly connect with myself anew and in ever greater depth. Through this direction of my attention, a deep sense of connection is formed.

Perception exercise

Contemplate the picture for a while with full concentration.
Shut your eyes. How much of the picture is retained
in the memory? Now open your eyes, and try
to imprint on your consciousness
the areas that were missing. Shut your eyes again.
Is part of the picture still missing? Look at it again.
Quietly and patiently, you let your attention travel to the
picture and back to yourself again.
Your relationship to the picture continues to grow.

JULY
Selflessness becomes catharsis

Letting go of our image of ourselves is like a leap over the abyss, leading to an intuition of our true selves. Suddenly something can come to meet me from without, which I prevent so long as I continue to hold on. A process of purification takes place.

Perception exercise

Contemplate the picture,
allowing yourself to comment spontaneously. (Do I like it?
The previous picture was better! It looks like ...)
Then let yourself become quite quiet, still and relaxed.
Contemplate the picture again.
Wait.
Does the picture tell you its story?
How has your first impression changed?

AUGUST
Compassion becomes freedom

By turning to an object, allowing my feelings to respond to it and experiencing compassion, I open myself to what things are trying to tell me in a way that goes beyond their physical appearance. If I pay attention to the after-image that is created in this state of mind, reality reveals itself to me from a new angle. Through the self-created after-image, a new dimension of relationship comes about.

Perception exercise

Look at the picture with full concentration.
Stay with it for a while.
Then direct your gaze to a white surface.
How do the colours appear on it?

SEPTEMBER
Courtesy becomes tact of the heart

It is not difficult to complain of discourtesy, or to observe the egotism that is at large in the world. How can I change this, without myself becoming too demanding, or remaining stuck in rigid, insincere conventions? How do I behave, so that people will respond to me with understanding? There is a key to be found in the symmetry of response. Finding one's own rhythm, of opening up and staying within oneself, allows connections to develop. In this way I can become the shaper of my relationships.

Perception exercise

If the red could speak, what would it say? The colours and surfaces that surround it approach it tactfully.
They ask, »What do we have to be,
to permit you to express yourself?«
The colours conduct a mutual dialogue. What do they say?

OCTOBER
Contentment becomes composure

I am myself responsible for my inner state at all times. I cannot make changes to my surroundings, but I can at any time see to it that I am content. In this state I can look at my surroundings with composure and confidence.

Perception exercise

For a moment, become perfectly still and relaxed.
Enjoy the picture. Let a sense of contentment come about, allow yourself to feel it. Stay with it.
Sense how pleasant this state of composure is. What kind of connection do you feel between yourself and the picture?
Does it reveal itself to you inwardly
for a moment?

NOVEMBER
Patience becomes insight

To understand anything, I have to have patience. Patience is the process of maturation to which all becoming is subject. If I subordinate myself to this, I can begin to see through the appearances of things.

Perception exercise

Describe the picture as you would to a blind person. What colours and forms can be seen, and how are they arranged? Describe for the blind person what feelings are produced by the various colours and features of the picture. Monitor these feelings, and keep on monitoring them as long as is necessary, until your inner images are in harmony with the outward picture. Do you find your insight has grown?

DECEMBER
Mental discipline becomes the sense of truth

With the courage I have already developed, a courage that enables me to take myself seriously as an object of contemplation, I observe my thoughts. My capacity for drawing distinctions and my sense of truth grow as my power of concentration increases.

Perception exercise

Imagine for a moment that you are the red in the picture. What would you say? Formulate a sentence in the first person. Check the sentence. Is it correct?
Are you in harmony with the picture?

PAINTINGS ON THE ZODIAC
Rolf Janssen

1998. 100 x 100 cm. Oil lazure with pigments.

For the occasion of the 25 year anniversary of the Christian-Morgenstern school in Reutlingen, Germany (a school for children with learning difficulties) I was asked to make paintings of the Zodiacal moods for the entrance hall. As a starting point, Rudolf Steiner's verse *"The stars spoke once to man"* became important for me. The circular architectural shape of the entrance lobby offered itself beautifully to create and position the paintings following the movement/course of the sun through the year. Guiding principles were the four elements of earth, water, air and fire:

Earth: Taurus, Virgo, Capricorn
Water: Cancer, Scorpio, Pisces
Air: Gemini, Libra, Aquarius
Fire: Aries, Leo, Sagittarius

I began with the painting for Libra, the breath of God, air sign, Michaelmas, working at the same time forwards, to Scorpio, and backwards to Virgo, etc. Thus the last painting was for Aries, the fire of purification, renewal, Golgotha, the Lamb of God.

My time of creating the paintings started at Easter, and they were then completed and exhibited at the time of Michaelmas. As the paintings were created in a number of thin layers, they had to dry in between. This enabled me to work on several paintings at the same time, meditating their deeper meaning while adjusting their colouring and compositions.

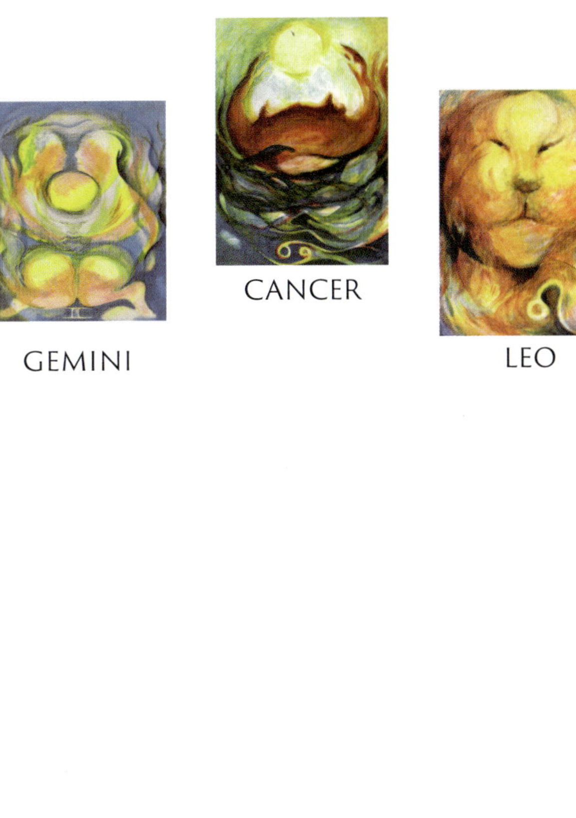

GEMINI

CANCER

LEO

TAURUS

VIRGO

ARIES

LIBRA

PISCES

SCORPIO

AQUARIUS

SAGITTARIUS

CAPRICORN

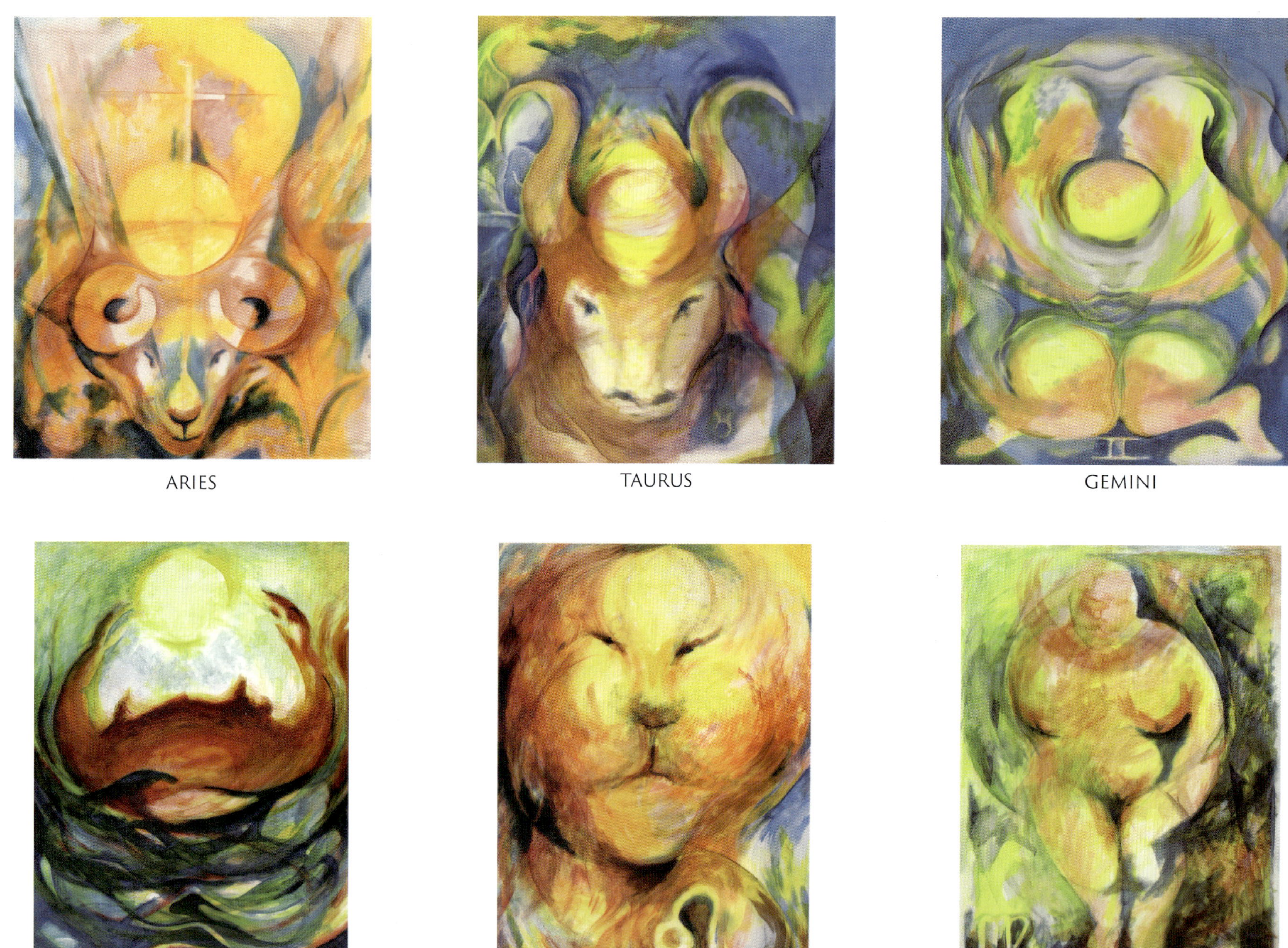

ARIES
TAURUS
GEMINI
CANCER
LEO
VIRGO

LIBRA

SCORPIO

SAGITTARIUS

CAPRICORN

AQUARIUS

PISCES

ZODIAC
Doris Harpers

1993. 70 x 100 cm. Watercolor and Pastel Crayons.

Doris Harpers' Zodiac paintings are based on Rudolf Steiner's indications concerning the colours of the signs of the Zodiac for the eurythmy gestures. Rudolf Steiner, the founder of anthroposophy, had taken up and developed Goethe's Theory of Colour, showing how every colour brings its own nature and power to expression. Spiritual investigation into the powers of the Zodiac can indicate the colour atmosphere most suited to reveal their qualities.

The human form is consistently represented by forms relating to a eurythmy gesture which seeks to show the special character of the sign and the way in which people whose sign it is relate to the world. (In eurythmy, the aim is to bring the sounds of words and of music to expression in physical movement.) The Zodiac does not exist, however, to show separate special characteristics but as a challenge to us all to overcome bias and arrive at a balanced harmonious whole that allows us to create community with others. The colour white therefore appears in every painting, representing the highest spiritual aspect of man to which we may refer in our search for harmony.

GEMINI
CANCER
LEO
TAURUS
VIRGO
ARIES
LIBRA
PISCES
SCORPIO
AQUARIUS
SAGITTARIUS
CAPRICORN

ARIES

TAURUS

GEMINI

An atmosphere of interpenetrating lines of forces, suffused with light and colour, recalls the radiating, formative qualities of the quartz crystal silica.

In Rudolf Steiner's description of the evolution of the earth, he emphasises how the human being gains his vertical, upright position through the formation of the nerve-sense organisation in the head and the vertebral column, in order to become the carrier of his spiritual essence, his "I".

This forms the basis for his capacity to think and to counteract the forces of gravity.

The painting shows us movements from within outwards, like concentric waves, permeated with colour. In the constellation of Taurus, the origin of sound and the word have their domain: the word of our larynx, as expressive of the movements of soul, from within outwards, from mouth to ear, from soul to soul.

Among the four symbols of the evangelists, Taurus represents St. Luke, the therapist, the author of the Gospel of Love.

The forces from the constellations of Gemini give us the symmetry in our whole body – a precondition to experience oneself on the earth, giving us the sense of solidity in ourselves.

On this foundation, we can open ourselves towards the world, which gives this sign a double movement: physical solidity and a levity of soul.

These polarities are represented in the painting through a centre, from which the energies from within enliven and lighten the circumference in yellow tones, freeing themselves from the weight of physical matter.

CANCER

Through the constellation of Cancer, a gesture of drawing inwards is experienced, expressing itself in the ribcage which houses heart and lungs. The great universal rhythms become concentrated and individualised in our middle region.

We take about 18 breaths per minute, which comes to 25,920 per day. It takes the sun 25,920 years to go through all the zodiacal constellations to return to the same point of her rise on the 21st March. We call this a platonic year.

The image in the painting gives this sense of isolation through a centre light in a green surrounding. It is the light arising in us with the realisation that we are individual spiritual beings.

LEO

This representation strikes us through its rhythmic colour movements which unfold like a vortex of warmth from the middle region of man.

It is the warmth of enthusiasm and courage for an ideal, which opens our heart to the world. Not the cold intellectual thoughts that flow into our actions, but a "knowing heart", which reflects what lives in the human soul. True free deeds can be born out of a knowledge of the spiritual laws. Our will to move in harmony with the world, brings our individual creative contribution to it.

From this "knowing heart", the old law of an "eye for an eye" can transform into a "turning of the other cheek", towards a creative, artistic collaboration with the divine.

VIRGO

This image for Virgo is characterised through an intense spiritual blue light, born out of a devotional inner atmosphere. In this inner light, the self finds in silent dedication its own spiritual dimension.

In man, the region below the diaphragm with its mysterious and wisely working organs of our digestive system works according to universal cosmic laws.

The gesture of Virgo encloses something precious, in the way the womb encloses the growing embryo.

LIBRA

Through our pelvis and hipbones, man is enabled to feel his balance and is firmly rooted through the gravity of the earth. Right and left, front and back, above and below find their equilibrium between levity and gravity through the firm foundation of the pelvis, which carries our vertebral column.

In the painting, we see the human figure in a gesture of balance between the light and the dark colours, between the rising and descending forces.

The Autumn Equinox brings us a predominance of earth forces, a retreating of the earlier cosmic forces of spring and summer.

SCORPIO

In this painting we see above a white bird in flight like a metamorphosis of the human figure.

The forces of sexuality carry life as well as death in their possibility to bind us too strongly to the earth and our egotism.

It is man's task to transform these forces and re-connect himself with higher spiritual spheres for which he is predestined.

SAGITTARIUS

Here we see radiating forms of light prevailing through the painting. Out of an atmosphere of darkness, shafts of light emanate, in which the human figure itself places itself in a radiant gesture.

Older representations of Sagittarius show us the centaur, with the body of a horse out of which a human figure emerges, holding a bow and arrow.

This image can be understood as a symbol of taking a measured decision out of oneself.

CAPRICORN

In nature, we perceive the (animal) goat high up in the mountains between earth and sky as a highly skilled climber and jumper, always up to new horizons and destinations.

This dynamic expresses itself in those of man's life forces, which bring fluidity and movement into stagnant tendencies, bringing harmonious cooperation between both forces into our whole organism.

Like the plant is able to harmonise all its different paths between its root, stem, leaves and blossom, man searches to balance in himself the spiritual world and the earth.

AQUARIUS

The forces of Aquarius enable man to move freely and lightly among men and the world.

In the painting we see man in an atmosphere of life, where air and water intermingle in a harmonious balance between inside and outside.

Through our spiritual essence, our I, we can bring order and clarity into our uncertain and nebulous feelings to direct our actions towards a right and good goal.

PISCES

In a concluding gesture of prevailing dark colours, the painting develops an impulse of light and life.

Something which is prepared in the dark silence manifests itself in life, taking on form. *"The event becomes destiny"* ... Rudolf Steiner's words for this sign. The symbol of Pisces stands for the Being of Christ.

Man's feet with which he walks his destiny on earth, are created out of the forces of Pisces.

ZODIAC
Marije Rowling

2018. A4. Coloured Pencil.

How do you truthfully and artistically portray the Zodiac? As an artist I need to be inspired to get started, ideally by a subject and a medium. But the Zodiac is so far away, so big, so mighty and so all-encompassing!

For many years Nature's moods and gestures have given me that inspiration. I worked on the Zodiac before. That was done loosely following Rudolf Steiner's colour indications, non-figuratively on large canvasses. This time I wanted to go deeper, but how? For three months I studied many texts whilst trying out various approaches and techniques. But I could not see the correlation between my small artwork and the mighty heavens. It was quite a trial, and several times I felt like giving up.

Then one sunny Spring morning I took my daily walk beside a local stream. Wild plants were jostling for growing space and at that moment I saw the gracious gift of Aries in the plant world. From then onwards sign after sign started to link up with Nature's increasingly strong unfurling and growth. That process went on till the height of Summer when Nature's exuberant out-breath slowed right down. What was I to do now? Again it was a 'chance' observation - the first tiny seed that started the next phase. Nature during Cancer (the crab with its hard exoskeleton) started an in-breath. My drawings became round without me noticing it at first!

In the withering Autumn I was struck how mankind celebrates Death in so many different ways. And when all outer existence gets increasingly dark, there are more and more festivals of light. Nature's grand in-breath, with its call for inner light, created a colour image of a lemniscate in my mind. Rudolf Steiner's indications show the rainbow colours for the Spring, Summer and Autumn. But for the Winter months there is a mysterious sequence moving from a dark blue violet, through six increasingly lighter and more pink colours to a pale rose. During the Sagittarius time there is an up-building of an inner light (Advent). The new buds outside are there, quietly waiting.

Then during the Twelve Nights in Capricorn, just like the Goat which can suddenly jump straight up, a big Solar turnaround takes place. It starts with a change in the quality and quantity of light. Nature responds with the first upward-thrusting shoots of the flowering bulbs. Nature is waking up. In Aries (the thrusting pushing Ram) the new out-breathing is well on its way and the sequence starts again. Over the following Twelve Holy Nights I created the whole series day by day in transparencies, inspired by Prokofieff's book on this subject. (See chapter Working with colour during the Holy Nights of 2018-19, page 34)

To finish, I want to whole-heartedly thank Gertraud for gently prodding me into action with her inspirational work and words, and encouraging me to continue when I felt like giving up.

And I fully recommend all artists to try and find a personal approach to this most marvellous of subjects.

Quotations following the illustrations are taken from Steiner's Sun Line from the Verses on the Zodiac. They are followed by the characteristic gesture observed in Nature.

TAURUS
GEMINI
CANCER
LEO
VIRGO
LIBRA
SCORPIO
SAGITTARIUS
CAPRICORN
AQUARIUS
PISCES
ARIES

ARIES
'Arise, O shining light'.
Strong upwards growth.

TAURUS
'Shine forth, O glory of being'
Unfolding

GEMINI
'Reveal yourself, life of Sun'
Furthest into the Light

CANCER
'You resting, luminous glow'
First turning inward, first seed formation

LEO
'Invigorate with senses' might'
Greatest Summer expansion

VIRGO
'Behold the world, O soul'
Ripening

LIBRA
'The worlds are sustaining worlds'
Balance of Light and Dark, inwardness and outwardness

SCORPIO
'Existence consumes the being'
Dying back, Darkness and Weight, also Light Festivals
overcoming darkness

SAGITTARIUS
'Becoming achieves the power to be'
Building up of an inner life, seed-like

CAPRICORN
'May what is coming, rest on what has been'
A mysterious rebirth of the Earth and Man

AQUARIUS
'May what is bounded yield to the boundless'
Sap rising, life returning

PISCES
'In what is lost, may the loss find itself'
Plant life begins to respond to the upward thrust

SOUND IMAGES
Gerard Wagner

1993. 54 x 73 cm. Watercolour: plant-based pigments.
Rudolf Steiner's 'Twelve Moods' Paintings by Gerard Wagner.

The verses of the *Twelve Moods* were composed by Rudolf Steiner in 1915 for the new art of eurythmy. In this 'cosmic poetry' the sounds of human language are put before us as archetypes of creation intimately connected to the starry heavens. Here the colours of the cosmos become visible and reveal their relationship to the forces of the planets and the Zodiac.

As the seven colours of the rainbow correspond to the seven planets and the vowels, the twelvefold colour circle, created by Rudolf Steiner, has a direct relationship to the Zodiac and the consonants.

The *colours* of the **zodiac signs** with their corresponding sounds are:

Aries, *red*, "W"   **Taurus**, *orange*, "R"   **Gemini**, *yellow*, "H"

Cancer, *green*, "F"   **Leo**, *light blue*, "T"   **Virgo**, *indigo*, "B"

Libra, *violet*, "CH"   **Scorpio**, *dark purple*, "S"   **Sagittarius**, *light purple*, "G/K"

Capricorn, *peach blossom*, "L"   **Aquarius**, *light pink*, "M"   **Pisces**, *dark pink*, "N"

The *colours* of the **planets** are:

Sun, *white*; **Venus**, *green*; **Mercury**, *yellow*; **Mars**, *red*; **Jupiter**, *orange*; **Saturn**, *blue*; **Moon**, *violet*.

A further dimension of this colour cosmos reveals itself when we learn that every consonant, in its corresponding eurythmic gesture, is built up out of three colours given in a specific order. Rudolf Steiner characterises these three colours as: 1. Movement. 2. Feeling. 3. Character. For the consonant 'W'(Aries), for example, the colour of <u>movement</u> is blue, the colour of <u>feeling</u> is purple and the colour for the <u>character</u> is red. This threefold colour sequence then 'sounds' through red, through the Zodiac colour corresponding to Aries. This is how the 'W' of Aries expresses itself.

Gerard Wagner, as part of his colour research, worked with the colours of the eurythmy figures for many years. He painted first the colour of the zodiac sign as a background colour, and then painted the three colours of the consonant in the order given as: movement, feeling and character. The medium used was watercolour; the colours plant-based pigments. The two-dimensionality of the picture surface together with buoyant colour, not subject to gravity but ensouled and in movement, can lead the onlooker beyond the physical form into the etheric realm.

Working with the formative forces within the colours in this form can be a deepening towards understanding of human language and its cosmic origin. Here, where the creative forces of colour, sound and movement are united, we are given a sense of the dominion of the 'Cosmic Word' which sounded at the beginning of time.

Living with the *Twelve Moods* can given lasting 'cosmic nourishment' for the human soul.

Dornach, 25th February 1996 Elisabeth Wagner

GEMINI
CANCER
LEO
TAURUS
VIRGO
ARIES
LIBRA
PISCES
SCORPIO
AQUARIUS
SAGITTARIUS
CAPRICORN

ARIES
RED, "W"

TAURUS
ORANGE, "R"

GEMINI
YELLOW, "H"

CANCER
GREEN, "F"

LEO
LIGHT BLUE, "T"

VIRGO
INDIGO, "B"

LIBRA
VIOLET, "CH"

SCORPIO
DARK PURPLE, "S"

SAGITTARIUS
LIGHT PURPLE, "G/K"

CAPRICORN
PEACH BLOSSOM, "L"

AQUARIUS
LIGHT PINK, "M"

PISCES
DARK PINK, "N"

FIRST ZODIAC
Gertraud Goodwin

1987-88. 50-60 cm. Clay.

During my sculpture therapy training, (4th and 5th year), my teacher Reimar von Bonin spoke of the zodiacal form forces and we made a few very simple sculptural exercises. I did not really understand then, what he meant and the exercises did not make a lasting impression on me. After my training I taught in various places for seven years and opened my own studio in 1987, the Hoathly Hill Sculpture Studio where I worked and taught until 2018.

During my 7 years of teaching, I had hardly done any of my own work and now felt empty and depleted ... and was well aware that I had little language of form I could call my own. While teaching, explaining and demonstrating had left my own sculptural development far behind, in fact I sensed that I had not yet made my own what I had been taught during my training ... Where was I to begin?

It must have been a rare moment of a true imagination, which was a cry for help at the same time, in that I began to search for a language of form through the form forces of the Zodiac. I worked for a year on all twelve forms, with the background of the four elements, the planetary relationships and Rudolf Steiner's verses of the twelve moods for the eurythmists.

As a budding sculptress I asked myself what kind of forces make a sculpture. Living with this question I found more and more that the forces which form nature must have the same origin as the forces I experienced in my sculptural work. I discovered flat planes, angles, corners and edges in a multitude of different relationships in my sculptural work, all of which form the mineral world.

I found that differentiated convex formations in my sculptures appear in nature at the early stages of plant development as well as in the embryology of animals and man. I experienced, how the concave in sculpture invites me inside, showing me an inside world of soul gestures and interiors, which I recognise in everything, which I look at with interest and love. These findings made me feel at home in my sculptural work in the same way as in nature. I sensed ever more strongly, that the form forces which are creative in both have the same origin.

From medieval drawings, paintings and texts I learned that the whole build-up of man's body has its origin in the zodiacal forces, and that each particular part of man's body originates in one area of the Zodiac. By "Zodiac" here is meant not only the constellations in the sky, but that these areas/constellations are centres of particular forces which make, shape and create every living being on earth.

I realised that my early zodiacal sculptures were inexperienced, clumsy, young and heavy. The outer appearance of these forms was not successful, they were not beautiful and I knew it. They were never fired, all recycled. But they were the beginning of my real training, the sculptural ground to stand on and work from. Through their cosmic background, they gave me the fundamental mood and direction for my work of the next 30 years – the reason for including them in this collation as they were really my beginning. I could feel how each of the 12 moods stretched me in a different direction, teaching and guiding me towards my own sculptural expression. I felt part of a stream of form forces which slowly built up and internalised sculptural capacities which were outwardly and inwardly fulfilling me in such a way that I could feel that my art and my life were intimately interlinked.

GEMINI

CANCER

LEO

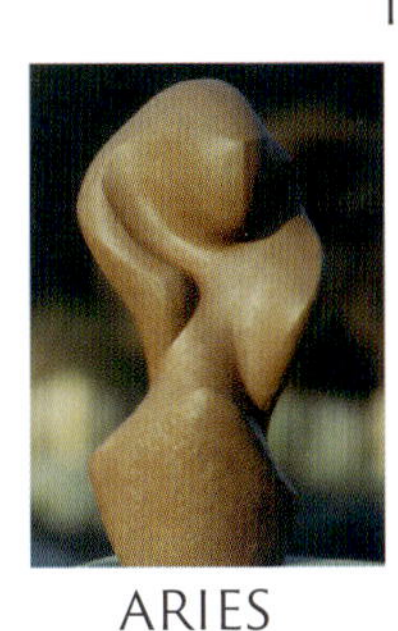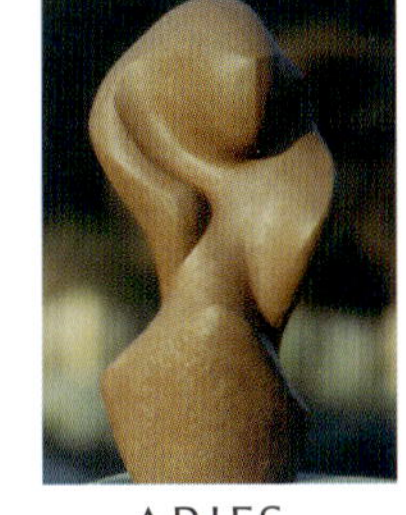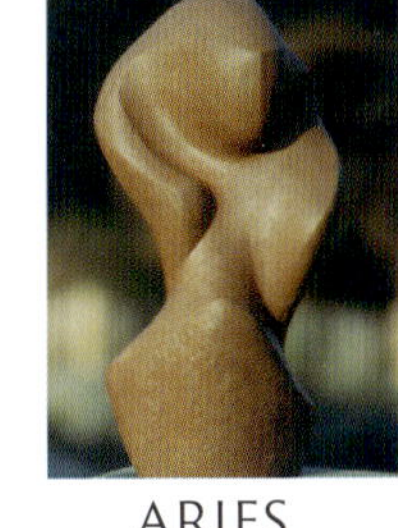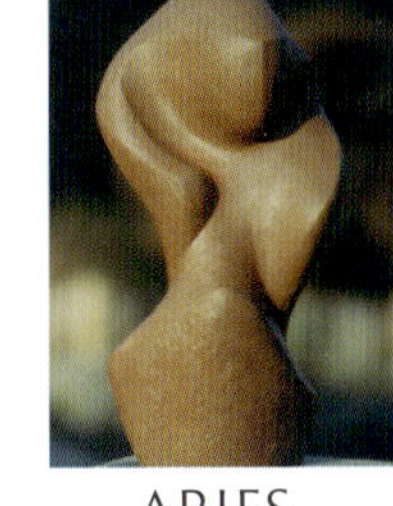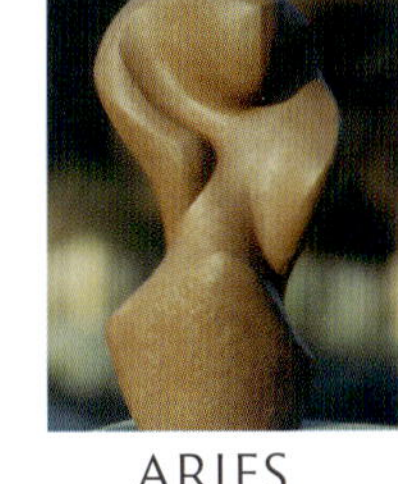

TAURUS

VIRGO

ARIES

LIBRA

PISCES

SCORPIO

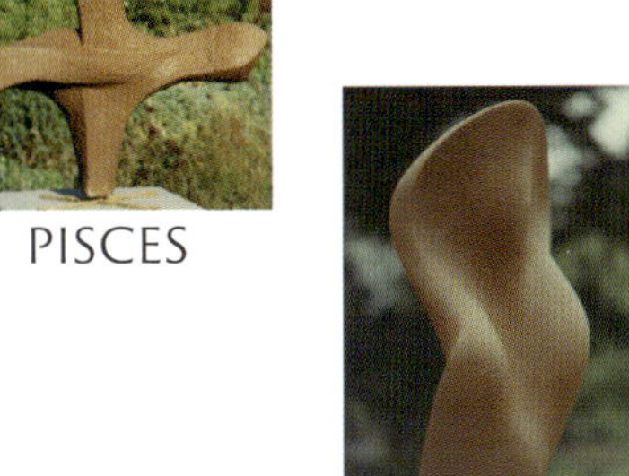

AQUARIUS

CAPRICORN

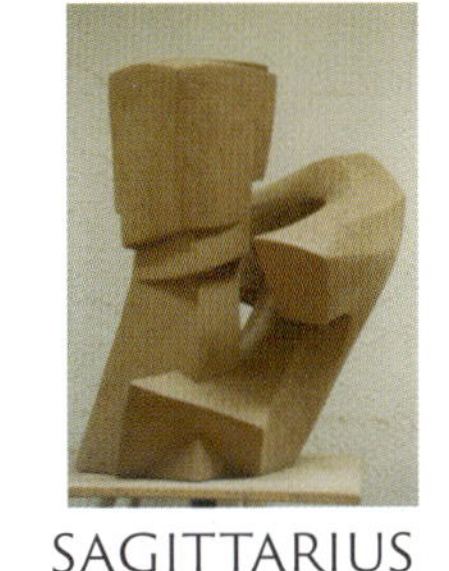

SAGITTARIUS

TWELVE RELIEFS ON THE MOODS OF THE ZODIAC
Gertraud Goodwin

1991-92. 70 x 110 cm. Patinated Plaster.

The relief work on the moods of the Zodiac was my second approach towards the theme. It took little more than a year and I tried to work on the Zodiac moods during their appropriate time, although this was not always possible.

I felt a stronger and simpler connection to each mood, so that their gestures have become more one- sided and characteristic. Yet again, I feel I have only discovered another side of each one. And new aspects would emerge, if the Zodiac would be worked on with the question of polarity, i.e. working on Aries and Libra, then on Taurus and Scorpio etc. or taking into account the Trigones, i.e. the relationship of always three of the Zodiac moods related to each of the elements. These aspects will be looked at at another time.

Here the exercise was to come to simple fundamental sculptural gestures, trying to find the underlying "alphabet of form" which is the basis of every living becoming thing in nature around us. But rarely we would find only one gesture at work—they work together in the most varied combinations, just like the alphabet is not yet poem!

During the work, the process of becoming of each relief was an experience of a true metamorphosis. This is not physically visible, as it is a process in time. But both forces—the form gesture, the forces of the Zodiac, and the process in time of metamorphosis – always work together: without the Zodiac forces no form would ever be visible – all would be a process in time like water and air! Without metamorphosis, we would have a never changing world of fixed and static forms without any change! The reliefs were originally all modelled in plasticine and then cast in plaster. Then they were painted with metal pigments according to their relationship with the planets.

The first four moods of the Zodiac – the Ram, Taurus, Gemini and Cancer have one common quality and that is that their form-gestures can be seen in the unfolding of the growing plant as it appears in time. But these form-gestures manifest in every living being in very individual ways and by no means in a time sequence which shows that the Zodiac constellations next to each other in space, i.e. Ram is followed by Taurus etc. In this sense, the plant organs are an exception as the character of appearance of the various zodiacal form-forces are totally individual and one-sided. But the twelve build a whole organism together, like a large alphabet of a cosmic script. The twelve different "letters" of this script form amongst each other the most varied poetry: the archetypal ideas of every living thing.

Into these great, timeless, cosmic special form-gestures, the processes of metamorphosis, of a development in time, works into it like the inner substance of the walnut is being shaped according to its shell – although the shell and the nut are quite individually shaped! But they are one in the idea:
"unity lies in the living becoming".

Thus, there is never a form without Zodiac gestures and there is never growth in time without the processes of metamorphosis: and both are intricately interwoven with each other. Thus, the Ram-gesture is present wherever a "head-formation" of one sort or another is present, the Taurus-gesture is always there where substance is spreading itself out into space, etc. It is important to see the archetypal universal gesture and then to study how it appears individually in every living being differently. In this sense, the description of the next Zodiac gestures is then not following the plant's next development, but looking at the individual form-gesture – wherever it appears.

GEMINI
CANCER
LEO
TAURUS
VIRGO
ARIES
LIBRA
PISCES
SCORPIO
AQUARIUS
CAPRICORN
SAGITTARIUS

ARIES

The motif of Aries is the beginning of the chorus of the twelve Zodiac moods—the overture with the theme: breakthrough towards the light! With enthusiasm and fire the Aries follows single-mindedly this purpose. In the physical birth, the head comes first—a deed in the truest sense. This pushing and reaching towards the light often goes against strong resistance and needs dedication and idealism to bring about this deed. And the strength of the will gains in the face of resistance, becomes stronger and doesn't break.

These were the principal qualities and guidelines to come to a sculptural gesture which is primarily a rising convexity from the bottom left to the top right, breaking through and relieved from its hold on the left side.

In nature, we see this force in the gesture and form of all buds and their striving to break through. Also, the uncurling fern and mushrooms, growing even through concrete or tarmac, illustrate the gesture of this deed.

TAURUS

Taurus carries the Aries theme forward into the gesture of "spreading life and substance outwards into space". Taurus forces are full of light, vitality and strength ever moving forward and outward, full of feeling and excitement for the love of the earth.

"...*it weaves the thread of life through worlds imbued with being in mindful revelation...*" we hear in Rudolf Steiner's meditation on the mood of the Taurus.

For the sculpture, these gestures manifested for me in forms of moving from inside out, forward and outward. In more differentiated forms, full of the juice of life, substance is being spread into space.

In nature, we can see this in all forms which spread themselves out: in the leaf to either side, in the plant as a whole, in the tree - everywhere where we have life pulsating through spreading substance.

GEMINI

In the beginning of Gemini lies the Pentecost experience, and at the end, the sun reaches its highest point. This highest time of the year is also full of tension, full of the mighty possibilities of unfolding. The plants reveal themselves fully, and they can do that through the typical Gemini of "*expansion and contradiction, held in symmetry*". Only the balance between right and left, and between centre and circumference makes it possible to hold the uprightness.

In the sculpture, this manifested in a form with two wings, spreading up and out—and held by a strong crossing and contraction below.

In nature, symmetry goes through every organism, in man and the animal in a particular way: in the crossing-over of the nerves lies the capability for consciousness, to be able to "lose oneself"—to "find oneself". In the plant, symmetry is visible in every leaf, but also in the whole of the plant: never is one side overcrowded so that the plant or tree would fall over. This would be a kind of living and moving symmetry.

CANCER

After the summer solstice, the great dying begins already in nature. All activity is turned inward to enclose what is the whole purpose of development: the blossom. All forces are being collected to be intensified and made inward - "*to meet with rigour each test*".
In man, the forces of Cancer build the shell of the chest and ribs which enclose heart and lungs. With each breath we take in, the jump from the outer to the inner world of our body has to be made, also from the old to the new.

In the relief, these forces manifested in a spiralling movement towards the within, closing itself off from the periphery. The three incoming waves are at a breaking point—thus the new seed can come into being in the inner space created.

LEO

Leo's relationship is with the sun: the sun being the heart for every growing life on earth. Through Leo, the sunforces manifest particularly where heart-qualities are present, our own heart being like a little sun in our own organism, where it relates between centre and circumference in an ongoing living rhythm. This faculty to relate between polarities, between centre and circumference, between concentration in a point and "*flaming enthusiasm*" is Leo's domain.

In the relief, the relationship between the centre and the circumference is also the main theme. The gentle rhythms emanating from the centre to the right side and then up, don't disperse outward, but are drawn back, and then over to the left and then down until they are gathered and called back into the centre.

Seeds are ripening in August: the plant has truly found its destiny and gathers all forces towards that aim. Leo's virtue is courage, and man needs this courage to make himself ready at every point in his life to take on his own karma out of the forces of his heart. This is how man searches with Leo forces, to unite himself (the microcosm) with his destiny in the macrocosm.

VIRGO

Virgo is always depicted with the ripe sheaf of grain as a sign for ripeness or ripening. In times of old, Virgo's cloak or mantle was seen as the whole of the Zodiac, holding all of the universal wisdom. All forces are turned inward to accomplish this deed of ripening. This Virgo wisdom knows all substances, tastes, divides, selects and separates them for their further aim in the cosmic order and harmony.

In the relief, I tried to indicate the vastness of the eternal plane out of which every relief comes, but which is particularly grand and cosmic in Virgo. In this vastness, an inner space of great intimacy opens itself up and invites us to admire its treasure: the seed. There is a feeling of inwardness and awe in that sign—maybe it is comparable to a mood when we watch a butterfly coming out of the pupa: if there is a great and sudden noise, the butterfly will die.

All of nature's greatest secrets are hidden to us either through a real physical sheath or through size, or both. The five-pointed star in the apple is one of these secrets.

LIBRA

In the time of Libra, we come to the equinox: the sun has reached a balance between her highest and her lowest point, and the quietness of autumn descends. This search for balance on every level is Libra's great domain: between levity and gravity, between giving and receiving, between inward and outward. In the great balance of polarities life unfolds and concludes.

The relief is spread out wide into the horizontal. Like two large wings the two sides reach out from the middle, where they are held in a conscious uprightness and an inner space, where the decision of all decisions is made—always moving, never still. The right side has the tendency downwards, the left side upwards—and maybe the moment of the change is depicted.

This search for balance it to be found everywhere in nature: the root is in proportion and size according to the whole of the plant, the branches are not too heavy for the trunk, etc. If a tree grows on a slope, its branches and roots grow in such a way that they build a counterbalance to the slope. This can be seen even in the cut trunk, where every ring of growth is widening and becoming narrower according to where the tree grew: the rings at the side of the slope are narrow and contracted, the wood is harder and on the other side the wood is wider and softer. Thus, the whole tree constantly balances itself to its surroundings.

SCORPIO

At the end of October, we are going towards the darkest time of the year. All of nature is penetrated by death-forces: the withering, wilting and falling leaves, all the life- forces, retreat into the earth. But as every falling leaf keeps the force of the new bud in the shelter of its former place of attachment until the spring, the spirit forces will transcend all dying in the seed. Scorpio forces work from the spirits of form, which work on the earth through the light: thus shaping, forming and finalising all shapes. In our ego, we have qualities of the dividing intellect and the recognising ego-consciousness present, which show us the polarity of the Scorpion - which kills itself when exposed to the light - and the eagle which unfolds its overlooking flight high up in the sunlight.

In the relief, these forces of polarity build the theme: down to the left sharp, cold hard and narrow contracted shapes and edges are finally stuck together, whereas up above a wing-like gesture lifts itself generously out and opens up to the right in open planes. Both polarities can only be held together by a great dynamic movement in between.

In nature, death and life are always very near together: in the dead hard crust of a seedpod, the seed is kept.

SAGITTARIUS

The Greeks illustrated the archer in the image of the centaur: an upright upper half of a human body comes out of a horse's body. It was the depiction of man's ego forces becoming master over the lower animal drives within himself. The sun reaches its lowest point, and we need all our conscious ego-forces not to die into the darkness of midwinter—but to keep spiritually awake and aware of our goal.

Thus, the sculptural theme became the battle between the horizontal, heavy pressing down forces and the vertical uprightness, which needs to be strong enough to be victorious over the horizontal. Both forces meet in the diagonal, which is held by verticality.

CAPRICORN

When we move into the time of Capricorn, the sun had reached her lowest point and is on her way up again. Into that tender hopeful sunlight in midwinter, the Christchild is born: the old year comes to an end and a new one begins. During the twelve Holy Nights, the twelve months of the coming new year are macrocosmically experienced in advance—the earth is spiritually open to receive a new impulse. Capricorn time is the time for new beginnings on many levels. It is the turning point of time and of the world! We are called on to go towards the future joy and enthusiasm but not escape from our present tasks and to take careful decisions on the basis of past experiences. We can have the tendency to hold on to the past, the habits and dogmas, and to be afraid of the future - avoiding the present by clinging on to the past. Inwardly awake and outwardly courageous we can master and prepare for the future.

The sculptural gesture tries to show these two one-sided qualities of clinging to the past in hard mineralised and fixed forms on the bottom left—and hurrying off to the future in dissolving waves on the right. In between is the space where in wakeful quiescence the "*I am*" can be born in uprightness, able to be in the presence and torn apart by the past—and future forces. In the Eurythmy movement of the sound "L" those polarities can be held in balance and related to each other in the flow of time.

AQUARIUS

The sun goes further upwards and one lives with hope towards the coming spring. In nature, it is the time when ice and snow begin to melt and all of earth's closed-off qualities of the wintertime get into a moving, melting and flowing process.
In Rudolf Steiner's meditation for Aquarius we hear about boundaries and boundlessness, about currents flowing further and sustaining themselves: man is caught in his own boundary of his skin—and part of the boundless cosmos. This asks for a constant seeking of balance between the danger of losing oneself in the boundless - and to stay stuck in oneself. The continuous striving throughout our life is to bring our thinking, feeling and willing into a balance. Thus, the Aquarian forces are the archetypal forces of the streaming life forces, the foundation for everything living, of streams meeting and working together in their very particular laws: the laws of the flowing water, moving in continuous rhythmical double-bent surfaces.

In the relief, we see a broad stream moving principally from left to right - but also up and down and down and up. All the movements pause and breathe out in the centre, a round space, but also incorporate it and move on.
In the Eurythmy gesture, we have the only movement in the circle of the other eleven still Zodiac gestures: a rhythmical movement of both arms undulating up and down.

PISCES

With Pisces, the circle of the Zodiac is complete. We have gone through the whole of our physical body, with the feet as the last parts being shaped by the Pisces-forces. With our feet, we walk the earth, we go from place to place, shaping our destiny. And in every destiny, we gain and we lose; and even when we lose we can accept the loss and thus gain in a new way, growing in our destiny. We hear about this gain and loss in Rudolf Steiner's meditation for Pisces, how the loss may be gain in itself. In our destiny, we feel that we are beings of two worlds: the physical and the spiritual. In the whole of the human form we can see ourselves standing on the earth and thus are firmly connected with the physical world. In our upright standing in levity we lift ourselves up into a different realm in our upper part, where we can perceive and think. This gesture is enhanced in the Eurythmy gesture for Pisces with our left foot firmly on the ground, the right foot touching the earth only with the toes. The left hand touches lightly the side of the pelvis whereas the right arm is stretched straight up. It is as though we are the bridge ourselves between these two realms!

The relief tries to show this movement up—and through a horizontal bridge into a new upper realm.

PENCIL DRAWINGS (TWELVE RELIEFS)

1991-92. A3. Pencil.

These drawings were carried out alongside the reliefs, doing sculpture in the morning and drawing in the afternoon. I tried to keep to the correct times during the course of the year, to imbue myself fully with the cosmic forces at work. Starting this process right away after the experience of the Twelve Holy Nights in Grindelwald, Switzerland, where my teacher Reimar von Bonin guided a small group of interested people through this very special time, had felt like a great gift, inspiring and deepening my imaginations ever since.

Being engaged in one of the meditations on the Zodiac by Rudolf Steiner for a certain time, sometimes days, sometimes a week, and sketching and working artistically alongside it—even if it was ever so simple – slowly a gesture started to grow inside me, which became deeper and more real as time went on. The importance for me was in the togetherness of the reading, the mediation and the artistic work. For each mood, a different key formed itself through this threefold working. In this sequence, the aspect of becoming, of a rhythmic flow of forces at work as a creative process was my emphasis.

Although the stars of the Zodiac are fixed stars and never change their relationship to each other, the experience of the movement of the sun going through this quiet twelvefoldness can be seen as a path from one to the other, where it is not arbitrary which ones are next to each other.

I saw the first half of the Zodiac to be more related to the outside development of the plant life in nature—from Aries with the opening of the buds, to Leo in August, where the seeds are dispersed and formed anew.

In the second half of the Zodiac I could see the relationship to the inner life of man in his search for himself through the darker part of the year.

This aspect of the movements through the Zodiac from one mood to the next is only one aspect and not its main quality which I see in this quiet giving and sustaining of qualities in their onesidedness. When particular qualities work together, they are the creative logos at work in the variability of all the life around us: mineral, plant, animal and man.

There is infinite depth and wisdom in that, and the exercises are a humble beginning to understand the langauge of the stars. And so, we can be aware as with learning of every language, that these exercises are like a first alphabet of a cosmic scrip and also that even when we know the single letters, we cannot yet form a word, nor a poem! And in every blade of grass the creator forces are "writing poetry".

In our time now, we need to understand and consciously strive out of ourselves through artistic creation and not rely any longer on our unconscious clairvoyance. Thus "*The stars once spoke to man*" will become a new possibility of man beginning to speak to the stars, recognising and acknowleging their forces. This should not sound ambitious, but a humble and simple beginning, which opens up a field of work that needs to be worked at so that we may make this step.

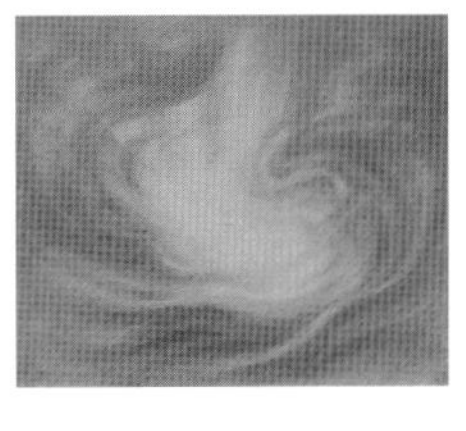

CANCER

GEMINI

LEO

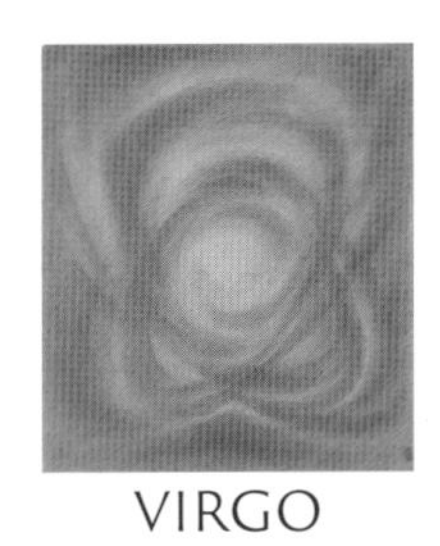

VIRGO

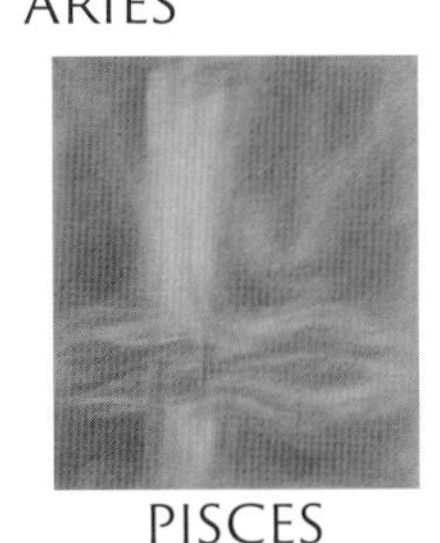

TAURUS

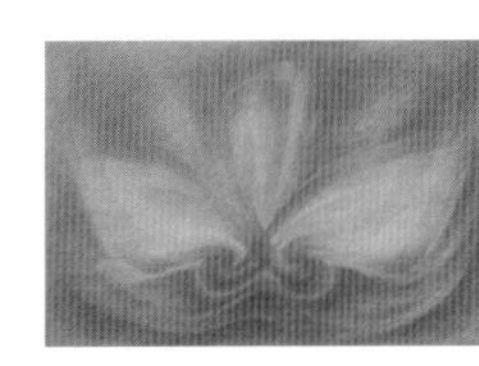

LIBRA

ARIES

SCORPIO

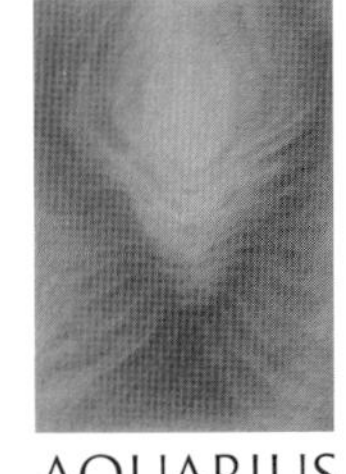

PISCES

AQUARIUS

SAGITTARIUS

CAPRICORN

♈ ARIES

The element of the fire, the rising and breaking through of the light in an upward and forward gesture became the main guidelines for the drawing. The light rises up, establishes itself, and imbues the circumference with fire's warmth.

Gentle horizontal waves begin to fill it as though the surface is being breathed through with the forces of a "W". Then out of this, the light, upright quality slowly establishes itself – being in a constant relationship with these waves during its rising process.

♉ TAURUS

Now the light pushes outward into the width in mighty forward gestures, thus involving the darkness to a much greater extent. In turn, the darkness becomes more active itself. It is a stronger working together of light and dark, full of strength and might and with a good relationship to the earth. The forces of Taurus guard the secret of life: how the heavy matter of earth can be brought into movement in such a way that one feels its strength as well as the overcoming of gravity.

♊ GEMINI

The next gesture shows the light's total expansion into the heights and breadth of space in an outward, symmetrical and wing-like gesture. This expansion can only be endured and held together because of a strongly held centre, and the symmetry. The light is grand and expansive, a joyful and summery gesture, pushing the darkness to the outermost edge: like the blossom of the flower, where matter has come to its physical boundaries in levity and thinness, which expresses the vast expansion of the flower.

♋ CANCER

Now, after a series of ever greater expansions, a strong gesture from within is manifesting itself in a roundish, caring gesture, holding the light, centring it and giving it a space to be. From there, the light settles, but also radiates out through the darkness. One can compare it to the concentration of fructification, in the calyx of the flower. It is the turning-point from the outer, greatly visible growth in the plant to the inner invisible transformation towards the seed and the fruit.

♌ LEO

From this new fructified centre, living and pulsating forces emanate: to the right, upwards, waves of darker grey move up and out, becoming ever larger and lighter, almost moving out of the picture – but then the darkness begins to hold them to slowly move them over and backwards, down to the left side, where they become ever smaller, sharper and darker.
Eventually, they get back into this heart-centre from where the rhythms emerge anew, invigorated. It is a constant and rhythmical exchange of expansion and contraction, of wide and narrow, slow and fast – of light and darkness, of breathing in and out.

♍ VIRGO

In the next mood, a quite different rhythm comes about: although moving, it is much quieter, even symmetrical, swinging in grander, more elongated gestures. The light-centre is held by loops of grey, which are intricately relating to each other and connecting to the circumference, the light being in between to shape and guide these movements. The light quality is more shining, from within, tender and holding the new inner seed which is forming itself.

♎ LIBRA

This mood deals with the qualities of weighing right and left, light and darkness, movement and resting, round and straight. A strong light expansion, like two wings, is moving both to the right and to the left. The darkness gives way, but also intensifies to hold together the crossing and the two spiral movements. The centre, upright, is holding the two polarities together. Thus, the upper left is connected with the lower right, etc., each movement trying to be aware and reacting to what another part of the drawing is doing.

♏ SCORPIO

Here a great battle is taking place, light and darkness are challenging each other. As they are both very strong in their polarity, this leads to confrontations and also enhancements; where the darkness pushes forward it is held by the light, thus forming sharp edges. The dynamic and movement are of great importance in that mood, otherwise it would freeze into a totally crystalline formation, and the light and darkness would be interlocked and dead.

♐ SAGITTARIUS

In the last mood the light was there to help the darkness to see its strength and sharpness, now the darkness is strongly supporting the light: in an upright gesture, the light gesture faces the right, the future and towards it light shapes are moving, supported by the darkness and strongly bridled by the shape and quality of this centre.

Again and again it is amazing how little physical space the light needs to be effective and strong! Even if surrounded by massive shapes of darkness, the smallest strip of light is enough to establish itself as a quality.

♑ CAPRICORN

Light and darkness are coming more together. They have not lost their identities, but are working together to create an inner space where they both are, and which can hold what wants to come as a new possibility.

From this inner quiet space, the light is pulling in its one-sidedness towards the future – to the right – trying to disperse into shapelessness. The darkness pulls towards the left in its own way, trying to hold everything in rigid, sharply outlined matter – to keep it where it always was, so as not to move.

♒ AQUARIUS

In Aquarius, great things are achieved by the light and the darkness together – a general relaxation and tranquillity, and acceptance of each other as well as listening and receiving of each other's qualities is the fundamental mood. In grand and quiet rhythms, the light flows down gently, is received by the darkness which comes towards it first from below and then gives way to it parting to the sides. But it could also be seen as though both qualities go through each other without losing their identity, the movement going both ways – up and down at the same time.

There is a great wisdom in this simplicity, like in the simplest of fluids. In the water lies the secret of all life.

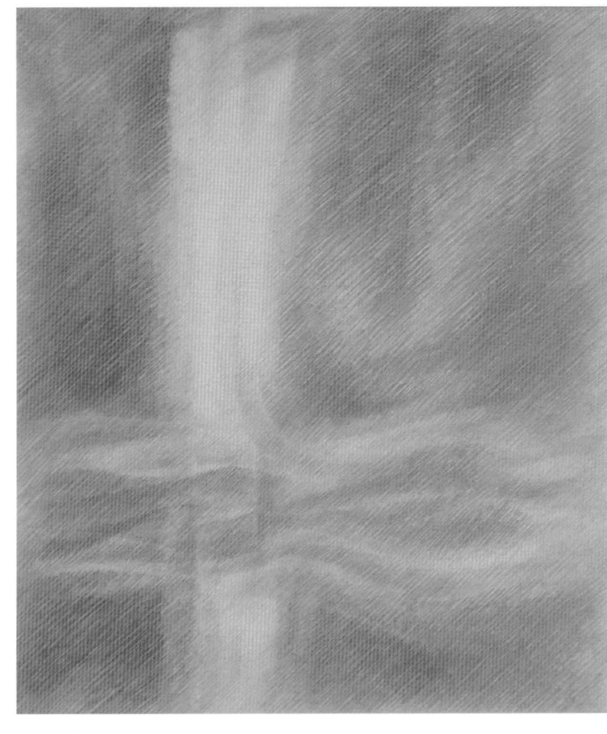

♓ PISCES

In the last mood, light and darkness are trying to come to an ultimate understanding of each other. It is like an end and a new beginning at the same time. The fundamental motif is the cross – or a light verticality, strong in its upright glory, meeting a horizontal flow of waves of darkness, which through the influence of the light, becomes more alive and wide in its gesture.

A GRAPHIC EXPLORATION
Gertraud Goodwin

2001-02. A5. Ink Pen.

We name things, as: "This is a tree". This gives us the entry to our world, a consciousness for the things around us, and our security. But it is only a first step. As we want to really get in touch with the inner nature of a tree, for example, we have to go beyond the mere name of the species and begin to ask many questions. These questions are intimately related to ourselves, and the answers help us to understand the world around us as well as ourselves. If we want to go beyond a materialistic worldview in which everything is explained through the DNA - then we begin to feel that there are higher super-sensible forces which are at work constantly to bring about and sustain all things around us.

The forces of the Zodiac were at all times believed to be part of man's upbuilding. But how about the rest of nature? Where do its forms come from? Exploring each single Zodiac force I began to see and observe more and more typical and one-sided form gestures occurring in the growth of plants. It became clear to me that I have a name, for instance "the gesture of Aries", which gives me another entry to the world around me: one which can give a possible starting point to explore and understand on another level how plants are made and what these forces really are.

It needs courage to make this step, to put a name to something which I have seen so many times and which neither a mere physical nomenclatura nor a scientific DNA description can explain to me in such a way that I would feel inwardly satisfied. As much as the specification "pine tree" only categorises and can separate me from the true pine-being if I don't go any further, as much can the realisation and acknowledgement of the specific form-building gesture of a Zodiacal force put me into a real at-onement with it. There, the naming and acknowledgement of a particular force/gesture opens a new door for me through which I can get in touch with how a plant is made, from where it really comes.

Then I begin to see how each shooting up vertically out of the earth towards the sun has to do with the force gesture of Aries - whether it be in a mushroom or a tree; that each spreading of leaves or branches, etc. has to do with forces of Taurus at work; that every symmetry - whether right/left or centre/periphery comes from the forces of the Gemini at work. Always, of course, there is more than one force at work, complementing and enhancing each other. And one begins to see and marvel at the wisdom of how the forces of each single Zodiac gesture are distributed around the year: this classification surely comes from a time when man was still in touch with the reality of the relationship between the earth and the cosmos.

The graphic depictions of the 12 gestures of the Zodiac are intended as a contribution towards the recognition of these forces. I have tried to concentrate each one into a sign-like, still-form gesture as a kind of archetype which would express itself individually in every form in a different way - man, animal and plant. The recognition of the archetype is a first step to then feel the whole plant-being, embraced and embedded in its cosmic origin.

The first seven gestures of the Zodiac, the "day rainbow", can be well followed in the upbuilding of the actual plant. They are physically visible and form the more material manifestation of the plant. The five following gestures, the "night rainbow", create much more inward and less outwardly visible form gestures. In the autumn and winter months, the plant undergoes fine chemical transubstantiations, in which the gesture is not so readily visible outwardly. From the study of these five Zodiacal forces as they work in the upbuilding of man's physical body, I slowly became aware of their working also in the world of plants. However, this is an attempt at a classification. Therefore, I would like to see it as a research and ongoing study which can be improved upon and changed in time.

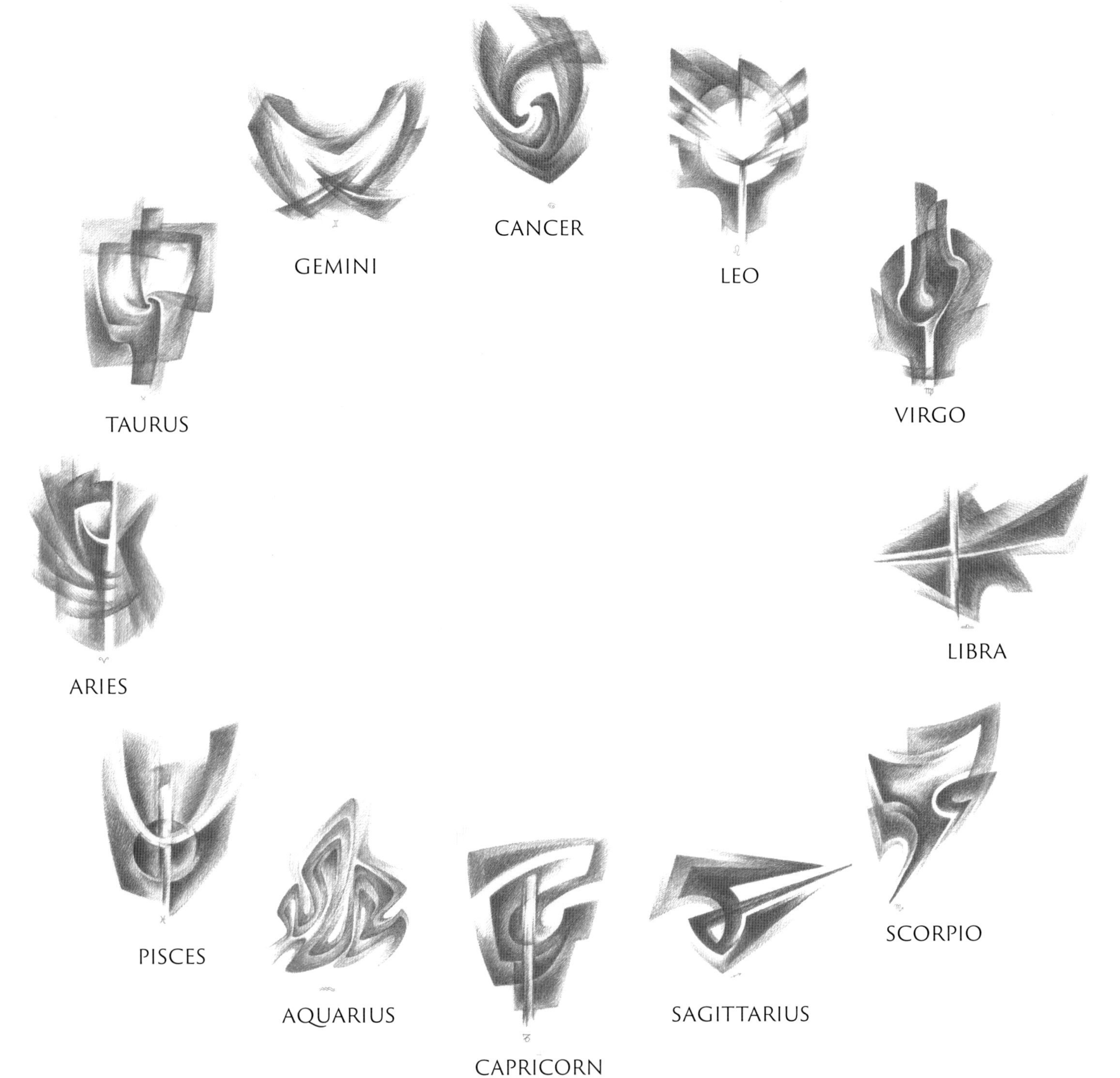

GEMINI
CANCER
LEO
VIRGO
TAURUS
LIBRA
ARIES
SCORPIO
PISCES
SAGITTARIUS
AQUARIUS
CAPRICORN

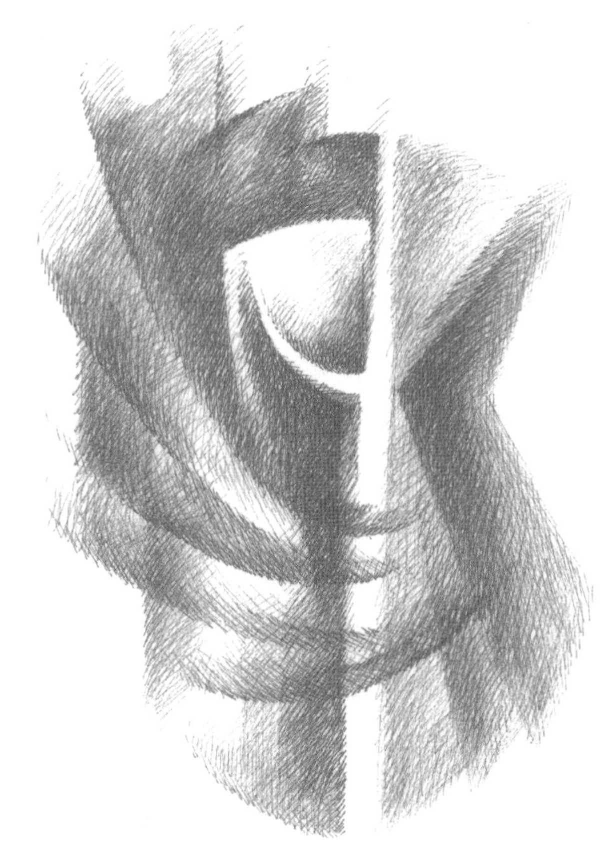

♈ ARIES

Vertically upwards. Growth upward, out of gravity into levity; pushing up substance in a convex gesture. Beginning of plant-life: shoots, buds, mushrooms, un-curling of ferns, pushing up of bud for the next year in the axel of the unfolding leaf, etc.

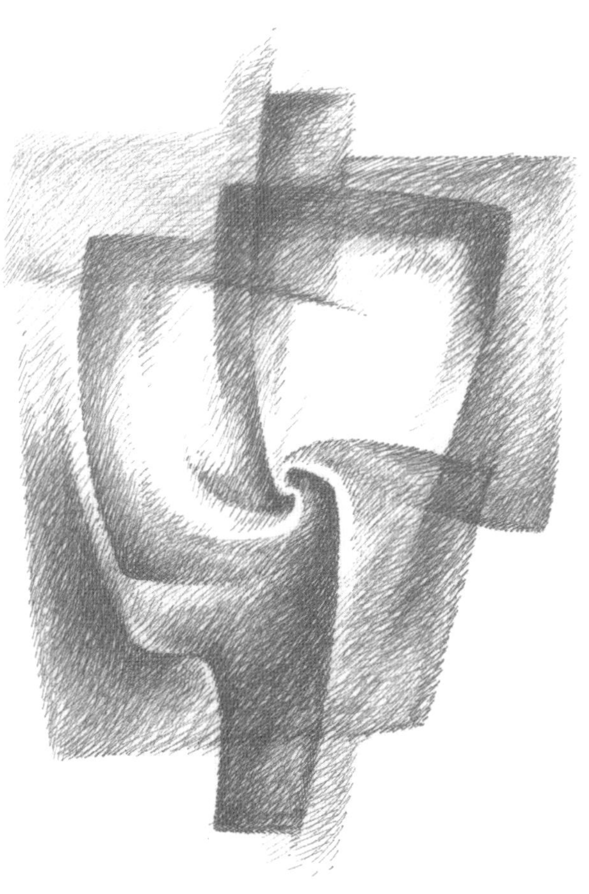

♉ TAURUS

From centre outwards towards periphery. Unfolding and spreading of leaves into the circumference, so that substance is pushed outwards.

♊ GEMINI

Finding inner balance and symmetry. Ordering between centre - stalks, trunk and periphery - leaves, branches, symmetry of leaves, bud, flower, fruit, etc. All symmetry - centre/periphery, right/left, front/back of leaves, the upbuilding of the whole plant.

♋ CANCER

Formation of an enclosing gesture, separating and defining between inner and outer. All building of an inner space - in the bud, the chalice, the flower, the fruit, the seedpod, in every detail of the plant.

♌ LEO

Most extended spreading - most contracted centring. Strongest extension of the fully grown plant in the spreading of pollen and scent and at the same time strongest contraction in the gesture of fructification.

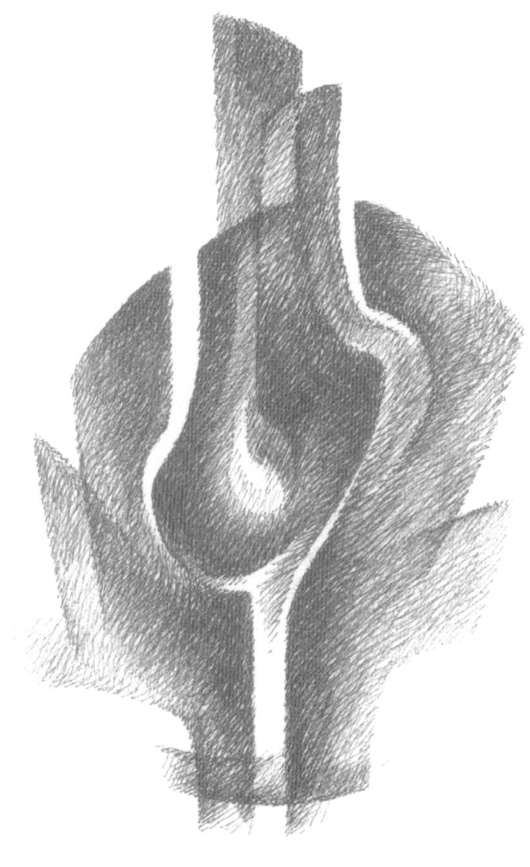

♍ VIRGO

Internalising and growing. Building of all fruit and seed in accumulating substance, flesh, and growth from centre to periphery.

♎ LIBRA

Keeping the centre and periphery in an harmonious balance. Gesture of keeping all the foregoing growth gestures in harmonious balance with each other, so that the whole plant can sustain itself. A too large blossom on a too weak stalk, too large and too far outreaching branches on a too slim tree trunk, all mean imbalances and a premature death of a plant.

♏ SCORPIO

Gesture of preserving and accumulation of matter, building in substance as in wood, maturing and hardening or seed: in it, its spirit being reaches its highest degree - all future possibilities are in it. If old matter does not fall way, the new can not go on into the future .

♐ SAGITTARIUS

Keeping continuity, aiming at the essence. Gesture of continuation of sameness and truthfulness of each plant to its own being: each cell "knows" always what, how and where to build in each part of a specific plant: a rose is a rose - will always be a rose. Over the death and hardening forces of Scorpio, Sagittarius becomes victorious: death here is not an end, but a gateway to a new life. Forms do not disappear into nothingness: they live on in the new forms into the future.

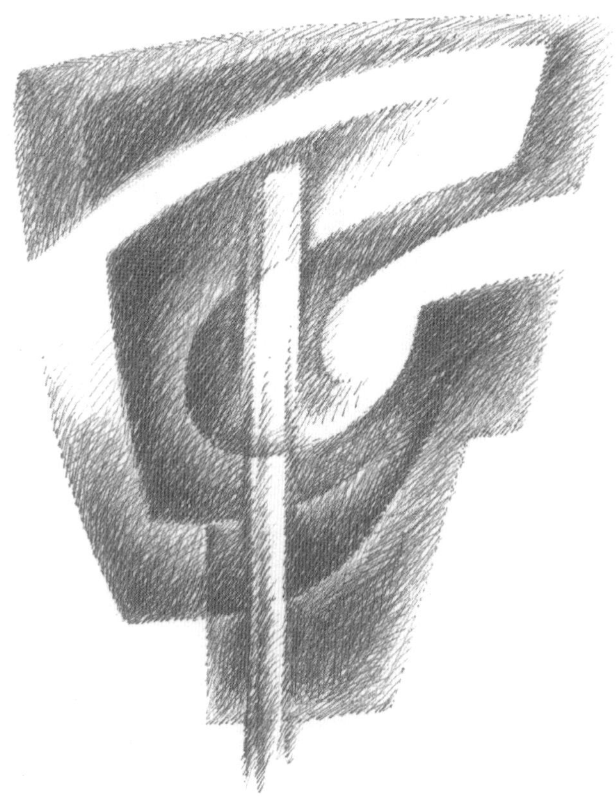

♑ CAPRICORN

Gesture of the plant as a time-being which grows in seasons in a development, between past, present and future.

♒ AQUARIUS

Interconnection between earthly and cosmic forces. The form forces of Aquarius are like a gate through which all other Zodiacal forces have to go in order to achieve a true plant-being. Also, through Aquarius, the plant is connected with seven planetary forces which bring all the 12 Zodiacal forces into a processual movement on the earth. The planetary processes themselves form the link between the cosmic Zodiac and the earth, so that the plant can become an earthly being.

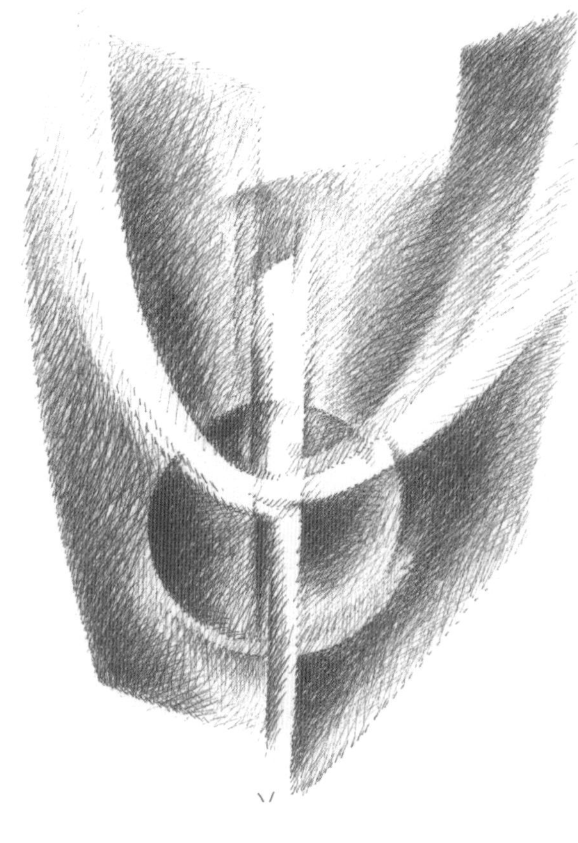

♓ PISCES

Our time today is the time of Pisces: 1413-3573. It is the age of the fall of the old form of consciousness. It also is a time of change and of new possibilities. Since only a relatively short time ago, we have the possibility to perceive the Christ in the etheric. The middle section of the rose-coloured window in the First Goetheanum shows how Christ's countenance can be perceived through the world of plants - meaning for me, that in all of creation the Christ impulse can be perceived if we let ourselves be touched and moved by what we see with our physical eyes. Through the forces of Pisces, the plant world is most intimately connected with the evolution of man and the whole earth.

MEDITATIONS ON THE ZODIAC
Gertraud Goodwin

2004-05. 45-55 cm. Patinated Plaster.

This is the third time within a 17 year period that I have worked on the Zodiac for over a year each time. It is a subject which is fundamental to my teaching as well as to my own free artistic work. For me it is the archetypal language of form, the sculptural alphabet so to speak. Each time I work with it the gestures become simpler and clarify themselves further. These gestures are the basis of form in every living, becoming being in nature around us, but rarely we find one gesture at work – they work together in the most varied combinations. In the human form these twelve gestures have created the most sublime symphony.

During the work, the process of becoming of each sculpture is an experience of true metamorphosis. This is not physically visible as it is a process in time. Both forces, the form gesture forces of the Zodiac and the process of creation in time, metamorphosis, always work together.
- Without the Zodiac forces – no visible form, only process in time like air and water.
- Without Metamorphosis – a never-changing world of static forms.

In the circle, everything comes to rest – and everything is possible. Life's beginning and end in endless variations of seeds, eggs and cells, it offers itself naturally to a subject of cosmic dimension. The cosmos in itself is circular, and is visited by the earth's circular motion in the cyclical movement of the year.

The symmetry of the circle holds centre and periphery at the same time, and within it this peaceful eternal rest. It is. It wants nothing and gives everything: focus, contemplation, stillness, holding, coming to an essence.

It offers itself selflessly to these Zodiacal, twelve gestures, which are imprinted on the circle as in a sign-like cosmic choreography. This twelvefold sculptural script can be thought of as the foundation for every possible physical gesture on earth in stone, plant, animal and man.
Working on the theme of "Resurrection" sculpturally, the last and most satisfactory part of a sequence on this subject impressed me in its clarity and simplicity. The circle within which it was held had, for me, an eternal peacefulness.

So I continued working with disc-like sculptural meditations, experimenting with symmetry and asymmetry. It was a new field for me to work with, geometry, simplicity and symmetry. And before long the arising gestures spoke strongly to me in a particular and more definite form language. I recognised the possibility of expressing the gestures of the Zodiac in this way.

I realised that this last disc for the theme of "Resurrection" had the right gesture for the expression of "Pisces"; the end of one group of work had become the beginning of a new group! This was a revelation. To be finally able to express so much with the greatest simplicity was like coming home.

This new-found simplicity within the circle has, for me, a strong biographical correlation to a new phase in my life.

GEMINI

CANCER

LEO

TAURUS

VIRGO

ARIES

LIBRA

PISCES

SCORPIO

AQUARIUS

CAPRICORN

SAGITTARIUS

ARIES

24th December 2004

The Upright

With the leading theme of "*Breakthrough to the light in the uprightness*", the forces of Aries make the overture to the twelve moods of the Zodiac. With idealistic fire this goal is pursued. Sculpturally this force concentrates itself into a triangle which breaks through the circle on top.

TAURUS

26th December 2004

Spreading, Enlarging

The forces of Taurus move and fill the earth forces with substance and strength in a life-filled gesture towards the outside and into space. In nature this inner fullness shows itself in the thickening and spreading of the buds and in everything which extends and broadens itself substantially in nature. The sculptural gesture is an earthen square which spreads substance into the circle, creating space and volume, pressing outwards.

GEMINI

Symmetry, Crossing

Through the forces of Gemini, complete unfolding is achieved, held in living symmetry. The sculptural gesture embraces a break-through, which is held symmetrically through a crossing.

CANCER

28th December 2004

The Spiral

The forces of Cancer bend themselves into two spirals towards within in such a way that they do not meet. In building an inner space together, they close themselves off from the periphery. Sculpturally the two spiral gestures begin to form an inner space.

LEO

29th December 2004

Periphery and Centre in Dynamic Tension

The forces of Leo form like the "heart core" of the Zodiac: sun-imbued extension into the periphery and contraction in the centre in dynamic tension have to be held together. Sculpturally, this is achieved through a vertical force, concentrated into a point. Whereas radial streams of forces reach out into the periphery.

VIRGO

30th December 2004

The Fulfilled Inner Space

The forces of Virgo harbour the fullness of cosmic wisdom and let them ripen with inwardness. Sculpturally, a half open, half closed, inner space embraces and shelters this abundance.

LIBRA

31st December 2004

Equilibrium

The forces of Libra hold the moveable equilibrium in the space between above and below, right and left, back and front. Sculpturally, the upper and lower half-circle are shifted slightly out of the circle; this tension is held in balance through a double-bent surface.

SCORPIO

1st January 2005

Healing the Split / Separation

Scorpio forces express themselves with great dynamic by means of separation, polarisation and even by death. All forms which have grown and become, achieve their ultimate materialisation – and through this also their death. But in every leaf axil of the dying leaf, there already rests the new bud for the coming year. Thus the forces of death are necessary to make room for new life. Sculpturally, the circle is divided into two halves; separating from each other they create a new space in between, full of tension.

SAGITTARIUS

2nd January 2005

The Diagonal

The forces of Sagittarius hold the dynamic between the forces of levity (movement) and the horizontal forces of gravity (rest), in the goal-orientated diagonal. Sculpturally, this dynamic tension expresses itself in a diagonal counter-movement; held and anchored on the bottom left, it presses upwards, penetrating the circle above to the right.

CAPRICORN

3rd January 2005

Connection Between Past, Present and Future

The forces of Capricorn mark the end of the old and the beginning of the new year. Into the turning upwards again of the sun, the Christ child is born. The forces of the old (left side) and the forces of the new (right side) "look at each other". In waking up to each other a fulfilled space arises between them: the vessel (the "crib") of the "present mindfulness" into which the greatest and highest that can develop between man and man, and man and God, can live and develop.

AQUARIUS

4th January 2005

The Double-Bent Plane

All other eleven Zodiac forces have to go through the gate of Aquarius "in order to become efficient on earth". The forces of Aquarius bring all the other forces to their full efficacy; they are made human. The manifestation of Aquarius in Eurythmy is the only moving gesture, whereas all the other eleven gestures are still, quietly held gestures. Thus Aquarius is the great move and mediator in the dance of the twelve, which creates the relationship between cosmos and earth. Sculpturally, this expresses itself in the standing wave, the double-bent surface. Responding to this all-encompassing efficacy of Aquarius, I have applied quite consciously, the double-bent plane in all the other eleven meditational discs.

PISCES

5th January 2005

The Cross

In our upright human form we walk the destiny of our life with our feet; vertical and horizontal forces interpenetrate in the cross. Christ has accomplished the greatest deed on the cross for humanity and the earth. In our own life, we constantly search towards bringing all the things to cross, to come together, to unite; matter and spirit, death and life, holding tight and letting go. Man is put into this polarity, equipped with all the faculties necessary to bring the poles together.

DRAWINGS

2004-05. A3. Ink Pen.

The expansive, white, flat surface of the paper can give another dimension to the expression of the Zodiac. The continuous plane allows the emerging theme to breathe beyond the boundary, to which the sculpture is limited. It allows the forces at work to be depicted, how they approach and condense themselves into the theme.

Our physical eyes can only see surfaces, the air around the objects is "empty" for us. The transmission and process of the forces of the Zodiac and the planets working into the elements and life-forces is not perceptible for us physically. Through practising observation, inner sensing, interest and openness, we can school ourselves towards a perception of these forces. In our daily life we unconsciously do much more of this kind of sensing than we are aware of.

Light and darkness shaded drawing lends itself particularly to tune into and depict a process of becoming.

I often feel the need to draw the same subject after a sculpture is completed. Through the sculptural process, the subject is incarnated, taken hold of.

Often already during the sculptural process, or after its completion I feel that the subject is "much bigger", as if it wants to expand again to reunite itself with the forces of its origin. Drawing it gives me a sense of this expansion!

Thus these drawings were carried out one by one, often while still completing the sculptures of the "Meditations on the Zodiac".

The basic compositions are similar, also based on the circle, but more simplicity was achieved through concentration on the interplay of light and dark. In the creative process, more and more layers of darkness are put on. The more intense the darkness becomes, the more the light gains strength too, creating together a particular constellation of forces. It felt as if light and dark tuned into each other to form a particular archetypal constellation together, moving, challenging and re-ordering the circle in a new way, thereby giving it a new creative force.

In the end, it is the light which emerges as the formative element, its power visible even through the darkest darkness. The darkness, even in its most intense layers, stays open for the formative and alive forces of the light – if too dense and solid, the darkness closes and isolates itself.

A mysterious and deeply intense mood can emerge out of the interplay between light and dark, a felt presence of an archetypal process of creation.

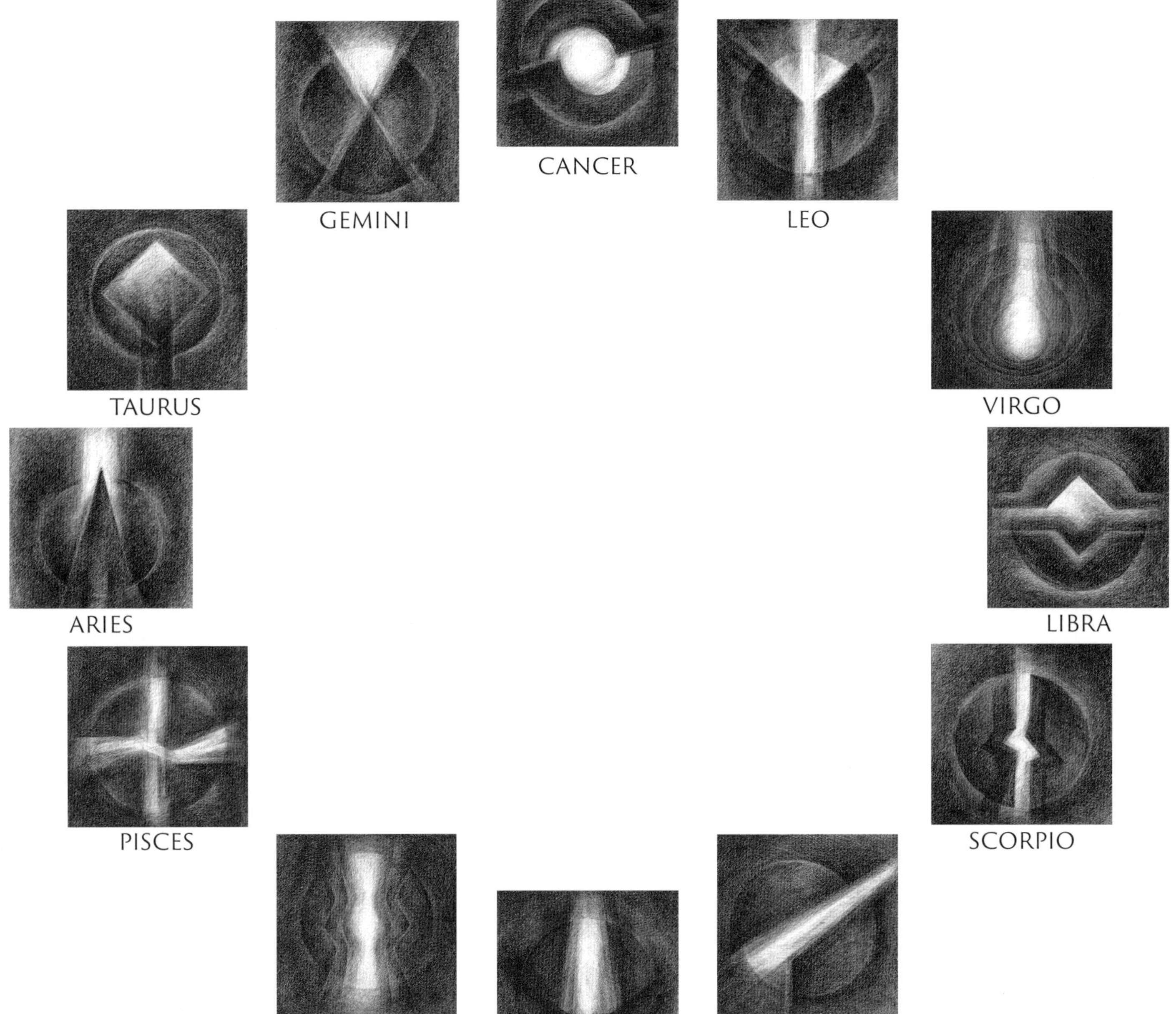

GEMINI
CANCER
LEO
TAURUS
VIRGO
ARIES
LIBRA
PISCES
SCORPIO
AQUARIUS
SAGITTARIUS
CAPRICORN

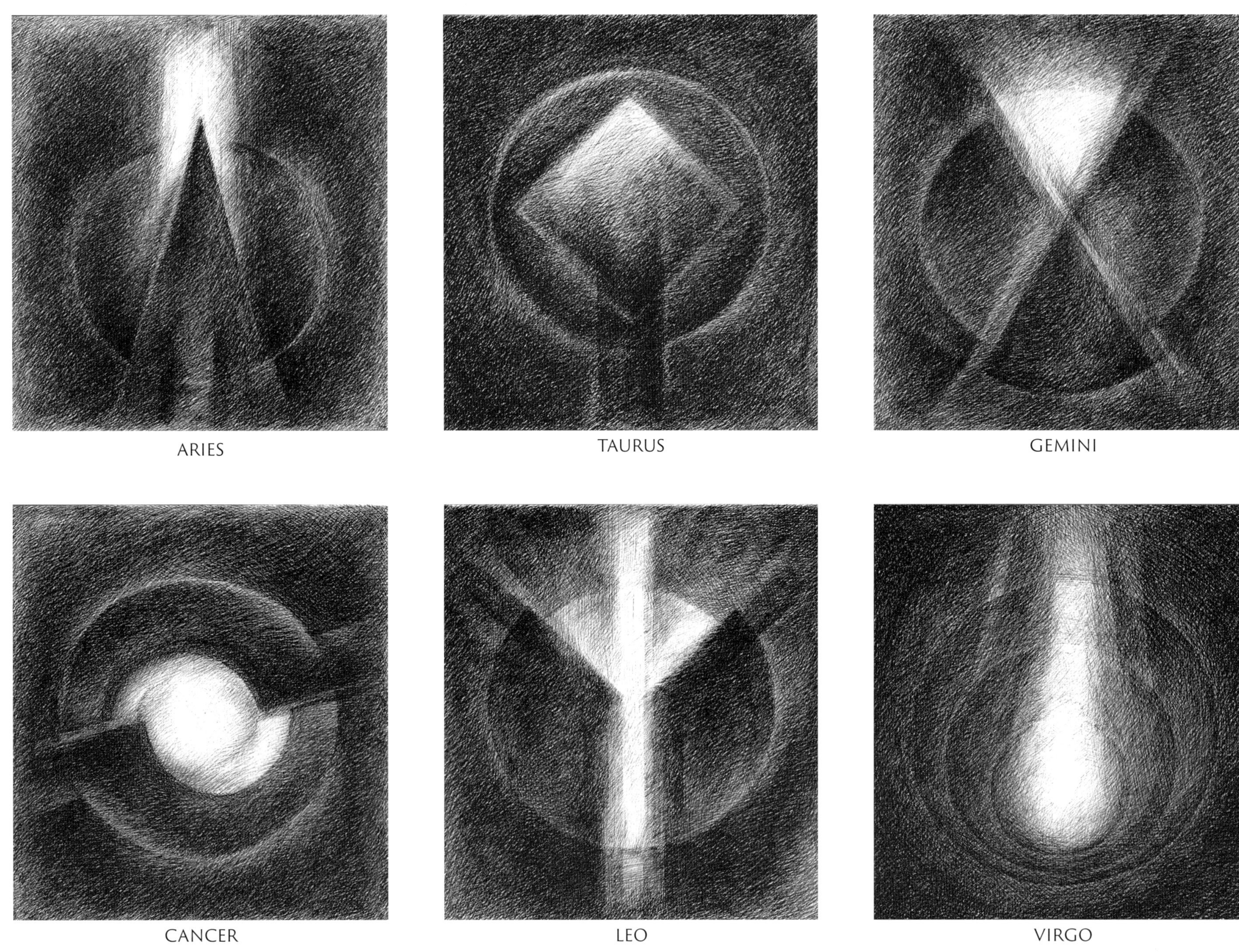

ARIES
TAURUS
GEMINI
CANCER
LEO
VIRGO

LIBRA
SCORPIO
SAGITTARIUS
CAPRICORN
AQUARIUS
PISCES

ZODIAC - SCULPTURES
Gertraud Goodwin

2016-18. 70-95 cm. Glass Fibre, Plaster & Wire.

During the Holy Nights of 2015/2016 I worked with the Zodiac again, this time with small wire armatures which I covered in plasticine and wire. Again, I sensed I was as if partaking in a big flowing movement through the 12 Holy Nights, the small models becoming one by one, day by day, part of a cosmic whole sculptural language. My longing was to refine and lighten their physical manifestation, to achieve a certain fragility and thinness, with open edges and breakthroughs. I wanted the individual zodiacal form forces like taking hold of matter, interpenetrating it, shaping it into a kind of instrument or vessel, which would resound in a particular gesture, showing these form forces like "at work": the rough surface and open edges seemingly unfinished, the process still continuing, unfinished, its traces strongly engrained where the wires show up clearly. This unfinished, incomplete, fragile and perishable quality has a special attraction and beauty for me, similar to nature's autumnal displays of seedpods and seeds. The Japanese term of "wabi-sabi" signifying a turning away from Chinese perfection and the splendour of previous epochs, comes close to what I searched for. "Wabi" means humbleness, moderation and the beauty of the eternally changing energy. The word "sabi" comes from 12th and 13th century poetry, points us today towards the transient, the patina, the mild mourning over the ephemeral process of things as a metaphor for our own existence.

Aspects of these qualities have always moved me, in nature as well as in life: I have to become still, be patient, look and perceive exactly and sense what moves me inwardly.

Rainer Maria Rilke formulates it in the first of his *Duino Elegies* in the following way:

> *For beauty is only*
> *the infant of scarcely endurable terror,*
> *and we are amazed when it casually spares us. …*

(Translated by Stephen Cohn)

The open irregularly textured surfaces create traces, evidence of a becoming, transient gesture "in process", contrasting the finished, slick and hard surfaces, which repel us in their impenetrable enduring finality. Becoming more aware of my own transience getting older, I sensed a longing for these more spiritual qualities in my sculptures, at the borders of impermanence and liminality.

Transposing the form from the small model to a larger armature and then adding fibreglass and plaster to it to create the sculpture, is much more difficult than working with clay – the soft, flexible material so willing and giving to search for the actual form. To arrive at the finished work, the patinated plaster and fibreglass sculpture, takes longer than the actual creation of the theme in clay from which the cast has to be taken. I realised that this casting process has too much of a craft aspect and takes so much time. I decided to leave the last sculptures in clay, a material in which they could not be kept because of the armatures inside.

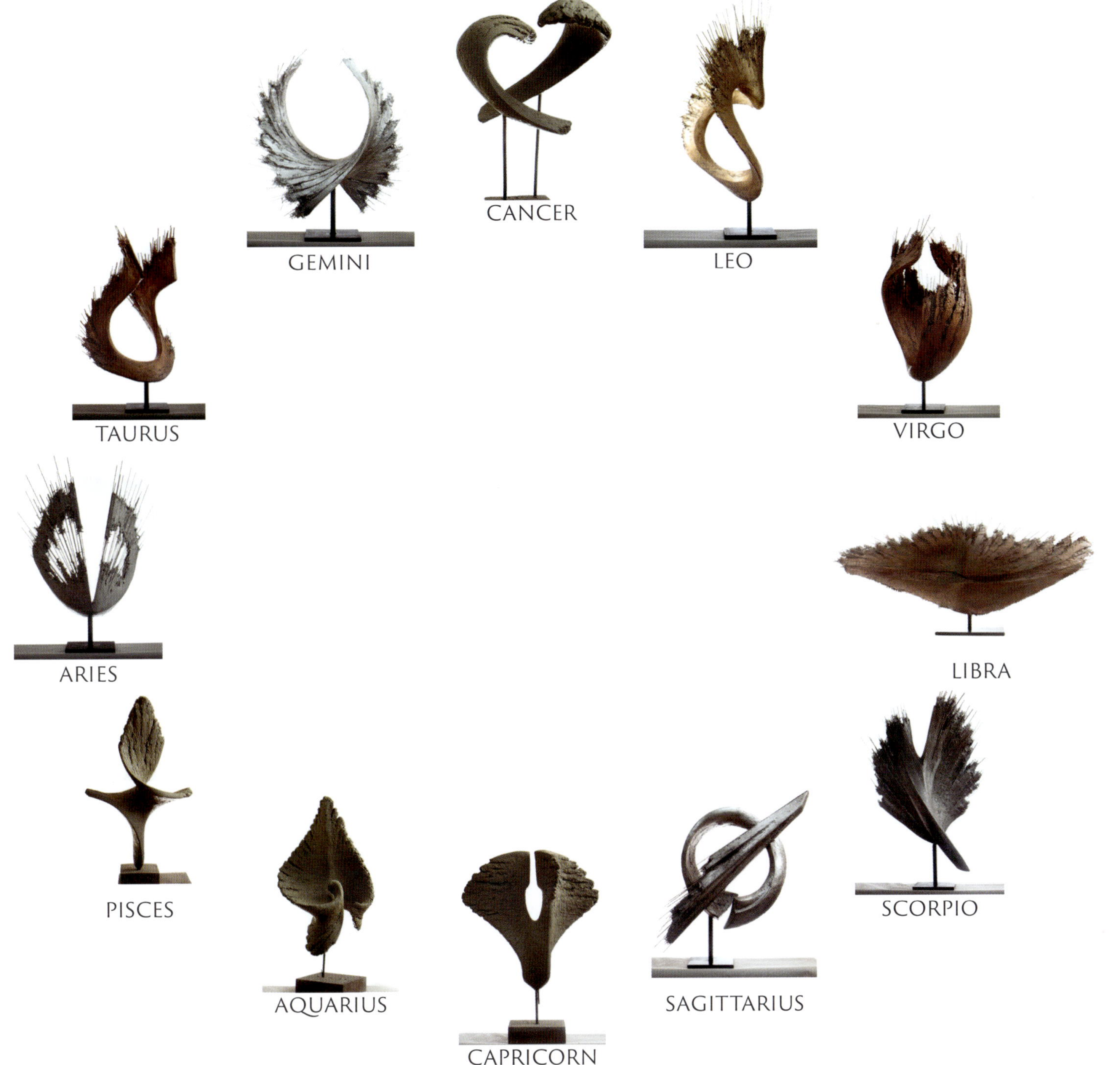

GEMINI
CANCER
LEO
TAURUS
VIRGO
ARIES
LIBRA
PISCES
SCORPIO
AQUARIUS
CAPRICORN
SAGITTARIUS

ARIES

♓

The straight wires radiate in from above and from a wide periphery, shaping and contracting on their way towards a point, a V-shaped shield: a receiving of cosmic forces is manifesting in matter in a condensed but open vessel, which resounds, materialises and protects these forces.

TAURUS

♉

The metal wires manifesting the formative forces begin to open and move in order to congregate into a forward moving spiral. Matter is moved, augmented and widened to embody and mould itself powerfully.

GEMINI

♊

The receiving metal wires spread themselves ever more into space. Wing-like and symmetrical, the gestures cross each other free and relying on each other at the same time. They form an inner space together, expanding and contracting with great dynamic.

CANCER

♋

Two separate spiral gestures move as if away from each other into opposite directions. Thus the space in between each other is moved and enlivened, communicating between the two gestures with inner warmth.

LEO

♌

A continuous circular spiral movement accelerates upwards and outwards, intensifying inwardly downwards. A pulsating expansion – systolic, and contraction – diastolic, embraces, enlivens and protects and inner space.

VIRGO

♍

A generous warm inner space is created by an embracing gesture. The movement gently spirals upwards where it is slowly and carefully released – and where new forces from above are received, and then protected below, in eternally exchanging motion.

LIBRA

♎

Wing-like, the double-bent surface spreads itself horizontally. The centre gently acts as a place of a sensitive exchange from top-right to bottom-left, and from the back to the front. The top edge is free and open to perceive, the wires guiding the forces to the centre. All activity is held and balanced by the quiet support of the bottom half.

SCORPIO

♏

From out of the greatest expanse of two wing-like, open, reaching upwards and outwards gestures, a sharply formed, concentrated and contracting spear-like gesture points diagonally downwards. The two polarities hold each other in great tension and awareness. Their one-sided capacities can be healing as well as destructive – if not coordinated and balanced out between each other.

SAGITTARIUS

♐

In an open, spiralling circle, a diagonal sharp "arrow" is held in check – which in turn keeps the circular movement open and in tension. The round and the straight are in a mutual understanding between each other.

CAPRICORN

With great dynamic and decisiveness the horizontal wing-like gestures receive, pass on, and are drawn out. Past and future reach out towards each other in a constant transition – a moment in time, a point of stillness in the open space, which holds and radiates at the same time.

AQUARIUS

These forces are the archetypal mediator in between. Between narrow and wide, thick and thin, open and closed, the double-bent surface stretches and contracts, always in movement and loyal to the laws of coherence.

Rudolf Steiner tells us that all the other Zodiac forces have to go through the gate of Aquarius to become capable to work on the earth. Thus the forces of Aquarius create the sublime harmony in the human being.

The eurythmy gesture is the only one within the twelve which moves the arms continuously.

PISCES

Tall, upright and open, the flexible centre swings out horizontally towards two sides – forwards to the future and backwards to the past. This creates a crossing as well as a cross which is held from the vertical centre, which gives and directs its forces into the horizontal.

ZODIAC - DRAWINGS "Every line a stroke of force"

2018. A3. Ink Pen.

When I work on the Zodiac sculpturally, a need to draw always follows: on the flat surface, I feel the possibility to depict the periphery of the forces at work in their creative process, shaping and moulding the gestures. It is as if the first pale strokes warming up the page, begin to gather, congregate in particular areas, concentrating themselves according to the forces at work for a particular subject. This is a slow and lengthy process with careful and delicate choices of slowly darkening certain areas, which brings out the light in other areas. This process is a creative manifestation of inner dialogue, through which many aspects of a theme are slowly eliminated, so that the strokes gathering intensity are more and more concentrating towards a simple, one-sided composition, expressive of an essence. This essence depicts naturally only a very small part of the cosmic wholeness of the zodiacal forces, which are all-encompassing, touching and creating every sphere of life. The build-up of the whole Zodiac then needs for me to form a cohesive whole, like a particular family of plants. Cacti and trees may then not be included, but maybe a family of twelve, grasses, as an analogy.

This desire for a wholeness within one particular depiction of the zodiacal forces has inspired as well as guided me throughout my work. In this particular rendering, to let the forces at work themselves speak, was my endeavour. How they enter the surface from far away, coming together from all sides to activate and enliven through their special dance a unique composition, was what I was looking for. I am well aware, that my own instruments - my physicality, my skill, my perception, etc., are very limited and allow only for certain insights.

This I experience as both, a strength and a weakness. My own repeated efforts on this subject and all the other artistic renderings in this book show the unfathomable heights of this subject and what the individual approach can contribute and bring to light to begin to speak to the stars, even if ever so much as a beginning.

Light and dark don't correspond for me with "good and bad". Rather they are both spiritual forces of equal importance but with different capacities and tasks: their working together, their mutual support, understanding and agreement is for me the basis of creation. It is fascinating and mysterious that the drawing begins with a pure white surface—pure spirit but invisible. Then the black strokes appear, take this purity away, and thus introduce matter and cooperation. The more darkness appears in a creative way, the more the light is helped to focus, to become active and be shaped into a composition. Both, the light and the dark, are inseparable and interdependent for any creation. The many shades of grey are an expression of their intricate, caring and intimate relationship.

Spirit is never without matter,
matter never without spirit.

From a verse by Rudolf Steiner, 24. Sept. 1919

As the creative lay at the heart of my efforts, the following drawings may sum these up:

GEMINI

CANCER

LEO

VIRGO

TAURUS

LIBRA

ARIES

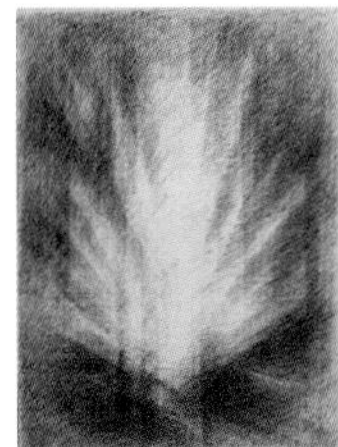

SCORPIO

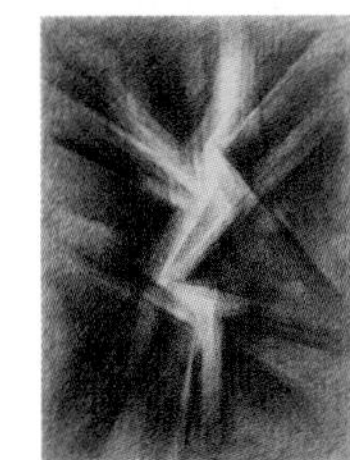

PISCES

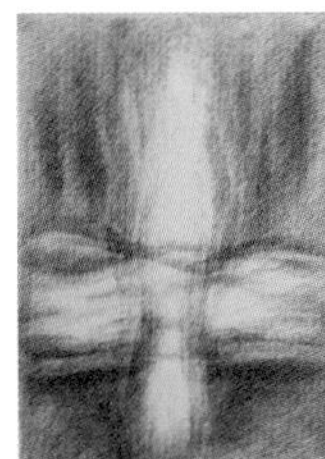

AQUARIUS

CAPRICORN

SAGITTARIUS

ARIES
emergence of light, rising upwards

TAURUS
gathering substance, spreading itself

GEMINI
extending itself into space symmetrically

CANCER
two counter-moving spirals closing themselves off
the periphery

LEO
double spiral of the heart

VIRGO
transubstantiating—outer world becomes inner world

LIBRA
seeking balance

SCORPIO
decisively separating

SAGITTARIUS
aiming through the centre

CAPRICORN
all streams past and future
come together in the present

AQUARIUS
movements and counter-movement

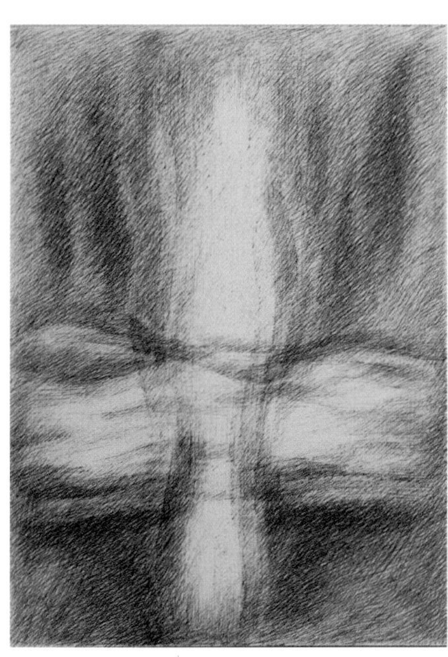

PISCES
interpenetration of verticality and horizontality

PISCES ZODIAC
Gertraud Goodwin

2006. 75 cm. Patinated Plaster & Gold Leaf.

In 1413 the sun moved from the sign of Aries into the sign of Pisces from where it now illuminates all the other signs of the Zodiac. This can be seen as a new gateway, through which all other Zodiac gestures may be understood in a new light. In the lecture cycle "Anthroposophy as Cosmosophy, Part II" Rudolf Steiner speaks about the Pisces-Zodiac as the Zodiac for our time beginning in the middle of the 15th century, since mankind entered the time of Pisces: 1413-3573. In the time of Pisces humanity makes the transition into intellectualism, undergoing a development towards abstraction in which we experience a quality of dissolving and fragmentation. It is a process from the light through darkness to a new-found light. It has become dark inside us and we need to set out to find the light again. This can only happen through our individual freedom. When we put ourselves under the guidance of Michael, we may reach the experience of the etheric Christ as our inner sun.

In the Aries-Zodiac, each sign is engaged in a one-sided gesture purely expressing its own being, whereas in the Pisces-Zodiac two polar opposite gestures work together. This interaction can only be achieved through METAMORPHOSIS. Through it, the great "rulers" and the great "movers" come together:

NO **FORM** WITHOUT THE FORCES OF THE ZODIAC
NO **MOVEMENT** IN TIME WITHOUT METAMORPHOSIS - THE FORCES OF THE PLANETS

The Aries-Zodiac with its individual forces and gestures is the basis for the Pisces-Zodiac. As they come together they influence and enhance each other, lending and transforming their qualities, together preparing a vessel into which a third element can incarnate.

Quite early on I felt that the gesture of each pair would have to work towards a similar goal, to receive the light and be a vessel for it. That, for me shone out as the all-encompassing task to be achieved under the guidance of Pisces. To do sculptural justice to the light aspect of the whole series, I decided to work mainly with crystalline and angular forms, as to me they feel to be sculpturally the most spiritual elements. During the sculptural conversation something happened which I can only describe as a coming into being of a third element which seems to become one of primary importance; it appeared as "a space in between" for which the two polar opposite gestures cared and took responsibility for as they created it. This space became their task, their reason for interacting. The Christ says: "Where two or three are present in my name, I am amongst them". The "Aries" Zodiac, with each of the twelve gestures standing on its own, resounded in me like an after-image, guiding me through my new step to bring the two polar-opposite gestures together.

The process of creating, shifting substance, putting on and taking off matter, had for me, a meditative quality. I sensed that my thinking and concentration on the new theme at first guided my hands, but soon my hands would lead my thoughts in such a way that I felt blessed, sensing that to work at this particular time of the twelve Holy Nights with this particular subject has a magic and a grace which I do not experience during the rest of the year.

I found that during this process, the virtues of the months developed further by Rudolf Steiner were of great help to me. The emphasis lies on the transformation, the process, the change. I felt that this provided exactly the right inner mood for the work on the Pisces-Zodiac, where the challenge is this transformation of each single sign through the working together with the polar opposite gesture. There can be no greater polarity and no deeper inter-relationship than between the straight and the round. These two form-forces built the overture to this new aspect of the Zodiac which has such significance for us today. The straight and the round are also the strongest sculptural polarities as well as its foundation. It is ultimately humanity's task to bring these together in ourselves and through our deeds in the world.

Standing and walking upright we carry our own cosmic origin within us at every moment of our lives, imbuing our horizontal life here on earth with this cosmic uprightness, bringing the two gestures into amalgamation through our deeds. Within our deeds, this crossing and interpenetrating takes place. I realised that the cross or crossing is our main task, our main obstacle as well as our main achievement. The motif of Pisces I find in the cross, as a reality consisting of horizontal, physical forces of gravity and of the vertical, cosmic forces of levity, direction and orientation, forces which have created our feet with which we walk our destinies on earth. The motif of Virgo, the eternally circling rounds, its cosmic wisdom of precision is so beautifully given in our digestive system, where the real transubstantiation, from matter, food, to life and spirit, is taking place.

The cross became the underlying theme for all twelve gestures working together in six pairs. Each pair creates a particular mood and sculpturally crossing and interpenetrating gesture. This becomes, for me, the inner space itself. Each meeting needs the protection and intimacy of this middle ground where it is held and becomes this new third quality. I have the feeling that this has to do with the thinking of the heart, a new quality which emerges in people now more and more out of an inner necessity. A new capability is being asked of us at a time when crossing the threshold takes place for each of us in different ways. It is a loosening of our loosely knit-together sheaths which can bring turmoil, illness and desperation, as well as new insight, and the task to take hold of ourselves in a new way. "FROM THE I". Those are the words which Rudolf Steiner gave to the Mercury column in the First Goetheanum. I see it as a breakthrough of the concentrated and isolated Mars gesture in the fourth capital to which belong the words "I" or "EGO". Here everything has been cut off, each gesture is on its own, cut off from its neighbour by vertical columns and cut off from above by a deep crevice. The stars don't speak to man any more, he is alone. This is an experience we can all have today. But in this loneliness ripens the longing to break through and free which man can do only "FROM THE I" out of his own free initiative, the metamorphosis to the next stage.

I see the Pisces-Zodiac as an expression of this metamorphosis, from the Mars capital to the Mercury capital. There, the breakthrough to a new gesture has occurred through the two moving snakelike gestures crossing and embracing a new vertical centre from two sides. The two snakes and the Mercury staff have been the archetypal sign of healing and transformation for millennia.

I chose a rectangular shape for the double reliefs, patinated with the metal iron. The rectangle is the most earthly of all angles, the most set, solid, quiet, rigid and reliable. It has the most sublime and also the most lifeless potentials within sculpture and within life. Within it is the cross! To bring about the meeting of polar opposites within this format would be a challenge and an opportunity. This was the choice to acknowledge and honour the Mars stage of our evolution, out of which this transformation can take place. Where the true meeting of the polar opposites takes place, it is as though the iron "blushes" with a new life and becomes golden. The meeting space is patinated with gold leaf, the metal of the sun and the heart, to warm and intensify the place of the meeting. The sculptural gestures are mostly crystalline and minimal in an effort to concentrate and to emphasise that in the most condensed forms on earth lie the most spiritual possibilities.

ARIES - LIBRA

The supporting gesture of Libra from below enables Aries to open up, offering itself to receive the light from above, which is then held and contained together in equanimity.

LIBRA - ARIES

Libra offers equanimity holding the balance between above and below, between right and left, between movement and stillness, so that Aries can become a light-bearer.

Virtues by Rudolf Steiner

♈ Devotion - becomes Sacrifice   ♎ Contentment - becomes Equanimity

PISCES - VIRGO

Virgos' concentric rhythmic circles succeed through tactfulness of heart to give an inner space for the cross of Pisces to hold the light in love. The Celtic sun-crosses have this theme in their relationship between the cross and the circle. It may become a transformed living reality for our time; internalised and intensified the circle with its conscious orientation of the cross becomes a moving spiral, a vessel to be filled.

VIRGO - PISCES

Through Love, the cross of Pisces comes out of its stern symmetry and angularity, inspired by the inner moving world of Virgo. They enable each other to engage in a moving spiralled dance, imbuing love and tactfulness of heart to the four directions of space.

Virtues by Rudolf Steiner

♓ Courtesy - becomes Tactfulness of Heart

♍ Magnanimity - becomes Love

TAURUS - SCORPIO

Taurus' square stretches, opens up and steps apart to receive the light; this progress helps Scorpio to order its own asymmetry towards the new task of creating an inner space, which is the new insight for both of them together.

SCORPIO - TAURUS

Scorpio offers its own in-between space to give Insight, opening up, making an inner space. This is held and protected. Progress is achieved.

Virtues by Rudolf Steiner

♉ Inner Equilibrium - becomes Progress

♏ Patience - becomes Insight

GEMINI - SAGITTARIUS

The square crossing over of Gemini opens up asymmetrically, faithfully, towards Sagittarius, preparing the space and direction for Sagittarius' diagonal gesture of light to be held and received. This new combined formation of an inner space for the light can be an experience of truth.

SAGITTARIUS - GEMINI

Sagittarius offers its capacity of the diagonal, the in-between of verticality and horizontality, as an experience of truth. This in-between space finds its new goal as an inner space. The new task achieves faithfulness for Gemini.

Virtues by Rudolf Steiner

♊ Perseverance - becomes Faithfulness   ♐ Control of Speech - becomes Experience of Truth

CANCER - CAPRICORN

The no-meeting of Cancer's two spirals experiences a catharsis through the offer of Capricorn to meet and, united, to work towards the creation of an inner space. Nature's building of inner spaces of blossoms and fruit and seeds in the time of Cancer is redeemed by man's soul-space at Christmas-time through which everything in nature can be experienced as Christ imbued (second coming of Christ).

CAPRICORN - CANCER

The receiving cradle of Capricorn offers itself for Cancer's two centres to move and become one to bring redemption in the inner space.

Virtues by Rudolf Steiner

♋ Unselfishness - becomes Catharsis

♑ Courage - becomes Force of Redemption

LEO - AQUARIUS

The centre of Leo offers itself in freedom to become the impulse and centre-giving force for Aquarius to create an inner space which is held and flows through from periphery to centre both ways at the same time. Meditative power is achieved by this quality of working together.

AQUARIUS - LEO

The sculptural double-bent plane of Aquarius offers its meditative power to Leo, so that Leo's centre and periphery flow freely in and out, out and in, achieving freedom.

Virtues by Rudolf Steiner

♌ Compassion - becomes Freedom

♒ Discretion - becomes Meditative Power

PISCES ZODIAC AND THE PRESENT AGE
John Salter

Sculptures: 2000-01. Approximate size: 26 x 24cm. Resin Bronze.
Drawings: 2004. A2 (59 x 42cm). Charcoal on paper.
Paintings: 2004. A2 (59 x 42cm). Watercolour on paper.

1. SUMMARY
The Zodiac handed down from Greco-Roman times has been traditionally related to the human form from Aries (forehead) to Pisces (feet). Rudolf Steiner's spiritual research points to a different configuration of the constellations in relation to the human being as being applicable in the current epoch of civilisation now under the sway of the Fishes. Following experience of working artistically with the traditional (Aries) Zodiac the attempt was made to elucidate some aspects of the present, Pisces Zodiac using artistic means.

2. INTRODUCTION
Whilst working artistically on the traditional Zodiac (described in Section 3) I was struck by Steiner's description of the Zodiac applicable now which resulted in a quite different general picture of the human being without, however, going into specific detail (1). What could this mean for us now? Did the qualities of the traditional Aries Zodiac no longer apply? Intellectual speculation led nowhere. Could the question be explored artistically, using artistic means for research purposes? Before that process can be described some minimal background is necessary. Section 4 outlines the relation of the different ages of civilisation to the constellations. Section 5 and Figs. 1 & 2 summarise the differing characteristics of the Aries and Pisces Zodiacs, whilst Section 6 discusses some aspects of the Pisces epoch. The working method and the means used are described in Section 7. The process is evaluated in Section 8 which appears to reveal a close relationship between the qualities of the Pisces Zodiac and the practice of the six basic soul exercises which should accompany esoteric work. Some positive and negative dynamics relating to this epoch are noted in Section 9.

3. PREVIOUS ZODIAC PROJECT
This exploration of the Pisces Zodiac grew out of and was founded on a previous project on the Zodiac. The earlier work was related to the traditional Aries Zodiac handed down from classical times. Starting with 12 sculptures in resin bronze it eventually also included 12 black-and-white drawings and 12 paintings.

The impulse for this work was not drawn from traditional images of the Zodiac, however, but from the modern art of eurythmy developed by Rudolf Steiner from 1912 on (3). This is an art of movement expressing the dynamics of speech. The consonants are related to the different constellations of the Zodiac; in some cases two closely related sounds belong to one constellation. The sculptures and drawings were developed from the movement for a particular sound and were taken through a seven-step process. This started with the expression of a simple dynamic in the clay or drawing, setting it aside and then developing further in a second, a third version and so on until a viable composition appeared in the sixth, seventh or sometimes an eighth attempt. Other factors were allowed to play into the process, such as the relationship of the constellations to the parts and functions of the human form.

The paintings went through a similar process but based in each case on a chord of three colours given by Steiner for each sound. Each work session was preceded by carrying out the relevant eurythmy movement and also by inwardly contemplating the dynamic to be explored. The sevenfold process proved invaluable in resolving discordant elements and producing an inwardly consistent composition.

CANCER

GEMINI

LEO

VIRGO

TAURUS

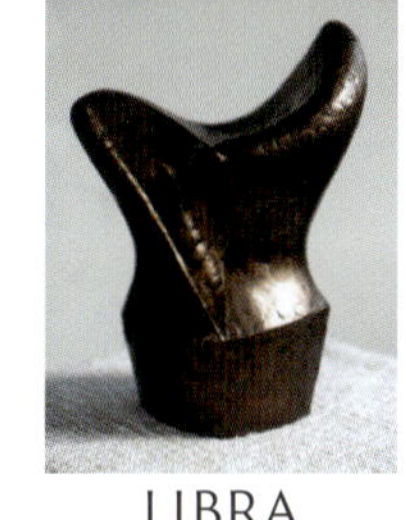

LIBRA

ARIES

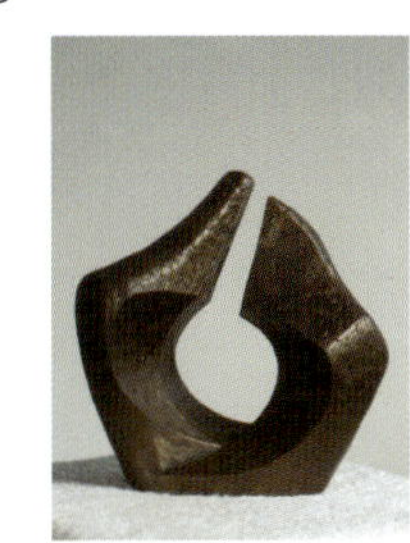

PISCES

SCORPIO

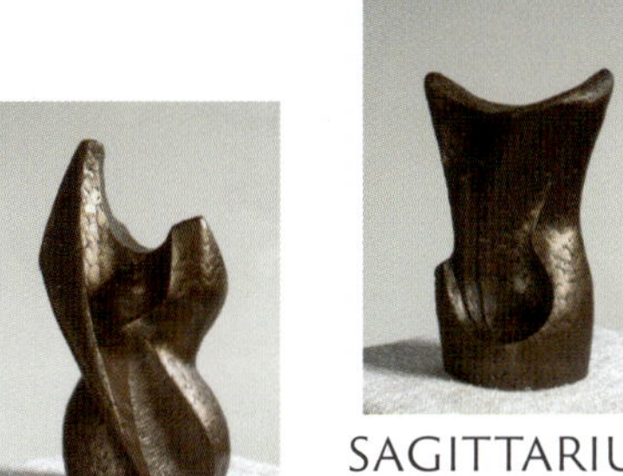

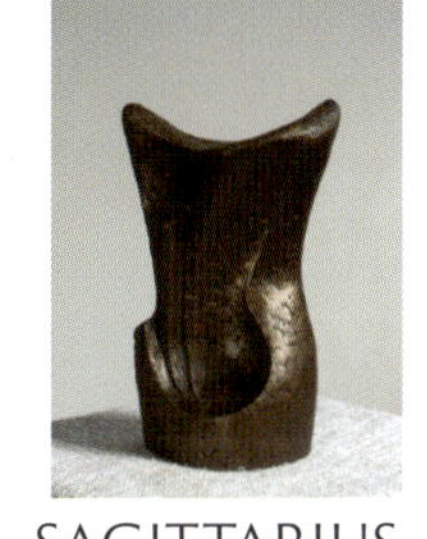

AQUARIUS

SAGITTARIUS

CAPRICORN

ARIES

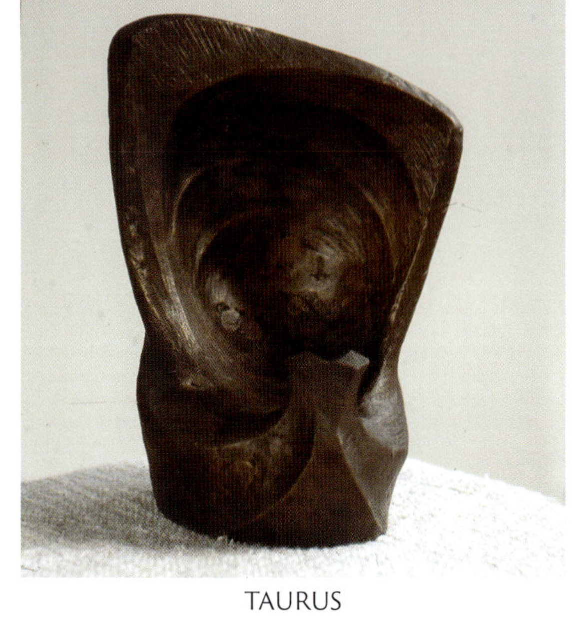

TAURUS

GEMINI

CANCER

LEO

VIRGO

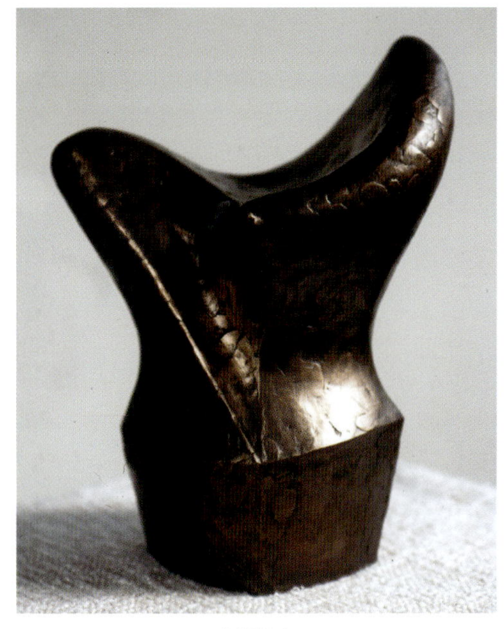

LIBRA

SCORPIO

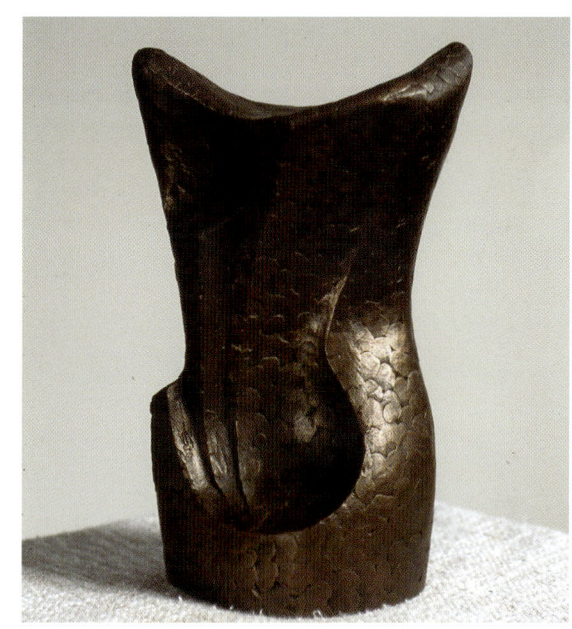

SAGITTARIUS

CAPRICORN

AQUARIUS

PISCES

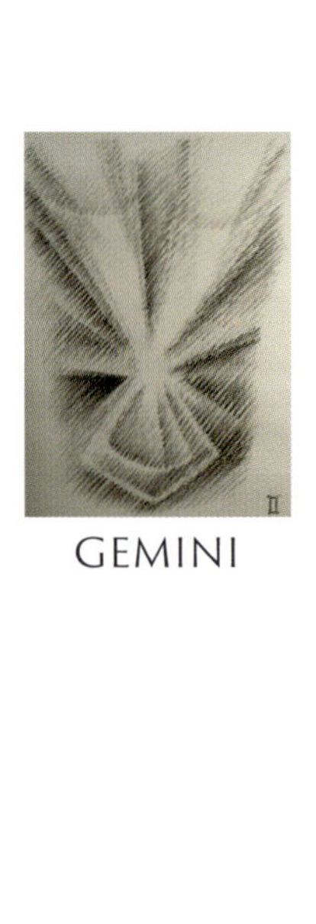

GEMINI

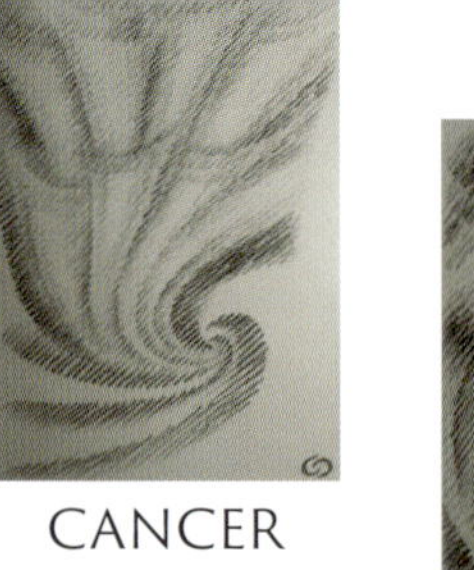

CANCER

LEO

VIRGO

TAURUS

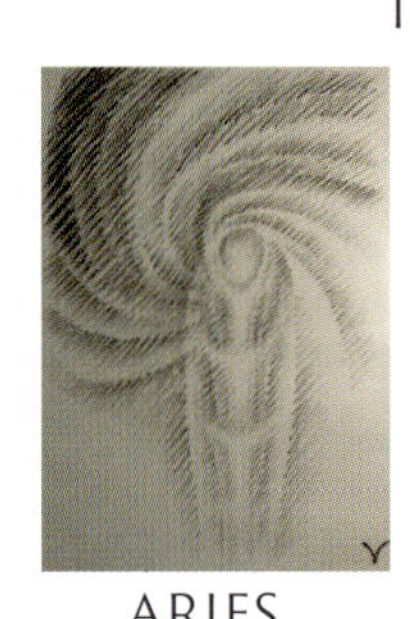

LIBRA

ARIES

SCORPIO

PISCES

AQUARIUS

CAPRICORN

SAGITTARIUS

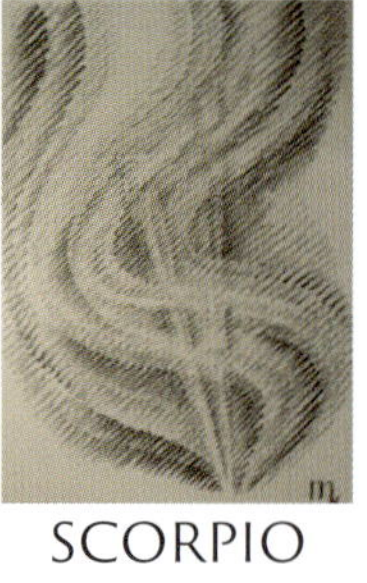

CANCER
GEMINI
LEO
TAURUS
VIRGO
ARIES
LIBRA
PISCES
SCORPIO
AQUARIUS
SAGITTARIUS
CAPRICORN

ARIES
TAURUS
GEMINI
CANCER
LEO
VIRGO

LIBRA

SCORPIO

SAGITTARIUS

CAPRICORN

AQUARIUS

PISCES

ARIES
TAURUS
GEMINI
CANCER
LEO
VIRGO

LIBRA
SCORPIO
SAGITTARIUS
CAPRICORN
AQUARIUS
PISCES

4. EPOCHS AND CONSTELLATIONS

The development of human civilisation as characterised by Steiner goes through major changes in a rhythm of 2160 years. This is indirectly related to the movement of the vernal point, where the sun rises at the spring equinox, against the background of the zodiacal constellations. The recent past and immediate future can be briefly summarised as follows:

Vernal Point enters Constellation approx.
Taurus: 4400 B.C.
Aries: 1800 B.C.
Pisces: 100 B.C.
Aquarius: 2600 A.D.

Cultural Epoch Post-Atlantean Periods
3rd. Egypt/Mesopotamia: 2907 B.C.
4th. Greece/Rome: 747 B.C.
5th. Present Epoch: 1413 A.D.
Next Epoch: 3573 A.D.

The cultural epochs start around the midpoint of the period that the vernal point is in in each constellation. Thus the Greco-Roman period begins in 747 B.C., the traditional date of the founding of Rome, about a millenium after the sun at the vernal point has moved into Aries and ends after the Middle Ages in 1413 A.D. The vernal point moves into Pisces around the time of Christ but our own epoch does not begin until the 15th century, the time of the Renaissance, and runs through to the middle of the fourth millennium. This according to Steiner is the true beginning of the Waterman (Aquarian) Age, although the vernal point will actually enter the constellation of Aquarius around 2600 A.D.

The change from the Aries epoch to that of the Pisces points also to a more far reaching change in evolution. The last Aries epoch marks the end of a great cycle starting with the previous Pisces epoch which took place before the beginning of Atlantis in the last period of Lemuria (1). There is, in addition, a very much greater cycle of evolution starting after the sun had separated from the earth. This cycle also started under the direction of Pisces when the cosmic forces working from the constellations over immensely long periods of time fashioned the human form from the feet up (2). Still an etheric form in late Lemuria the human being gradually took on physical form, becoming by Greek times fully at home on the earth. This last Aries epoch was also the time when the being of Christ incarnated upon earth to give a new impulse to the development of the spiritual individuality of man. From the new Pisces epoch on we have to begin the process of freeing ourselves from the danger of entombment in the physical and increasingly share in the full unfolding of our spiritual being.

5. CHARACTERISTICS OF ARIES AND PISCES CONSTELLATIONS

The traditional Aries Zodiac was related to the human being from the head (Aries) to the feet (Pisces) and was characterised at one time by Steiner as follows (Fig.1) (1).

In contrast to the Aries Zodiac the Pisces Zodiac of the present time has a radically different orientation to the threefold human being (Fig.2). The upper part of man, the head region, now runs from Pisces to Gemini, whilst the lower part, the limbs, runs through the polar opposite constellations, from Virgo to the Sagittarius. The middle man, the rhythmic system, now comprises the remaining opposite pairs of Cancer/Capricorn and Leo/Aquarius (1).

Constellations	Part of human form	Qualities
Human being formed out of the cosmos: head Aries Taurus Gemini Cancer	- head - neck - larynx - shoulders - arms - thorax - skin	- taking in the universe - looking out into the universe - taking hold of oneself
Human being formed from within: chest Leo Virgo Libra Scorpio	- heart - digestive system - pelvis - hips - reproductive organs	- actively filled from within - ripening - becoming part of inorganic matter - seeking balance - poison sting of ingested matter
Human being formed in relation to the earth: limbs, occupation Sagittarius Capricorn Aquarius Pisces	- upper leg: thigh and knee - lower leg: calf and feet	- hunter - animal breeder - tiller of soil - trader

Fig.1

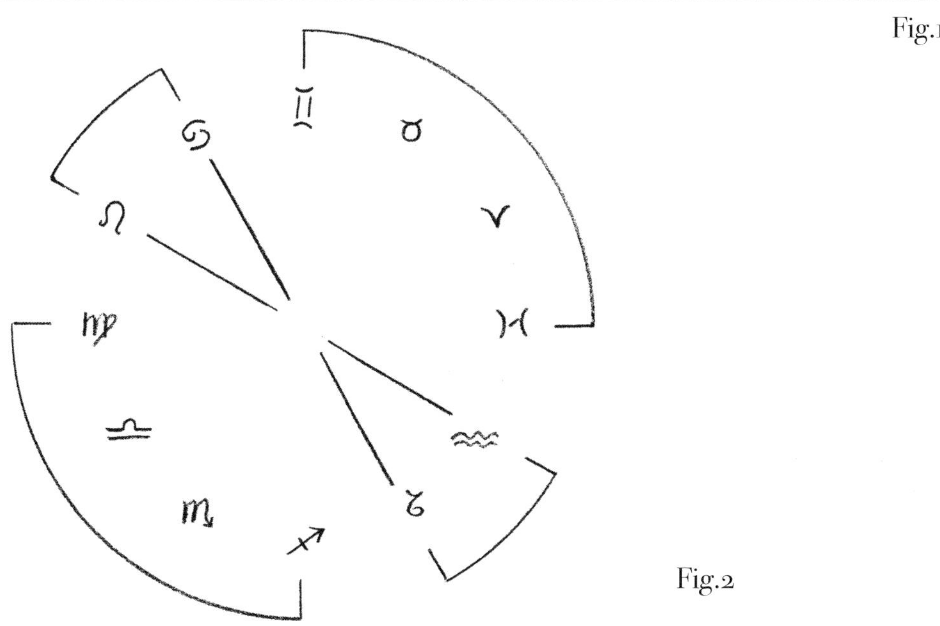

Fig.2

6. THE PISCES ZODIAC

Steiner's remarks concerning the Pisces Zodiac do not go into any detail regarding the part played by individual constellations. He refers to the development of the intellect and to the growth of industrialisation as processes of abstraction and to a kind of "dissolution" which will increase into the next Aquarian Age. This is in contrast to the earlier evolution of the human form out of its purely etheric condition in the previous Pisces epoch towards physical embodiment on the earth. The head region (Pisces to Gemini) has a dying quality that forms the basis for the inner life of ideas and images. The limb or will pole (Virgo to Sagittarius) is imbued with undeveloped life, is embryonic. The constellations in between (Cancer/Capricorn and Leo/Aquarius) relate to the rhythmical aspect of the human being which swings to and fro between image and embryo.

It seems clear that – whatever perspective one adopts – the human being had, after immensely long periods of evolution, fully arrived within his physical organism and was fully at home upon the earth by the time our present age opened in the 15th century. As man lost his earlier spiritual faculties his etheric body shrank closer to the physical form. References to "abstraction" and "dissolution" seem to imply that the whole process is going into reverse. The etheric body will now start to expand and mankind will be faced with developing new faculties. It will have to take an increasingly more conscious part in its own evolution. The present age of Pisces inaugurates another great cycle of development.

With this as background, how can one start relating to this new configuration of the Zodiac? I was still working on the earlier Zodiac project at the time and any speculation about its significance tended to be in terms of traditional ideas about the working of individual constellations and did not lead anywhere. However, I did briefly wonder what it would be like to place the forms of opposite constellations against one another. When the earlier project had been completed I began to look at the Pisces Zodiac without having any real line of approach. The Zodiac seemed to be all polarities or opposites: the "head" constellations ranged against the "limb" constellations and those relating to the "middle" man were split into opposite pairs. There seemed to be a pulling apart in all directions. Then I remembered my earlier intuition to bring together the opposite forms belonging to each axis. This would be too complex a task to do sculpturally, at least initially, but it gave rise to the thought that one could explore two specific movements in drawing and hope to come to some sort of resolution. The idea evolved of relating opposite pairs of constellations together in a series of drawings. But before proceeding to do this I felt the work needed underpinning with a comprehensive picture of the whole. This led to the concept of Wholistic Imaging with a descending order of relationships:

1. The Upper and Lower Pairs (Pisces to Gemini and Virgo to Sagittarius) working together in cooperative tension and harmonised in this by the remaining Middle Pairs (Cancer/Capricorn and Leo/Aquarius) : the whole Zodiac regarded comprehensively as an organism bearing the threefold being of man as an active principle.

2. Three sets of Crosses, two of which have Upper, Lower and Middle Pairs (Aries/Libra with Cancer/Capricorn and Taurus/Scorpio with Leo/Aquarius). The third Cross (Pisces/Virgo and Gemini/Sagittarius) are the first and last of the Upper and Lower Pairs (taking Pisces/Virgo as the first). Two of the crosses have the harmonising qualities of the Middle Pairs as it were built in, whilst the third lacks this support and remains within the Upper and Lower duality. It will be seen later that this has an important consequence.

3. Pairs of opposites or axes across the Zodiac; these are the smallest subdivisions of the whole and would be the subject of the sequence of six drawings. But it was felt important to bear in mind, throughout, the more inclusive relationships outlined in 1 and 2 above. The actual working process was based on experience with the previous Zodiac project. In this case the eurythmy movements for two consonants, relating to the two constellations concerned,

would be brought together in a sevenfold process aimed at producing an artistic composition as a result. The human form as something completed would no longer be relevant as a factor playing into the process as before. However, an awareness of the "Twelve Moods" by Rudolf Steiner, a compactly expressed poem on the twelve constellations, was present during the work (5). The process had both eurythmic and meditative aspects, as preparation for the actual drawing. Each work period was preceded by the following steps:

1. Performing the eurythmy gesture for the relevant pairs of constellations followed by

2. the eurythmy movement for the corresponding pair of consonants.

3. Dwelling inwardly upon the dynamics of the two movements that had to be brought together without, however, imagining a pictorial outcome. At a later stage of the sequence of seven drawings some aspect of the relevant poems of the "Twelve Moods" was allowed to play into the process.

In the first sketch both movements were expressed in the simplest terms; a second then played with the possibilities that emerged. As the interaction became more complex it often grew confused and it then became necessary to simplify and/or harmonise the working of the dynamics which had been set in motion. In most cases an artistically satisfactory composition resulted in the seventh attempt, although sometimes final adjustments required a further drawing. This process resulted in the six drawings described in the next section which relate to the six pairs of opposite constellations working together. Each pair of opposites will be referred to as an axis. (Note: it is obviously desirable to have had experience of the basic movements in eurythmy in class work with a trained eurythmist to carry out the above. However, descriptions of the relevant movements are given in Steiner's lectures on eurythmy (3) and are further explored in Margarete Kirchner-Bockholt's book on curative eurythmy (8). Werner Barfod's booklet (7) which brings together many different levels of experience of speech sounds in connection with the constellations and planets proved an invaluable companion in this and the former Zodiac project.

7. PISCES ZODIAC: WORKING TOGETHER OF OPPOSITE DYNAMICS

The development of the drawings for each axis will be described in turn but not in number order.

1. PISCES/VIRGO AXIS: N/B

Below, the dynamic activity living in the movement for B leads into the dark, warm, enclosed realm of Virgo. In this realm below the diaphragm the transformation of substances takes place to build up the human form. The enfolding, embracing movement leads into the realm of human will. Shielding, protecting a precious inner activity is the gesture which B brings from the realm of Virgo.

In this composition the lower, enclosed realm of Virgo is to be related to the dynamic of Pisces expressed through the movement for N. This has a lightness of touch, a touching and withdrawing, indicating something grasped in a flash before moving on quickly to comprehend something else. Several attempts which tried to penetrate too far into the realm of B had to be abandoned before arriving at the Pisces/ Virgo composition.

The enclosing movements which above have a looser relationship to the inner B realm have taken on the N quality of touching and leaving so that a zigzag path of light begins to permeate the hidden realm. The warm, dark space below receives a gentle awakening to new possibilities. Through the touch of the Fishes a new dimension awakens in the depths of the Virgin. The Gemini/Sagittarius axis which completes the Pisces/Virgo and Gemini/Sagittarius cross will be dealt with after the other relationships have been described.

2. ARIES/LIBRA AXIS: V/C

The weaving, welling, on-flowing movement of V streams across the upper part. In eurythmy this wave movement streams unendingly but provides a warmth shield around the human form. As a movement in drawing or modelled in clay it can shape itself into a holding form. In the wave or rounded form are reflected different aspects of thinking: concepts which are clearly defined in the rounded form (top left), thoughts which express movement in the weaving wave forms (top right).

From below work the dynamics of Libra, experienced in the movement for C (as in dance) which can be felt as if one went to pick up something heavy and finds that it is quite light and flies upward with ease: gravity mutates into levity. The skeletal organ of balance (pelvis) allows movement across the earth and freedom of movement in the upper part of the body. In the physical world balance is a state of rest; spiritually one feels it as continual movement balancing out imbalances.

The movement wells up from the base and rises in continually balancing sweeps to meet the weaving of Aries until a conversation arises between them.

5. CANCER/CAPRICORN AXIS: F/L

This axis belongs to the Middle Man and can be seen as particularly supportive of the Aries/Libra axis. Working into the dynamics of this axis led after some attempts at vertical compositions to prefer a horizontal format (which was also followed for the other "middle" axis of Leo/Aquarius). The realm of Capricorn is filled with the flowing dynamic of L, sweeping down, embracing, rising up. From small beginnings it can grow rhythmically to great enclosing arcs, filled by the buoyant forces of growing things. In the ancient mysteries the force of L was felt in the creative and formative element in all things which can overcome matter.

Now the fleeting movement of F belonging to Cancer has to find its relationship with the expanding, flowing L. In this image the deeply breathing, flowing movement is woven into the L so that some Cancer streams unite with the sweeping L and some preserve the in-and-out gesture of Cancer. The experience of F in the breath connects the wisdom inherent in the ether body with the source of wisdom in the cosmos, a relationship understood in ancient times through the being of Isis. The mystery of the Word was explored at Ephesus through the intimate experience of human speech upon the breath (4). Werner Barfod points out that the place name embraces F with the vowel E before and after the F: EF-FE-SUS (7).

The unaccustomed position of Capricorn in the middle system of the human being, compared to its role in the former Aries dispensation of the Zodiac, becomes clearer when the rhythmic life-sustaining flow of the L is allied to the rhythm of the breath in F. Combined they provide a powerful basis for harmonising the soul life and, in the axis comprising the other arm of the cross, enabling the rising will of Libra to play into the weaving thought-life of Aries in tranquil conversation.

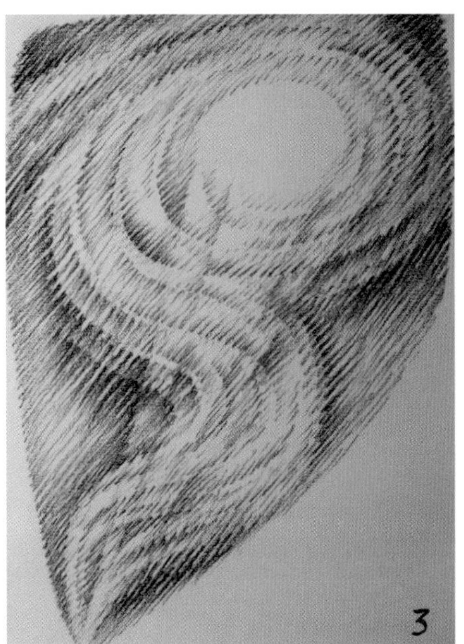

3. TAURUS/SCORPIO AXIS: R/S

Now we have to reconcile the rolling dynamics of R, for Taurus, with the powerful sweep of S, belonging to Scorpio. In this drawing a simple wheeling movement embraces a light-filled centre, recalling Taurus' role in the human being of moving with everything that flows from the cosmos: a gesture between surrender and standing firm. The powerful movement of S, like the sweeps of the magician's wand calming what is in turmoil, is focussed into the point of the sting. The earlier image for this constellation, the Eagle, speaks of the heights whilst the sting, which relates to the incorporation of matter into the human form, creates a tension between above and below.

A powerful ambiguity can be experienced where the strong movement of S stands between good and evil, between the use or abuse of power. In the combined dynamics of R and S, the latter is drawn into the circling, upholding quality of R. The light realm of Taurus, which in this instance is functioning within the upper region of the human being, now streams down, illuminating the sting of Scorpio.

Whereas in the Aries/Libra axis a conversation is inaugurated, here in the Taurus/Scorpio axis something more like an interaction appears to take place.

6. LEO/AQUARIUS AXIS: T/M

In some ways this was the hardest to bring to a satisfactory artistic conclusion. The powerful vertical of T streaming down from above into the depths of the human being is allied with Leo's joyful, expressive gesture of enthusiasm. The dynamic of Leo moves through the rhythmic pulse of the circulation, harmonising head and limbs. In T lives a feeling for the TAO, indicating all that radiates from heaven to earth behind nature and pointing to the upright posture of man within creation.

Finding the right expression for the movement of Aquarius and M in a horizontal composition in which the dynamic of T had to be central presented some problems. M has the quality of penetrating everything with understanding together with the dynamic of a reciprocal forming movement. This reciprocal activity appears in the human form particularly in the fore-arm where the radius and ulna have their "knobs" at opposite ends (formed under the sway of Aquarius).

Eventually two horizontal interlocking movements appeared that stream from infinite distances and move around the central T gesture. The constantly flowing reciprocal movement forms a shape like the standing wave which forms above a submerged rock in a flowing stream. The image arising from combining the movements of T and M, Leo and Aquarius, has a certain inner strength in the midst of constantly harmonising movement, reconciling the distant periphery with the centred posture. This strongly supports the dialogue of R and S, of Taurus and Scorpio, which constitutes the other part of this cross in the Zodiac.

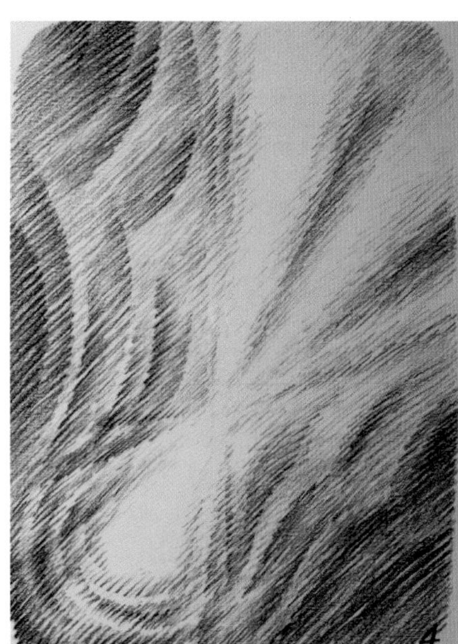

4. GEMINI/SAGITTARIUS AXIS: H/G

The darker, surrounding gesture grew out of the movement for G, belonging to Sagittarius. This movement presses back a surrounding world that is felt to be oppressive or creating revulsion; in fending off the outer world a protected space arises within which the soul's inner forces are consolidated.

The shining awareness of H, belonging to Gemini, has been drawn into the inner space of G. After a number of experiments the gesture for Gemini came to rest within the protected space of Sagittarius. The movement for H has a dual character: initially contracting, a gathering together of forces which are released in joyful expansion. The symmetry of Gemini in the human form allows the hands to touch each other, awakening the sense of self which is enhanced by the focus of the eyes on an object.

The combined dynamics of this composition brings the sequence working through from the Pisces/Virgo axis (which forms the third Zodiac cross with Gemini/Sagittarius) to a certain conclusion. From the gentle awakening in Pisces/Virgo (Drawing 1), through the thematic conversation of Aries/Libra (Drawing 2) and the more interactive gesture of Taurus/Scorpio (Drawing 3) we now arrive at a complete integration of the Gemini/Sagittarius motifs. The shining radiance of the H streams out from the inner space of G (Drawing 4).

8. EVALUATION

The Aries epoch marked the end of a long period in which the human form was fully developed as a physical organisation on earth. The forces associated with the Aries Zodiac obviously continue to support the human form and work into every embryo that is conceived but different influences are called into activity by the configuration of the Zodiac in the Pisces epoch. This age is concerned with the loosening of the soul from the physical and the development of new spiritual faculties. It therefore appears appropriate to concentrate attention on soul faculties and their development. In this case the upper motifs would apply to the faculty of thinking, the lower to the activity of will and the middle motifs to the harmonising and purifying of the realm of feeling. In this context the way in which the upper and lower motifs increasingly interact makes one aware how thinking and willing play into one another; thinking requires a certain amount of will to keep it on track and willing needs the clarity of direction given by thinking.

This perception soon leads one to recall the six basic inner exercises which should accompany the life of meditation as described in several of Steiner's basic books. The next section outlines how these six exercises can be related to the six drawings and the relevant constellations. The book by Florin Lowndes entitled *Enlivening the Chakra of the Heart* (9) is invaluable in deepening one's understanding of these exercises, both individually and as an organism. It also throws up an interesting relationship between the six exercises and the six positions of the basic eurythmy exercise "I think speech". In the ensuing discussion the theme of the 12 Virtues which relate to the 12 constellations is introduced. Each of these lead on to the development of a new ability. This is recorded in *Reminiscences of Rudolf Steiner* by Ilona Schubert (10).

THE SIX BASIC EXERCISES AND THE PISCES ZODIAC

1. Control of Thinking: dwelling for a few minutes upon a particular object without deviating from it trains one to think consequently. The accent is mainly on thinking but requires the steady support of the will to do it. In Drawing 1 the upper motif lightly touches the lower which provides quiet support. The upper motif relates to Pisces whose Virtue is Magnanimity; this quality is required to bring into the thought process manifold aspects of the object of contemplation. Practice of this Virtue leads on to Love. The lower motif relates to Virgo and the Virtue of Courtesy leading to Tactfulness of Heart. This inner tact helps order the different aspects brought together through the Magnanimity of Pisces in shaping the exercise towards clarity and coherence.

2. Control of Will: the carrying out at a specified time of a simple act which is not required by the normal demands of life. The will is called into action by a thought that tells it what should be done. This helps develop the ability to carry out one's intentions. In Drawing 2 the upper motif formulates its gesture quite clearly and hands it down, as it were, to the lower. The "conversation" brings a formative element into the lower motif; the thought provides a motif for the will, calling it into action. The Virtue of Devotion, belonging to Aries which in time leads to the ability for Sacrifice, is a necessary ingredient in the education of the will whilst the Virtue of Contentment, belonging to Libra which becomes Calmness, also supports the will exercise.

3. Control of Feeling: this is not the suppression of feeling but the disciplining of emotional displays and the cultivation of sensibility; an inner composure and balance is gradually established. Now we move to Drawing 5 relating to the Cancer/Capricorn axis. Here, in the middle realm, the two motifs work together bringing harmony into the flow of breath and the life of feeling. Cancer points to the development of Selflessness, which can become Catharsis, whilst Capricorn can give us Courage, leading to the power of Redemption. These are the very qualities that can strengthen and purify the life of feeling. In a certain sense these three exercises mutually support each other in bringing about a basic inner discipline. The first two need the help of the third and the Cancer/Capricorn axis can be regarded as lending its support to the first two axes. The remaining three exercises can be experienced as transformations of the first three; the fourth of the third, the fifth of the second and the sixth of the first (9).

4. Positivity: looking out for the positive qualities in what appears at first sight to be destructive or unwholesome, seeing some aspect that is beautiful in what otherwise at first appears completely ugly. This brings a certain liberation from the constraints of sympathy and antipathy and an education of the life of feeling in relation to the world, a turning outward of the equanimity gained through the third exercise. Now we turn to Drawing 6 for the other middle axis, Leo/ Aquarius. Here there is an opening out, as it were, from the realm of the heart towards the world around. The realm of feeling takes on a wider and deeper resonance. For Leo the Virtue of Compassion leads most interestingly to Independence, a quality supportive of the judgement which grows out of the exercise of positivity. This is further enhanced by Discretion stemming from Aquarius and leading to the power of Meditation.

5. Openness: establishing the faculty of openmindedness, not immediately dismissing something because it appears impossible, and developing an attitude of trust toward the future. This has an inner connection with the second exercise but now through the application of will, good will, towards the world and the future. This brings us to Drawing 3, the Taurus/Scorpio axis, where the lower motif is drawn into the movement of the upper, strengthening it, whilst the upper motif pours its enlightening energy into the lower, clarifying it. The Virtue of Taurus is Equilibrium, producing a sense of Progress, whilst Scorpio contributes Patience which can become Insight, all qualities which seem to go along with the development of openness and a trust in the future.

6. Balance or the harmonisation of the preceding five: this means carrying out exercises 1–5 in different groupings and becoming aware how each can support another and how gradually they form an organism of self-sustaining thought. This not only integrates all the separate exercises but becomes the fulfilment of the first exercise, control of thinking. We now come to Drawing 4 where the upper and lower motifs are completely integrated. From Gemini we gain the Virtue of Endurance which can become Faithfulness; from Sagittarius we should learn Control of Thinking which leads in time to the Sense for Truth.

If this process through the six exercises is grounded in reality it outlines a path which grows out of Love (Pisces) and ends with the Sense for Truth (Sagittarius).

9. POSITIVE (PISCES/VIRGO) AND NEGATIVE (GEMINI/SAGITTARIUS) DYNAMICS

There are a few instances where Steiner refers to the positive influences emanating from Pisces and Virgo together; this seems to indicate that there is validity in working with the opposites together. The most extensive description occurs in the last of three lectures given in November, 1917, and collected in the volume, *The Reappearance of Christ in the Etheric* (6). These three lectures deal mainly with occult brotherhoods whose work takes different forms of opposition to the being of Christ. In the third lecture Steiner points to the possibility of research in which scientists take the spiritual world seriously even when working in the laboratory. Experiments could be conducted in such a way that cosmic influences of morning and evening (dawn and dusk) are accepted whilst those of midday and midnight are excluded. Forces emanating from the axis Pisces/Virgo are favourable and would assist work being done with sunrise and sunset conditions. He did not distinguish between the influences of these two constellations.

In the case, however, of the other pair of constellations (Gemini/ Sagittarius), which make up this cosmic cross, a distinction was made. Influences from Gemini would bring negative forces relating to the poles of magnetism which would be effective at midday and would be of use to certain western brotherhoods in their opposition to the being of Christ. In the case of Sagittarius with its traditional picture of a centaur, the upper part human and the lower an animal form, the as yet untransformed animal nature of man is portrayed. This latter negative element is effective at midnight and would assist the activity of eastern occult brotherhoods.

From these indications it seems that the favourable forces of Pisces/Virgo operate mainly at sunrise and sunset; perhaps from the evidence of the first drawing one could ascribe Pisces to the sunrise (light increasing) and Virgo to the sunset (darkness increasing). Gemini and Sagittarius have their negative effect at midday and midnight respectively.

At sunrise and sunset there is a transition between the realms of day and night, between waking and sleeping. Midday and midnight present a strong polarity, the extreme of each condition. It is, therefore, interesting to note that Gemini and Sagittarius both display polarities or dualities. Of the Twins (Gemini), Castor and Pollux, one is mortal and the other immortal. In the human form the symmetry of left and right is displayed. The eurythmy movement for H shows both contraction and expansion. In Sagittarius the duality of the human/animal form is vividly present in the centaur, whilst the bow he holds is strongly drawn back to project the arrow forward. It may be that the strong internal tensions represented by these dualities relate to the negative aspect of this axis.

As already noted these four constellations comprise a cosmic cross. This is not in itself a negative relationship as witness the cosmic cross formed by the two axes Taurus/Scorpio and Leo/Aquarius. With Scorpio considered in its earlier image of the Eagle, it appears as the totality of the human being in the Sphinx and as the fourfold characterisation of the Gospel writers. In the configuration of the Zodiac that we are here considering, the axes of Pisces/Virgo and Gemini/Sagittarius form the beginning and the end of the sequence represented by the four drawings (1 – 4) relating to the working together of the upper and lower motifs connected to thinking and will. Whilst hindrances and adverse forces can make their mark from any direction and at any time, the complete integration of thinking and willing posited by Drawing 4, which requires the most effort to achieve, indicates the point of greatest vulnerability. In addition, the other pairs of upper and lower axes (Aries/ Libra and Taurus/Scorpio) have as their counterparts in cosmic crosses the middle axes (Cancer/ Capricorn and Leo/Aquarius) and their directly supporting activity. The Pisces/Virgo and Gemini/Sagittarius cross do not have this direct support and have only their participation in the harmonising effect of the middle axes as part of the dynamic of the whole Zodiac. It seems as if the whole process might come unstuck from the Gemini/Sagittarius axis.

10. CONCLUSION

The attempt to work artistically on the dynamics of the Pisces Zodiac was an open-ended exploration. Carrying out the artistic activity required to produce six compositions and the reflections arising out of and subsequent to the work, led to the perception that the six basic inner exercises appear to have an intimate connection with the present configuration of the Zodiac and that the 12 Virtues associated with the constellations have a role to play. This would indicate that whatever is working from such cosmic regions is growing more dependent on human activity for its fulfilment. The forces may stream towards us but can only be really fruitful through our own efforts. The human being is increasingly called to be an active partner in evolution. Of course, what has come out of this study is but a small fraction of a much greater potential which would include very different processes and influences.

Bibliography
Works by Rudolf Steiner
1. *Cosmosophy Vol.2* (October±November 1921) GA 208, Gympie, Australia 1997 (Lectures 4 & 6)
2. *Egyptian Myths and Mysteries* (September 1908) GA 106, New York 1961 (Lectures 7 & 8)
3. *Eurythmy as Visible Speech* (June±July 1924) GA 279, (Lectures 2, 3, 10, 15)
4. *Mystery Knowledge and Mystery Centres* (November±December 1923) GA 232, London 1973 (Lecture 6)
5. *Twelve Moods* (August 1915) GA 40, Spring Valley 1984
6. *The Reappearance of Christ in the Etheric* (Selection 1910, 1911 & 1917) New York 1983 (Lecture 12)
Works by Other Authors
7. Werner Barfod: *Consonants and Vowels: Rudolf Steiner's Characteristics for Eurythmy*, Eurythmy Association (updated)
8. Margarethe Kirchner-Bockholt: *Fundamental Principles of Curative Eurythmy*, London 1992
9. Florin Lowndes: *Enlivening the Chakra of the Heart*, London 1998
10. Ilona Schubert: *Reminiscences of Rudolf Steiner*, London 1991

THE BLUE WINDOW IN THE FIRST GOETHEANUM
Torsten Steen & Gertraud Goodwin

A window separates and connects. It is part of the outer wall of a building. It allows daylight from outside to enter into the building. Whoever is inside the building can see the outer world through the window. Transparent glass allows separation and connection from inside and outside at the same time. If it is coloured glass a formation is introduced which enables the depiction of a spiritual nature in artistic form through the light from outside. The master builders of the Gothic cathedrals have interpenetrated the walls with stained-glass windows. Out of them spoke the figures and events of the Old and the New Testaments, the saints and donors. They spoke to the people in the space inside of the spiritual world through coloured light and form. In the Goetheanum building the glance should also not direct itself from inside to the outside onto the four kingdoms of nature, but the spiritual world was to reveal itself in colour and form. There were nine coloured-glass windows in the First Goetheanum: four in the north and four in the south of the large dome, each in the form of a triptych with a larger part in the centre and two small parts to either side. There was also a window in the West.

Whereas their colours were symmetrically opposite to each other in the large auditorium of the First Goetheanum, two green, two blue, two violet and two peach blossom, their subject matter changed from one to the next. The motifs of each triptych had its own inner relationship. The First Goetheanum burned down on New Year's Eve 1922/23. Rudolf Steiner was able to create a model for a second Goetheanum building before his death in 1924. He gave the windows in this new building a different form. Instead of the triptych there now was one tall window. Maybe he would have also designed new motifs for these windows? As he was unable to do this it was decided to use the old motifs and adjust them to the new dimensions of the window: the larger centre panel of the earlier triptych was now placed on top of the two smaller side panels on the bottom.

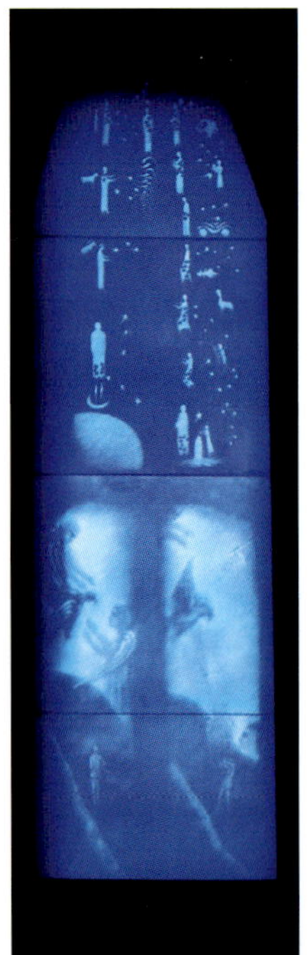

Window in
The Second Goetheanum

To find an entrance to an understanding of the motifs in the coloured-glass windows, a knowledge of Anthroposophy is helpful. Rudolf Steiner founded Anthropo-Sophia – "the wisdom of man" – at the beginning of the last century. It is a path of knowledge, "*which wants to lead the Spiritual in man towards the Spiritual in the Cosmos*". (R. Steiner) (See also: R. Steiner, *Knowledge of the Higher World and How to Attain it*. And *Occult Science*.)

In the motifs of the glass windows we see the experiences of man striving towards higher knowledge. (See also publication on the glass windows at the end of this chapter.) Amongst the windows was one, which depicts the theme of the Zodiac, the cosmic forces which radiate towards the earth and man, whose human form is built out of these forces.

The colour blue, particularly in its transparent radiance, creates a magical depth, which speaks to the depth of our own soul. W. Kandinsky formulated it like this:

"*The deeper the blue, the more it calls man towards infinity, awakens in him the longing of purity and finally the supersensible. It is the colour of the sky as we imagine it when we hear the sound of the word heaven.*"

(W. Kandinsky: *The Spiritual in Art*.)

Rudolf Steiner formulated it like this:
"*When one lives in the colour blue and gradually finds oneself in it, one will find that the blue has something which attracts the soul. Our soul would like to lose itself in it, it has a continuous longing for it. Then one will also find how figures emerge, figures who express the secrets of the cosmos, who express the soul of the cosmos.*"

(GA 287).

Etching by Assja Turgenieff

157

THE MAIN MOTIF

The light and dark of the whole window is strongly formed and shows contrasting silhouettes. We see twelve human figures in a tall elongated circular composition. With every figure a number of stars around the human figure correspond to a number of stars inside the human figure. The stars around it are light on a dark background, the stars inside are dark on a light background. In each figure the stars are positioned in particular regions of the body, going from the head to the feet according to the zodiacal regions.

Aries – figure on left side, centre

The ram behind the head and the rays of the stars in front of the brow transmit the impression of focussed concentration and sparkling clarity of spirit manifesting in the head. The ram jumping forward from behind underlines this impulsive vitality in this realm of thinking. The rest of the body stands full of peacefulness and stability, its arms in a gesture reaching out into the world showing that here are not only abstract thoughts emanating, but decisions for deeds are made.

Taurus – above Aries

Peaceful and sedate is the body posture of this form, quiet and comfortable also the animal at the back. The stars in the neck, breast and region of the larynx enliven even the arms, which vigorously seem to reach out. The stars from the periphery radiate widely from the front below out of spaces near the earth.

Gemini – above Taurus in top-left corner

A fully convex chest underlines the breathing experience of the human figure, which is covered with stars in the region of the upper arms. The stars from the periphery seem to concentrate their radiation in the region of the clavicle. Almost like a distant echo the other twin appears behind the figure, as if supporting it in its verticality.

Cancer – in the centre on top

Beneath the human figure we see circulating spiral movements in giving and receiving gestures; from above radiate the stars, three stars in a diagonal line. A fourth star in the above central breast area allows the figure to hold an open tension and balance within itself. The four stars above the figure almost mirror the ones inside.

Leo – in the top-right corner

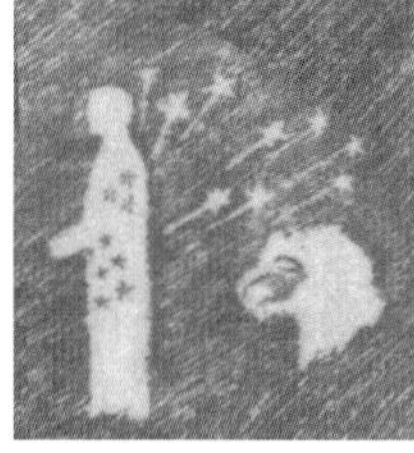

The nine stars within the figure seem to pulsate through it with sounding fanfares, receiving the sounding of the stars from outside in the region of the heart and the solar plexus. The figure has an aura of dignity and nobility, inspired by the lion from the back.

Virgo – underneath Leo on the right

With an intimate inclination of the head, the figure lifts its arms reverently. It radiates conscientiousness and trust, enlivened by the eight stars in the region of spine and diaphragm. The eight stars from the periphery shine in an orderly parallel fashion. The figure behind carrying an ear of corn accompanies like a quiet ideal.

Capricorn – below Sagittarius

We see a kind of elemental Pan-like roguish being behind the figure, and not a mountain goat. The influence/effect of the stars from behind concentrate themselves towards the region of the knees so that the figure strongly bends its knees. With a relaxed spring-suspension the figure reacts, holding itself in balance with the gesture of its arms.

Libra – underneath Virgo on the right

The figure's bowed head seems to direct its attention within towards the region of the hips. Above and below are in balance. The three stars in a diagonal slanting line are held in balance by the three upward slanting stars from outside, a fourth star within and without acting like a fulcrum. A scale-like image gives assurance as well as seeking a living balance.

Aquarius – below Capricorn

As a next step in giving impulse to the limbs of man, a steadfast, earthly peacefulness takes hold of the figure. It seems to move up to its knees as if through water. The figure behind is also immersed up to its knees, a third figure administering a baptism. The image of the baptism is unusual for Aquarius. (One could think of a quote by Rudolf Steiner, in which he tells us that all the Zodiac forces have to go through the gate of Aquarius in order to become effective for the earth, a baptism of a very particular quality.)

Scorpio – underneath Libra

From low down at the back of the figure, a half daemonic, half animal-like being shoots into the picture along the line of two raying stars. With a secure sense of the body the figure reacts and gives way, stepping forward. Despite a certain heaviness, there is gracefulness in this movement, sensing itself well without getting lost. There is also a relaxed sense in this spontaneous and hardly conscious appearing reaction.

Pisces – below left above the earth

A readiness to plunge into all the depths of existence as well as an openness towards the heights goes through this figure. Stars from above and from below radiate in up to the feet of the figure. Two fishes are directed upwards towards the feet of the figure supported by the waning moon, which approaches the earth below. A mystical image emerges, through which the feet approach the earth like magically enchanted.

Sagittarius – underneath Scorpio

Compared to the figure of Scorpio, this figure is dramatically enhanced in its movements, which seem to be directed towards far away goals. The stars from outside give impulse and enliven the whole figure from the back. The centaur behind the figure emphasises the direction of "up and forward" through its elongated neck and strong brow.

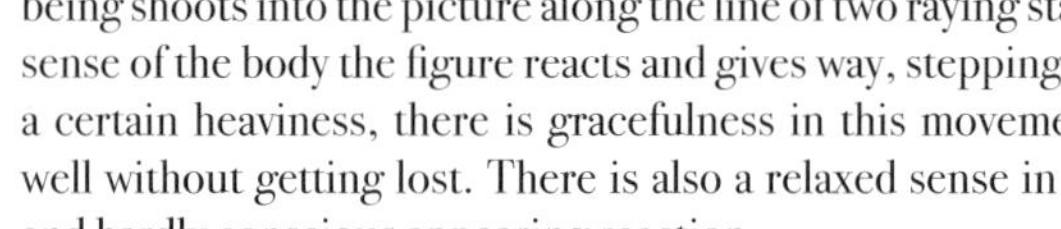

The twelvefold appearance of the human figure astonishes. The twelve build an elongated circle around an empty centre. Almost all figures look towards this centre, thereby underlining an experience of outside, of the periphery, maybe a cosmic periphery. At the same time they are human figures which definitely have taken into themselves the mirror images of the stars from this cosmic periphery.

The light stars from outside mirror themselves as dark stars inside the figure. Thus the macrocosmic Zodiac receives a microcosmic relationship. Rudolf Steiner's words for this window were these: "*The outer world in decision.*"

One can recognise that the concentrated will of the world creates a "world within a world" in the human being, in which the cosmos mirrors itself, thereby becoming the outer world. This creative outer world, the efficacy of the outer cosmos, concentrates itself in man like in a focal point, becoming his body, his gesture, causing his destiny. In this sense this blue window is like psychology in imaginative form, representing that which impulsates man's destiny through his astrality. (Greek. *astra* = star)

A powerful reality is brought into our experience through this magnificent circle of these twelve human being. The earth on the bottom left, only partially visible, and the motif of the ninefold vortex, underneath Cancer, suggesting the chakra of the larynx are pointing towards a mysterious formula: the invisible I of man which is working in the composition as a whole.

References and Further Reading

Bargum, Erika, *Der Weg der Glasfenster im ersten Goetheanum*, Verlag Die Pforte
Glöckler, Michaela, *Die Glasfenster – Motive des Goetheanum als Leitbilder der menschlichen Entwicklung*, Raffael Verlag
Hartmann, Georg, *Goetheanum Glasfenster*, Verlag am Goetheanum
Rath, Wilhelm, *The Imagery of the Goetheanum Windows – An interpretation in verse form*
Steffen, Albert, *Zu den Farbfenstern des Goetheanum, Verlag für schöne Wissenschaften* ISBN 3-85889-087-1
Turgenieff, Assja, *The Glass Windows of The First Goetheanum* (out of print)
Die Goetheanum-Fenster. Sprache des Lichtes. Entwürfe und Studien
Mit Wortlauten Rudolf Steiners, Berichten über die Arbeit an den Fenstern und Radierungen von Assja Turgenieff, sowie einer Fotodokumentation über die Entstehung der Fenster im ersten und zweiten Goetheanum, herausgegeben von Walter Kugler.
Zwei Bände im Schuber, Grossformat 23.5 x 30cm, Rudolf Steiner Verlag, Dornach 1996.

CARVED RELIEFS OF THE ZODIAC
Reimar von Bonin. Text by Gertraud Goodwin

1978-81. 28-53 cm. Wood.

Not much is known about the circumstances in which these carved reliefs came into existence, though the impulse for a sculptural form-circle on the basis of the Zodiac has lived in Reimar for a very long time. The reliefs must have been carved between commissions and periods of teaching over a longer period of time. Reimar's carved reliefs have an expressive sculptural eloquence which brings his research on the etheric and astral form-circles, as he described them in his notebook, to a culmination. They have become a sculptural language, expressive of each one of the twelve zodiacal forces.

From his diary, around 1978:

"There exist two form-circles, an etheric one and an astral one. The etheric corresponds to the building of all the shapes of the letters of the alphabet, their build-up out of the straight and the curved lines in all their variations and relationships. The formative impulses of the astral condense these cosmic forces into sounds. Out of the realm of the I being above it, comes the impulse to form the human language. With gestures of sound, the events of the world can be expressed and interpreted. The sculptor has to work his way through these stages in order to go beyond a silent pointing, then a stammering, to ultimately arrive at an eloquent sculptural language. On every stage, the appropriate elements have to be first experienced."

Reimar chose the woods for his carvings according to his own insight and research of the Zodiac in the small domed space of the First Goetheanum. His understanding is beautifully described in a piece of writing: in a conversation between two friends, who similar to the two main protagonists in the First Mystery Drama, observe and point out to each other the different form gestures in this small domed space. It is meant to stimulate an experience of the language of form in the small domed space. (From STIL, Johanni 1996/97, Heft 2. Only in German). From this piece of writing it becomes clear that Reimar understood the two-times-six symmetric columns as the aspects of all twelve Zodiacal gestures, starting next to the Group Sculpture with Aries on the north side, and ending with Pisces next to the Group Sculpture on the south side. (See illustration on page 169)

As there are two-times-six columns with the same design and twelve differently shaped reliefs of the Zodiac gestures, this means that two of the Zodiac gestures share the same columns. How can this be understood? In the conversation mentioned above, Johannes in his quest to understand these forms perceives various elements of form for each gesture of the Zodiac from different parts of the column, from the thrones at the bottom to the architraves above. Maria answers him by telling him, that every form has at least two expressions of forces, and actually much more. Giving the example of the fourth throne in elm wood in the north, which Johannes saw as related to Cancer – this would be the realm of Sagittarius in the south, showing its entire spiritual force of direction as well as its discrepancy, its being present in the now and aiming at a goal in the far distance.

This shines light on how the small domed space has many more dimensions, which can be taken into consideration. Its whole gesture is of a more vertical spiritual dimension and a strong relationship to all four directions of space, where everything is connected and interrelated with everything else.

Looking at Reimar von Bonin's carved reliefs related to the whole world of form in the small domed space, can become a meditative joyful exploration. Each person will discover different relationships and congruities, bringing both to life for her/himself.

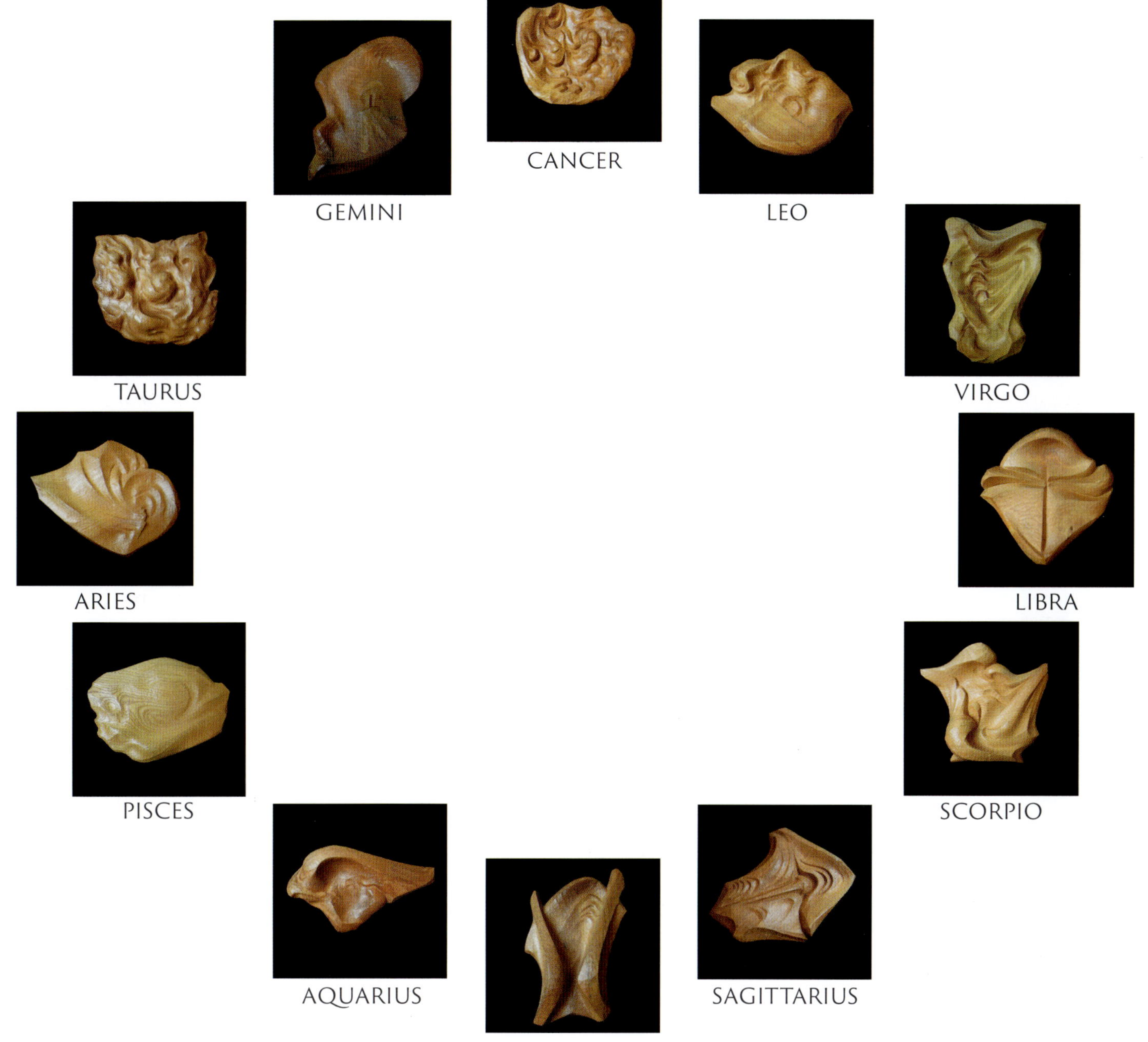

CANCER
GEMINI
LEO
TAURUS
VIRGO
ARIES
LIBRA
PISCES
SCORPIO
AQUARIUS
SAGITTARIUS
CAPRICORN

ARIES / ASH

There is great dynamic and movement: from the left, diagonal planes sweep downwards, concentrating themselves in rhythmically structured impulses which are received and embraced by three rhythmical concentric round gestures. The outermost embracing gesture is impulsated from above threefold, as in a counter wave. The light coloured ash wood counters the sculptural movements with its grain, and supports it with its lighter and darker colours: this emphasises the dynamic greatly.

I can see a similar dynamic in the capital of the first column of the small domed space: between the two small, pointed triangular gestures facing each other on the vertical edge. The large, convex, downward swinging gesture creates a space for this impulse, accentuating it through the contrast of small and pointed versus large and round.

41 x 33 cm

TAURUS / CHERRY

The whole relief is taken hold of by vibrant vivacious, alive movements, pressing onwards towards, with and against each other with great force. A burgeoning and becoming of intensified life-forces manifests itself.

In the second capital of the small domed space, this actio- and re-actio of forces is brought to a point in a clear simplicity: from above a powerful convex is pressing downwards, impressing and also being met by a strong gesture from below. This encounter takes place on the vertical edge, which accentuates its power, and opens up the space of the panel, creating a contracting and expanding flow within the negative space.

29 x 29 cm

GEMINI / OAK

In its darker and quiet mood, this expression gives us an unusual insight into Gemini: the one which Rudolf Steiner also emphasises in his indication for the eurythmy gesture, where man is standing upright, both hands holding the upper arms of the opposite side. In the relief we see an inner symmetry, held by a centre verticality, which radiates upwards and towards the right where it is held. This contrasts with the more open and rhythmically articulated left side. The Mercury theme resounds in a more sincere tone.

This sincerity is taken up in the third capital of the small domed space in the symmetrical gesture establishing itself in the centre of the panel. Its open gesture receives the triangular sharp impulse from above with great certainty and strength. Here, the relationship is more between above and below, whereas in Reimar's relief it is more between centre and right and left: both are mercurial archetypes.

28 x 37 cm

CANCER / ELM

The dark and colourful vibrancy of the elm wood gives this relief an inner intensity: all the smaller and larger movements spiral back to themselves, forming inner spaces. As a whole the relief is self-contained, as if deep inside something is mysteriously shaped and worked on.

In the fourth capital of the small domed space, this "something" manifests itself, descending seed-like into the space on the panel, watched over and protected by likewise budding "sentinels" on either side.

31 x 29 cm

LEO / MAPLE

The light, golden maple wood supports the rhythmic flow around the centre: breathing in, open and diastolic in larger open spaces, from left to right, breathing in systolically from right to left on top in wave-like powerful rhythms.

This contracting and expanding gesture is expressed in the fifth capital of the small domed space in a powerful vertical gesture, occupying almost the whole of the panel. It reaches out horizontally, to the right and left forming a strong link, joining up with its neighbour. This horizontal link, formed in rhythmic togetherness, enables a seed-like shape to be held as though in suspense on the vertical edge.

41 x 31 cm

VIRGO / BIRCH

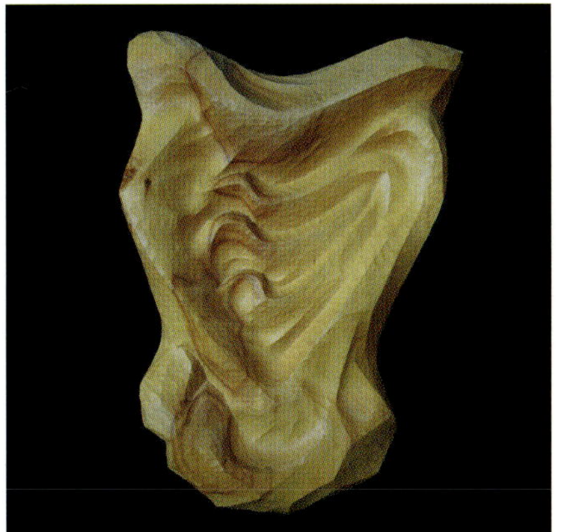

Birch wood gains a golden sheen with age, has a lightness and is soft to carve. Supported from the bottom of the relief, several rhythmic movements take their origin from the left to swing up diagonally to the right. There they are received, held and returned to swing back again. Above these rhythms a quietly accompanying large wave frames this happening, giving the whole a threefold formation and order into a bottom, middle and top as well as a right, middle and left. The main emphasis seems to enable and support the rhythmic centre with intimate inner warmth.

This rhythmic movement and order also weaves through the whole capital of the sixth column: in the up and down full-bodied, strong zigzag movement swinging around the whole capital. Virgo forces work like an ever giving and receiving wise peristaltic rhythm of life.

27 x 43 cm

LIBRA / BIRCH

The challenge for the second half of Reimar's carved reliefs is to perceive their relationships to the same capitals, which have already been "allocated" to the first six reliefs. I draw my support from Rudolf Steiner who said that there is also symmetry in the Zodiac. (Where?)

Birch wood darkens with age when exposed to light. Reimar chose a piece of wood which is much more evenly coloured than the more vibrantly coloured piece he used for the Virgo relief. This more evenly coloured wood lends itself to the almost symmetric formation of the Libra relief: a centre slim, concave vertical acts like a fulcrum for the horizontal gesture swinging up gently and clearly to the right and to the left. The vertical rests on a triangular formation on the bottom of the relief, into which it seems to stretch itself while over its top a protective canopy arches itself, amalgamating to a mobile balance seeking itself ever anew.

The capital of the sixth column with its zigzag movements which connect all round the capital through double-bent surfaces depicts this constant sensitive and fine tuning of an invisible inner fulcrum constantly seeking balance through movement and counter-movement.

34 x 35 cm

SCORPIO / MAPLE

From the top right, a straight diagonal impulse moves to the bottom left where it is gathered, augmented and passed on upwards in rhythmic gestures. It culminates into another fully convex gesture coming from the top left, meeting a smaller wave-like movement originating also from the top right. Great decisiveness and dynamic weave through all movements and counter-movements, also some controversy and opposition, characterising qualities of Scorpio.

In the capital of the fifth column there is also dynamic and decisiveness, but in a more held back archetypal manner, depicting more the aspect of power and inner strength of Scorpio.

36 x 34 cm

SAGITTARIUS / ELM

The dark elm wood underlines the earnest decisiveness, governed by the centre diagonal arrow-like gesture, expressing the tension and power of holding the bow just before or at the moment of releasing the arrow. This tension and counter-tension is expressed in small, accompanying rhythms.

This decisiveness is expressed in the fourth capital in all formations pointing sharply upwards. From the common foundation, vertical spearhead-like gestures rise upwards along the edges of the panel. In the centre of the panel, drop-like forms are held as though in suspense and tension between the rising gestures. I sense a more archetypal and held back aspect of the tension and counter-tension of Sagittarius.

35 x 45 cm

CAPRICORN / OAK

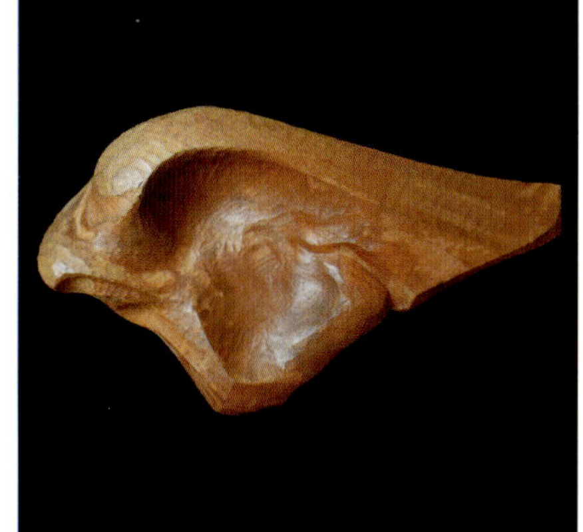

27 x 41 cm

The dark oak relief is dominated and guided by two powerfully swinging in curved arches from right and left. These two arches seem to come from way beyond the relief for a particular purpose: they come close together in the bottom half of the relief, building a chasm together, which opens upwards. This gesture releases the plane between them which extends itself eagerly and rhythmically upwards.

In the capital of the third column, the action is similarly poignant and brought to a point: the symmetrical twofold energetic gesture lifts itself up decisively into the centre of the panel ready to listen and answer to the triangular wake-up call from above.

In both Reimar's relief and the motif of the third capital I sense the wakeful, attentive earthly qualities of Capricorn, ready for immediate action.

AQUARIUS / CHERRY

53 x 32 cm

The colouring of the wood has lent itself beautifully to the in-and-out breathing of this generous wave at rest: from the top right, the long horizontal movement streams in to descend on the left, in order to be held, intensified, and returned below. Offering up small ripples, this in-breath re-joins the large movement on top again to complete the cycle.

The formations of the second capital can also be seen as undulating wave-like from the top downwards and upwards again, creating an in-breathing space on the panel. The potential power of the thrust downwards is felt by the gesture below, reacting to it by receiving it.

PISCES / ASH

48 x 36 cm

The light, golden ash wood with its marked grain supports the open gentle streaming through this relief. From the left, small wave-like ripples are received, tenderly collected in the centre and passed on and released to the right. This movement can also be seen to go from the right to the left, the sculptural flow as well as the grain of the wood suggesting as if both movements flow through each other: a movement from the past to the future, from left to right, and a stream from the future into the present, from right towards the left.

In the capital of the first column, a wave-like movement goes through from the top downwards, in alternating more contracting and expanding rhythms. The large round and relaxed movements expand on the panel, whereas the smaller, sharp triangular gestures move downwards on the edge, wakeful towards perceiving similar gestures from below.

Thus a rhythmic exchange between a more expansive, dreaming-sleeping and a wakeful, contraction is created. This quality goes through Reimar's relief as well, a mood of life's weaving from sleeping to waking, and life to death and rebirth.

EXPLORING THE RELATIONSHIP BETWEEN REIMAR VON BONIN'S CARVED RELIEFS AND THE CAPITALS OF THE SMALL DOMED SPACE OF THE FIRST GOETHEANUM

Gertraud Goodwin

It is a great and mysterious challenge to perceive two quite different sculptural reliefs through the same archetype of the capitals in the small domed space! It would mean that Aries and Pisces both have their origin and archetype in the first and twelfth column, that Virgo and Libra have theirs in the sixth and seventh column, and so on. (See illustration opposite)

In nature, we see individual expressions of the archetype "plant" in million-fold ways – filling us with wonder and awe. This book wants to celebrate and honour the so individual and different perceptions and expressions of these archetypes which are the foundations and makers of all form. This encourages us to see ever new aspects of the same theme, never settling for one particular answer!

Another challenge is the allocation of the planets and their derivative trees to each Zodiac mood. The woods Reimar chose for his reliefs derive from their relationship to the woods in the small domed space in the First Goetheanum. Elsewhere the following particular planets are associated with the Zodiac:

Aries – *Mars*	**Taurus** – *Venus*	**Gemini** – *Mercury*
Cancer – *Moon*	**Leo** – *Sun*	**Virgo** – *Venus*
Libra – *Venus*	**Scorpio** – *Mars*	**Sagittarius** – *Jupiter*
Capricorn – *Saturn*	**Aquarius** – *Saturn*	**Pisces** – *Jupiter*

I am reminded of the verses of the "twelve moods" which Rudolf Steiner gave to the eurythmists in 1915 – see chapter 'The Twelve Moods/Introduction to Rudolf Steiner's Verses'. Each verse consists of seven lines, each one as if "spoken" by one of the seven planetary forces. This reveals the sevenfold aspect of each of the zodiacal forces and their being incarnated and made alive on and for the earth through all the planetary forces. Only through their working together can each of the zodiacal forces come into their full effect. The fixed stars and the planets enable each other to be creative on earth.

That Reimar was fully aware of this is shown by this little story I experienced in 1984 when I was a guest teacher at his sculpture school in Munzingen near Freiburg, Germany. Reimar and I stood on a balcony overlooking the school yard, where Edwin Böck was building up the exhibition of his third year final thesis, the Zodiac shown in this book. (See Edwin Böck's own chapter). Reimar said to me: "*Here you see the Zodiac from the point of view of Leo and the Sun.*" I did not really understand at the time what he meant as I created my first circle of Zodiac sculptures only in 1987/88.

Based on Rudolf Steiner's indication, there is also symmetry in the small cupola, Reimar von Bonin took up this challenge, and carved his wooden reliefs accordingly. I am attempting to find out if I can also see this connection. Reimar was my sculpture teacher during my training and I trust him completely. In my observation I was not so much looking for outer similarities in form, but rather for related dynamics, movement and mood, respecting and wondering at his individual and free approach and grasp of these archetypal forces. Reimar gives us an entry into this relationship through the choice of wood for each of his Zodiac reliefs, which is the same as the wood of the whole column. Reimar had great experience with wood, his first training was in figurative wood carving in Oberammergau. I sense that in these carved reliefs a great insight into the individuality of each tree has been manifested, letting the wood resound in its originality, enabling it to connect to its archetype – the Zodiac.

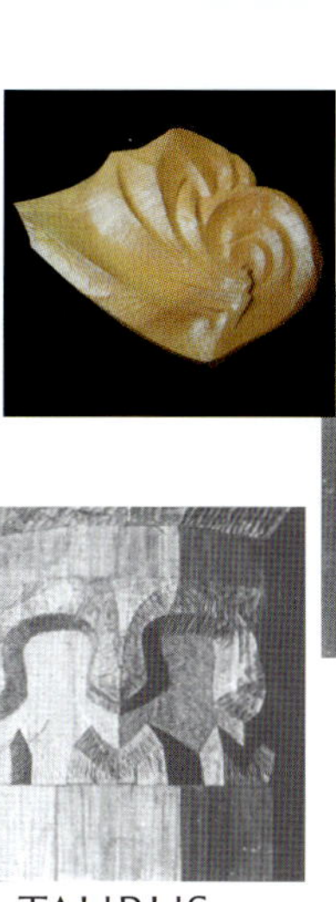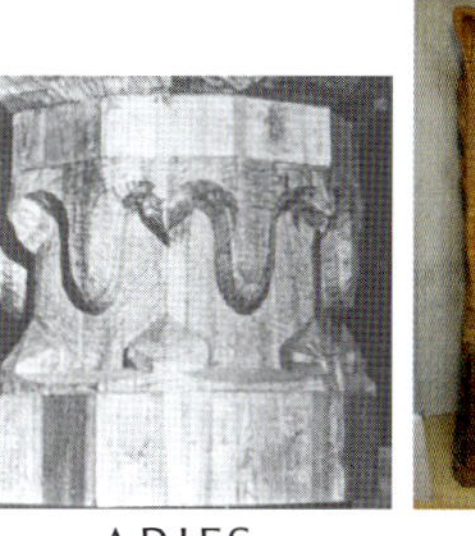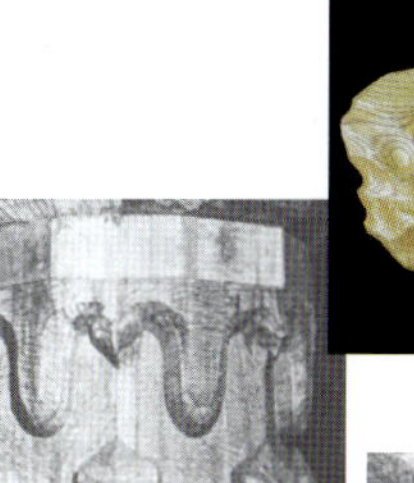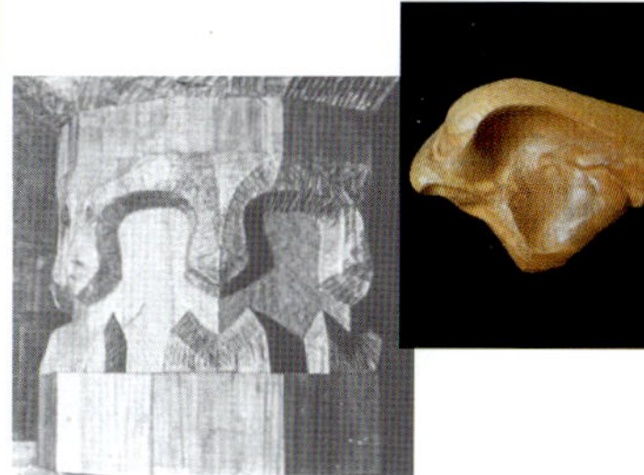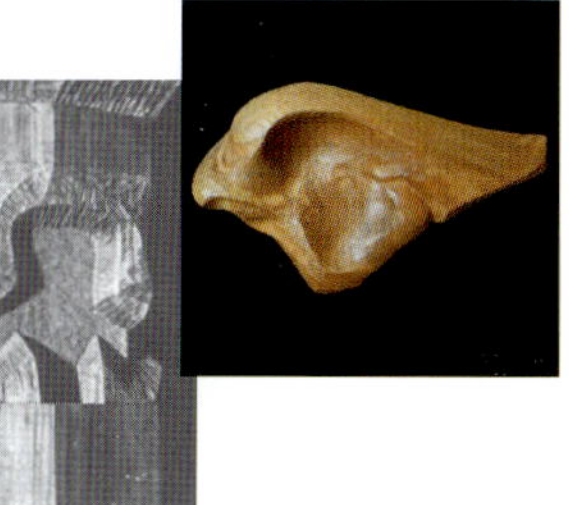

ARIES

PISCES

TAURUS

AQUARIUS

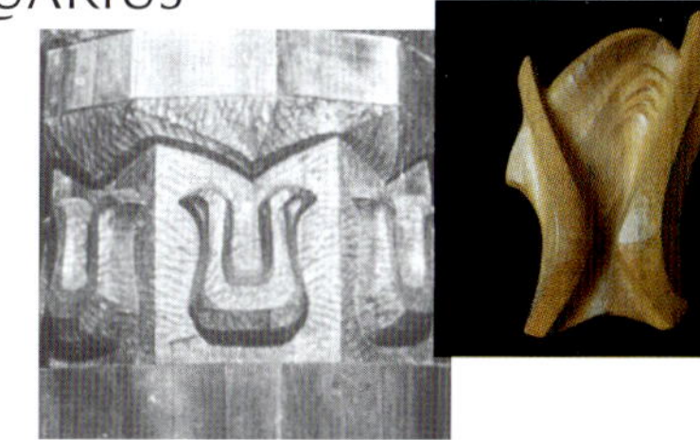

GEMINI

CAPRICORN

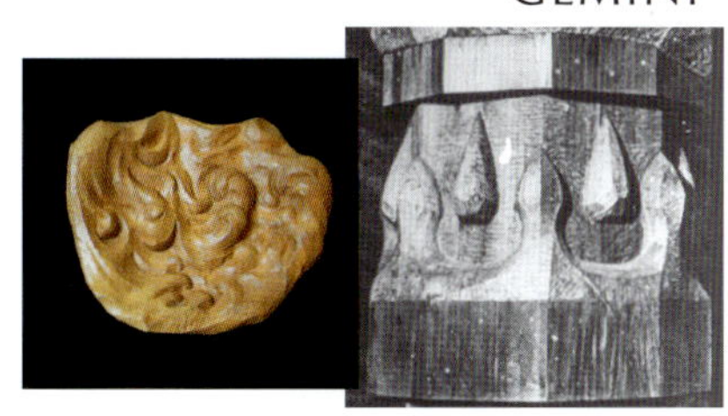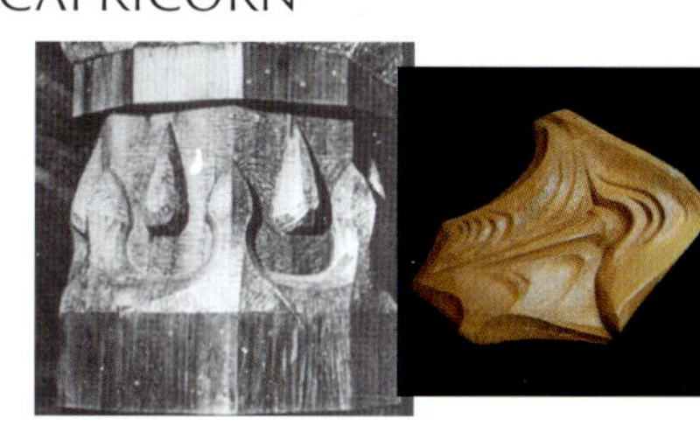

CANCER

SAGITTARIUS

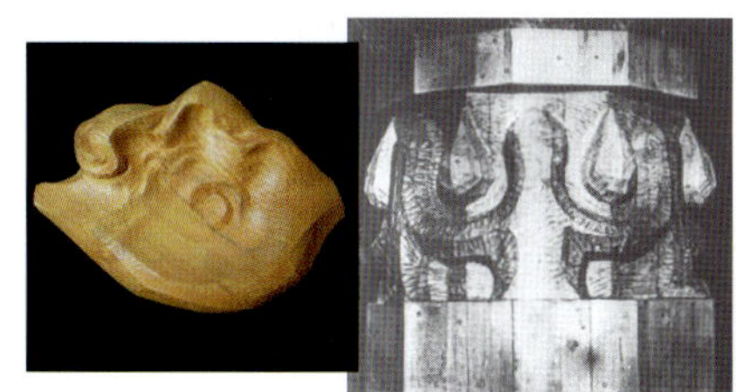

LEO

SCORPIO

VIRGO

LIBRA

THE FORMATION OF THE CAPITALS OF THE SMALL DOMED SPACE AS VIGNETTES
Gertraud Goodwin

For the programme of the Theosophical Congress in Munich in 1907, Rudolf Steiner made five drawings. About them he wrote in the magazine *Luzifer Gnosis*: "They are the motifs of the first five of the seven capitals, transposed into the form of vignettes." In the following years, the sixth and seventh were added. These drawings are known as the planetary seals. Please also see the chapter on "The Seals" in my book, *Metamorphosis, Journeys through Transformation of Form*.

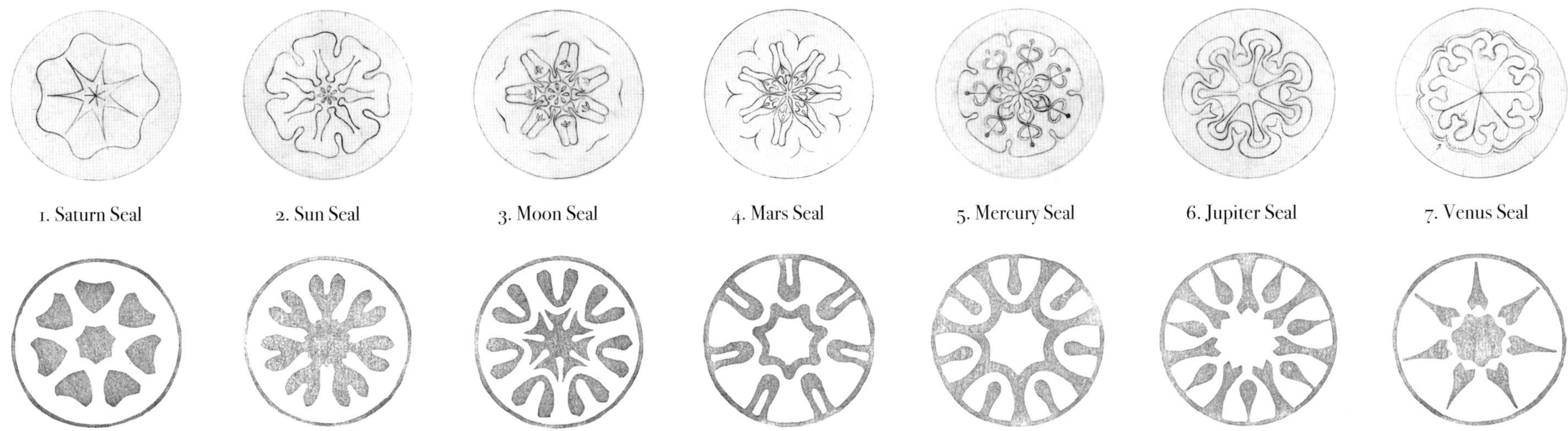

1. Saturn Seal   2. Sun Seal   3. Moon Seal   4. Mars Seal   5. Mercury Seal   6. Jupiter Seal   7. Venus Seal

Woodcuts of the 7 Seals by Carl Kemper

Much artistic consideration was given to the seals; they were worked on, studied, drawn and sculpted by many artists and by goldsmiths in their appropriate metals. Carl Kemper made sketches to transpose the formations of the capitals of the small domed space into two-dimensional vignettes, to be carried out in woodcuts. It is interesting and revealing to look at the different moods and characters, comparing the vignettes of the small cupola space to the seals of the large cupola space. The seals of the capitals from the large cupola space can be characterised as softer, younger, flowing and becoming, rhythmically acting and reacting with each other.

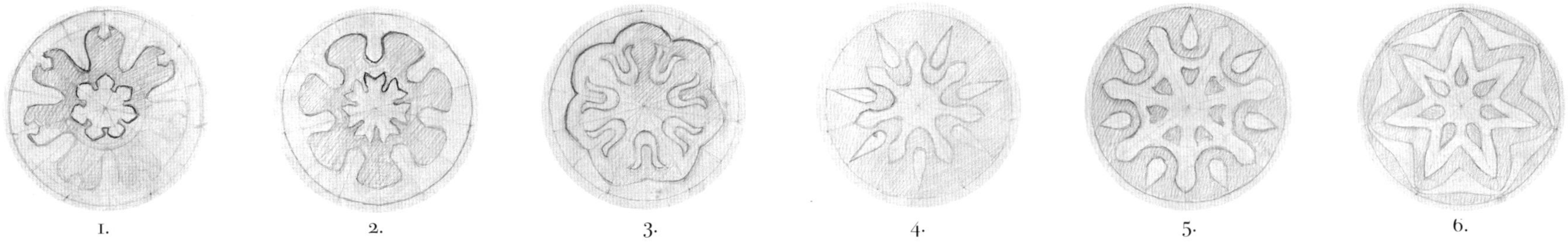

1.   2.   3.   4.   5.   6.

Vignettes - Sketckes by Carl Kemper. Transposed from the capitals of the columns from the small domed space.

The vignettes can throw a light and another aspect on to the less known formations of the capitals in the small domed space. In Carl Kemper's sketches, he lightly shaded in the "background" in between the motifs of the carved capitals. How he intended to carry out the woodcuts, is unclear: was he marking the space to be carved out, like he did for the seals, or would he have carved out the motifs themselves, leaving them light, thus treating the vignettes of the small domed space differently? I became intrigued! I tried it both ways, darkening the background and darkening the motifs themselves and was amazed at the different (messages) results: it is remarkable how the dark form, surrounded by white, seems to have diminished in size considerably, while the same formation in white, surrounded by black, seems to have expanded, seems much larger.

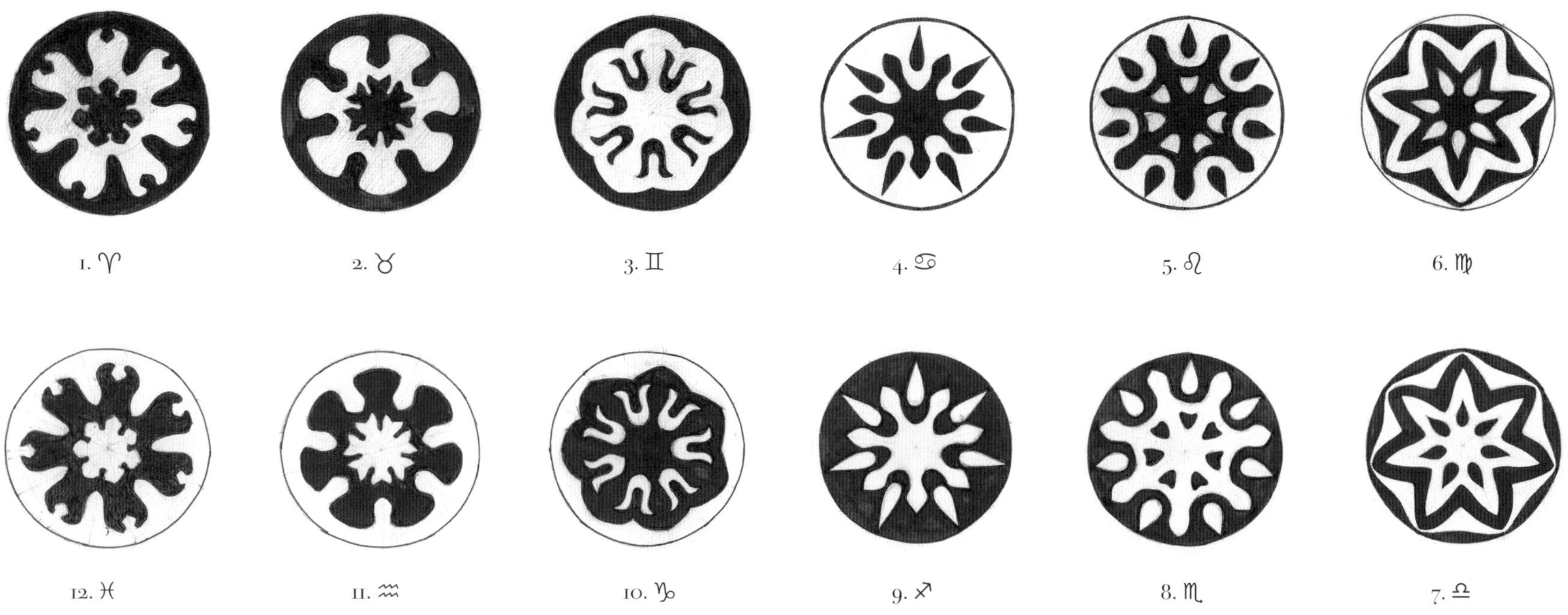

The motifs arising from below upwards in the carved capital are placed in the centre of the vignettes, pointing outwards: the motifs reaching from above downwards in the carved capital are radiating towards the centre from the periphery of the circular vignette. Thus, the conversation between the top and the bottom in the carved capital has become a relationship between the periphery and the centre. This is the same as in the "seals". But the emphasis in their two- dimensional, flat, planar depiction rather than in their linear or sculptural rendering already makes a big difference: the linear and sculptural depiction of the seals emphasises their rhythmic movement and enhances their transformative quality from one to the next.

In the depiction of the seals as woodcuts, these qualities are like lost, replaced by a more static and lifeless quality which seems to go against their planetary nature and their potential. Whereas in the woodcut depiction of the vignettes, a new quality comes to light which seems to me to reveal a further attribute not present in the linear drawing nor in the carved capital: they seem to be imprinted in a kind of eternal cosmic form, boldly unmoving, preserving, holding and protecting a cosmically wise, all-knowing fundamental law!

This surprised and moved me as I had never given these vignettes much attention. And it was in keeping with the intimations I had all along of the form- forces of the small domed space as the space of the Zodiac! Carl Kemper's choice to recreate them as woodcuts then seems to me to be a very fine and appropriate artistic choice! As we do not have his artistic rendering of the vignettes in the woodcuts, the unsolved riddle still is what he would have carved out: the motifs or the background? Could it be that both possibilities are a potentiality, maybe even a necessity, as the twelve-foldness of the Zodiac would ask for two-times-six views?

Reimar von Bonin's (see his own chapter) twelve carvings show how he tried to draw from the wisdom of the two-times-six columns, seemingly the same, by changing his point of view for the second set of six columns, thereby opening up and discovering their "other" message for himself. In my description of his work I tried to sense towards this mysterious and intriguing aspect. It is often thus, that seeing a problem from an opposite and unusual angle throws a completely new light on it that bears the potential to be a solution.

After I had finished colouring in both sequences I was amazed how harmonious each one looked as a whole - even with each single vignette showing a certain one-sidedness. What is convex in the actual carving is black in the top row, the background is white. We see what is meant, what is physically visible as in writing. This gives us the sense that the actual activity is within the black, whereas the white is "in between", more a reaction to the black. If I assume that the forces of the Zodiac are the

TOP ROW

1. Aries ♈
Reaching from the periphery far in towards the centre, dark convex gestures initiate the centre to diversity into bud-like creations, echoing and answering their partners in the periphery.

4. Cancer ♋
A new centre radiates out, creating spaces to hold the seed forms desending and receiving from the periphery.

2. Taurus ♉
Powerfully pressing inwards from the periphery towards the bud-like creations, encourage these gestures from the centre to open up.

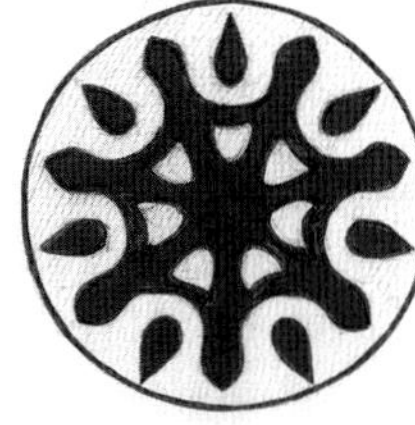

5. Leo ♌
The centre has made spaces in itself, white, swinging up further towards the periphery to receive the seeds into itself.

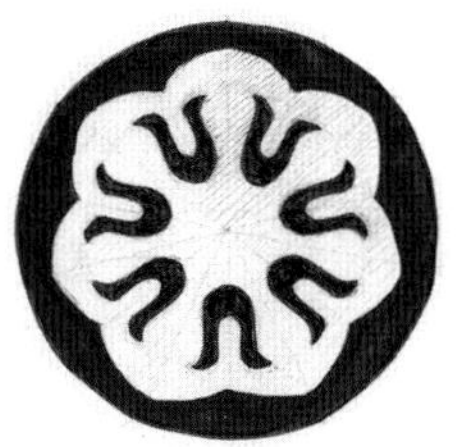

3. Gemini ♊
Symmetrically shaped and individualised gestures have moved outwards towards the periphery, their opening expectant and directed towards a point from the periphery.

6. Virgo ♍
The seeds have been taken inside for ripening, star-like the formations swing in and out in harmony with their counterparts from the periphery.

foundation of the columns and the vignettes, and making the same relationship as the illustration shows on page 174, I can sense a particular aspect of the zodiacal forces emanating out of the vignettes. I had a feeling that the top row expresses more the spring and summer half of the year, the bottom row more the autumn and winter half of the year. I am well aware of the dangers of over-interpreting, of reading something into a design which never was meant, thus making a particular view fit. My findings would like to be a beginning, an opening towards an understanding of these vignettes, which can be approached in many other ways as well. I tried to formulate my short observation of each vignette in such a way that an aspect of the respective zodiacal force becomes visible.

In this sequence, bottom row, the "in between" shaded spaces are now black as an experiment. Following Carl Kemper's sketches for the woodcuts, it is open for us to anticipate, if he would have left the shaded areas standing or if he would have cut them out.

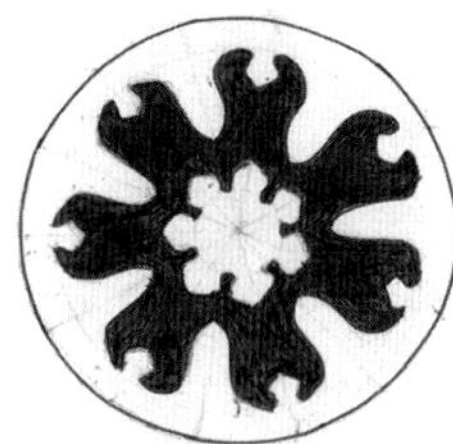

12. Pisces ♓

From the centre, small, bud-like shapes point out-wards, in between them, the small dark space is like preparing the way for the large white gesture swinging in from the periphery: giving and receiving, holding and releasing, seeking to bridge polarities.

9. Sagittarius ♐

Sharp and purposeful the seeds from within and with-out may have united together, radiating and shaping the star-like, white, receptive formations.

11. Aquarius ♒

With joy and exuberance, the white formations from within and from without strive towards each other, the black formation in between rhythmically expanding and contracting.

8. Scorpio ♏

The seeds are now more individualised and open to the periphery, sensing the archetypal drop form, white, in the periphery.

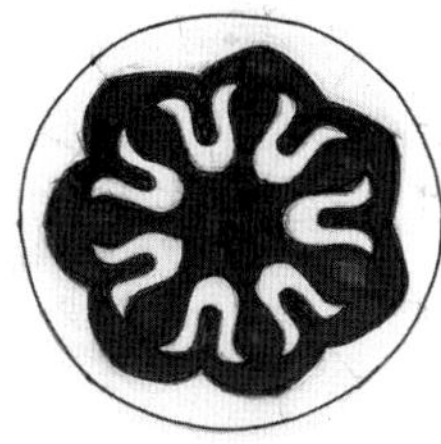

10. Capricorn ♑

The white shapes are like suspended in their gesture, re-lating to each other on either side as well as being open to the above, receptive of a new impulse. ("Janus head", new impulse: Christ's birth.)

7. Libra ♎

The seeds around the centre are now black, contracted, like waiting and maturing in the white space, held and protected within a threefold black-white-black undulating gesture.

In the year's course, the sun moves through each of the zodiacal constellation, her light moulded and individualised by each zodiacal force. The plants grow, unfold and metamorphose themselves with each of these forces. It is a complex cosmic process of the greatest wisdom. An aspect of receiving, a becoming, transforming and metamorphosing lives within the zodiacal force—therefore a developmental nature is inherent in the description of the vignettes from one to the other. That does not mean that the forces themselves change or metamorphose from one to another. It means to me that both the planetary and zodiacal forces always work with and through each other as the creator forces of all things on earth.

THE SMALL DOME OF THE FIRST GOETHEANUM
Gertraud Goodwin

The Sculptural Depiction of the Zodiac in the Capitals of the Small Cupola of the First Goetheanum

Studying the form and colour relationships of the small domed space, their immensity and complexity becomes ever more apparent. Slowly these intricate relationships reveal themselves to the observant eye and the open heart: both are needed to realise the intricacies and complexities of their mutual and interdependent organisms – just like in a living body, where all organs work interdependently together.

The two-times-six columns, which held up the small cupola of the First Goetheanum, stood on the ground with two-times-six so-called thrones, each shape carved individually. The top of the columns, the capitals, were also carved individually, towered by carved architraves, which related in their formations to each column as well as impulsating the space in between each column. The half-sphere cupola was painted with the representatives of the cultural epochs and their spiritual guides. A vast *Gesammtkunstwerk* opens up where none of the formations can be understood without their relationship to all the other parts: each column, throne, capital, architrave and section of painting above it relates and sounds together like a mighty chord, at the same time relating to all its neighbours and the auditorium as in a huge orchestral symphony. The proportion of the relationship in which the two domed spaces were integrated with each other, had a particular and harmonious measure, able to express a Christian element. Had the two spaces been pushed into each other more closely, a luciferic element would have dominated. Had the two spaces been further away from each other, an ahrimanic element would have made itself felt.

"The difference in the sizes (of the two cupola buildings) *only means, that here in the large cupola space the physical aspect is larger and that it has been tried in the small cupola space to make the spiritual aspect predominant. But a lifting up to the spirit is already expressed through the form."*

–Rudolf Steiner, 16th October 1920

Here I will concentrate on the sculptural compositions of each column, leading the observant eye from the bottom of the column, the thrones, to the capitals and the architraves. I will only list the paintings of the cupola as their content has been masterly researched and described by Hilde Raske in her book, *The Language of Color in the First Goetheanum*. The relationship between the large and the small spaces has been described in the chapter entitled, 'The Mystery of the Columns and Capitals in the Smaller Dome' by Christian Thal-Jantzen in my book, *Metamorphosis – Journeys Through Transformation of Form*. Here it will suffice to just briefly indicate this relationship as far as it is needed for my attempt at deciphering the form-language of these capitals.

The graph shows the geometric relationship between the in-between spaces of the columns of the large cupola to the places of the columns of the small dome. A relationship that is made manifest in the use of the particular woods used for the columns.

Carl Kemper's deciphering of the formation of the capitals of the **small domed space** is entirely based on this relationship between the columns of the two spaces. He takes his starting point from Rudolf Steiner's lecture of 16th October 1920:

"That's why the motifs of the capitals in the small cupola space are not held in their developmental form like here (in the large cupola space), *but they are held in such a way that they are the parts of a single beingness so to speak, which opens its arms to that which rushes towards it in its development."*

–Rudolf Steiner, 16th October 1920

The evolutionary metamorphosis of the capitals of the **auditorium** shows the formations from above and below in a constant exchange of forces, influencing each other, transforming and developing with and through each other. The formations from above and below in the capitals of the **small domed space** stand quietly opposite each other in space.

The change of forms in the capitals of the **small domed space** occurs in a circle of two-times-six columns in polarities. There is a quietness between each of the motifs, and not so much of a horizontal movement and development in time as in the **auditorium**. Here, in the **small domed space**, we have a next-to-each-other in space. This brotherly togetherness of the twelve was to have the thirteenth in its midst in the sculpture of the Representative of Man. I have not yet seen a deeper decoding of the sculptural language of the formations of their capitals.

In deciphering the form-language of the capitals in the **small domed space**, Carl Kemper indicates "similarities" and "congruences" in relation to the capitals of the **auditorium**. The forms of the **small domed space** are received, like a radiation out of the formations of the **auditorium**. Also an unexpected new living symmetry along the north-south axis becomes visible and important.

"You go into the building through the gate in the west and walk towards the east: there you can sense that which makes a man into a human being: he congregates the good, the formidable of all the individual cultures in this soul ... so that it will symphonically sound together, we hope, in the second, smaller building, in that which is underneath the second, smaller cupola."

—Rudolf Steiner 19th October 1914

"The alive element in our building expresses itself thus, that the one cupola has in a certain sense its conscious mirror image in the other. That both cupolas mirror each other."

—Rudolf Steiner 4th January 1915

This inner relationship expresses itself also in how the different woods are used. The puzzle begins right away as we see two-times-six columns which mirror each other in their position and design symmetrically. One of the workers once asked Rudolf Steiner why there weren't twelve different capitals in the small cupola, representing the Zodiac. Why symmetry? Rudolf Steiner answered: "There is also symmetry in the Zodiac!" This answer gave me a lot to think about and for many years I could not find a satisfactory entry to this question. Having worked artistically on the Zodiac a number of times over 30 years, the individual form-gesture of the "twelve moods" crystallised themselves ever stronger so that the thought of a symmetry was extremely hard to grasp for me. In 2005/2006 I attempted to work with the polar opposite gestures of the Zodiac for the first time. (See chapter on "Pisces Zodiac".)

In 1413 the sun moved from the sign of Aries into the sign of Pisces from where it now illuminates all the other signs of the Zodiac. This can be seen as a new gateway, through which all other Zodiac gestures may be understood in a new light. In the lecture cycle *Anthroposophy as Cosmosophy* Part II Rudolf Steiner speaks about the Pisces-Zodiac as the Zodiac for our time beginning in the middle of the 15th century, since mankind entered the time of Pisces: 1413-3573. In the time of Pisces, humanity makes the transition into intellectualism, undergoing a development towards abstraction in which we experience a quality of dissolving. It is a process from light through darkness to a new-found light. It has become dark inside us and we need to set out to find the light again. This can only happen through our individual freedom. When we put ourselves under the guidance of Michael, we may reach the experience of the etheric Christ as our inner sun and our new guide.

In the Aries-Zodiac, each sign is engaged in a totally one-sided gesture purely expressing its own being, whereas in the Pisces-Zodiac two polar-opposite gestures are brought together. Could it be, that Rudolf Steiner created a Pisces Zodiac for our time in the **small domed space**? I felt it worth while to look at the six capitals in this way and will attempt here to explain my approach.

In the Pisces Zodiac, two polar-opposite gestures work together to create a new whole. What comes into being when all twelve Zodiac gestures work together in their most sublime creation is the form of the human being.

As two polar-opposite gestures of the Zodiac come together, they influence and enhance each other, creating a space in between each other. This space is like a **third** element, for which the two polar-opposite gestures care and take responsibility. "*Where two or three are present in my name, I am amongst them.*" The ten-metre-high carved sculpture was to stand in the middle and end of the **small domed space**. This sculpture can be seen as a key to all the (formations) choreography of the **small domed space**.

I sensed, that the order of the Pisces Zodiac would start with the relationship of Aries and Libra next to the sculpture of the Representative of Man. In the cycle of the year there is an ascending impulse from spring to autumn, and a descending impulse from autumn through winter to spring. I could feel that the forms in the capitals from above downwards had a different thrust than the forms from below upwards. Rudolf Steiner answered the workman's question, why there were only six columns, symmetrically the same, with this: that there was also symmetry in the Zodiac. This made me sense that the forces of the ascending and descending year always balance each other, thereby creating a living balance within the year, a living etheric symmetry which is not static and the same on either side.

All twelve of the zodiacal form-forces radiate their individual powers out into the cosmos. These powers are enlivened and rhythmically moved by the planetary forces which make the zodiacal forces accessible to the elements and the forces of the earth. It is a very complex and highly sophisticated process of creation in which many different spiritual forces work together. To slowly learn to perceive and understand just one of these forces is like learning a new language: first the alphabet of this cosmic script has to be deciphered, in order to sense a word of this sounding of the 'Harmonies of the Spheres'. Perceived in this way, I could sense the possibility to always see two polar-opposite zodiac forces working together in one of the capitals of the **small domed space**: the one sounding forth from above, the other, polar opposite, from below. In between them, the space is mightily moved, receiving these forces at work, passing them on like the still water of a lake is moved by the pebble thrown into it.

For me it was important to bring these forms to life for myself. In my effort to decipher them I was not concerned with who is right or who is wrong. Rather each approach sheds a different light onto those still mysterious formations, and other, new perceptions still to come will eventually enlarge the picture.

The observation of the sculptural formations of the **great auditorium** principally leads us through three-times-seven sequences of metamorphosis – from the bases up to the capitals and to the architraves, from east to west in great rhythmic movements. I sensed that this movement has a horizontal gesture, whereas the sculptural formations of the **small domed space** opened up for me when I observed them in a vertical way: each column standing individually for itself in its build-up from the thrones at the foot of the column, up to the capital and further up to the architraves and the motifs of the cupola painting above.

This is not meant as an either-or, but as an inner main movement, as both the small and the large domed spaces have both a horizontal and a vertical aspect in their sculptural gestures and will reveal particular aspects of themselves when looked at in different observational modes. As I have chosen to look at all the metamorphic sequences of the auditorium in their horizontal aspect (see my book, *Metamorphosis – Journeys Through Transformation of Form*), I am choosing here to look at each column individually in its vertical aspect: from the thrones at the base of the column to the capital, the architrave and the painting above.

At the east end of the **small domed space** in the centre stood the ten-metre-high sculpture of the Representative of Man carved in oak. This is like an overture to all the other sculptural formations: the figure of Christ standing on both feet in between taking a step, holding both Ahriman and Lucifer at bay, seeking equilibrium in the asymmetry.

The intricately rich carving has been described in a number of publications, which are mentioned in the list for further reading at the end. I will therefore not go into it in detail, but begin to concern myself with the columns.

Above the carved statue, which was housed in a kind of alcove, in the region of the architraves, we see the last step of metamorphosis of the *Hauptmotiv*, which started its development above the entrance in the west. (See chapter on the Main Motif in my book, *Metamorphosis – Journeys Through Transformation of Form*.) The ultimate culmination of this main motif has here its strongest contraction in the centre in a pentagonal form, holding together its widest soft expansion of reaching out. At the same time it gives itself completely, initiating and protecting all sculptural gestures of the whole of the **small domed space**. It is as if it has reached its highest sculptural consciousness in this space, like a wise director leading his orchestra. Above this mature main motif, the painting of the **small domed space** shows again the Representative of Man between Lucifer and Ahriman.

For all images and descriptions of the paintings in the small cupola, please see the excellent book by Hilde Raske, *The Language of Color in the First Goetheanum*, Verlag Walter Keller.

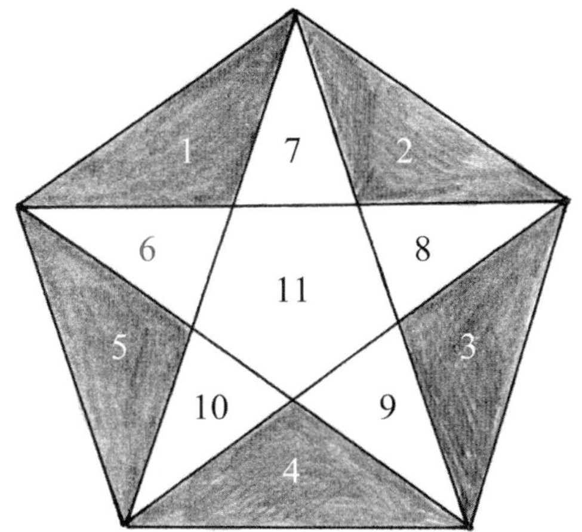

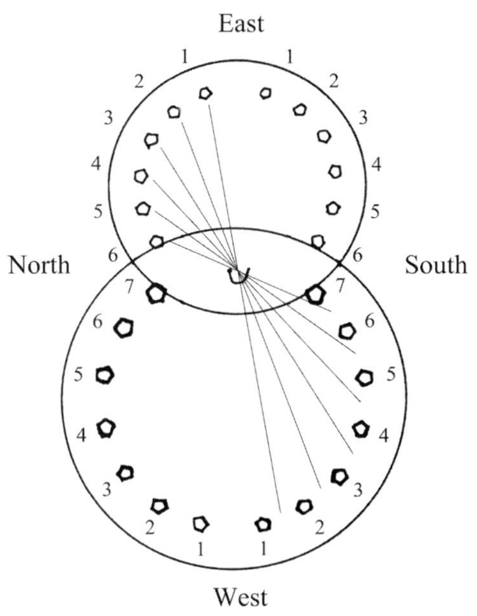

The columns begin on either side of the sculpture of the Representative of Man. All columns were laminated in a pentagram of eleven pieces.

The first column reflected in its materials both the Saturn and the Sun column of the great auditorium: its inside was made of hornbeam, its outside was made of ash. I sensed a movement from the west to the east, and a response from the east towards the west, culminating in their centre, the speaker's rostrum. The outside becomes the inside as in a lemniscate, both loops giving to and receiving from each other.

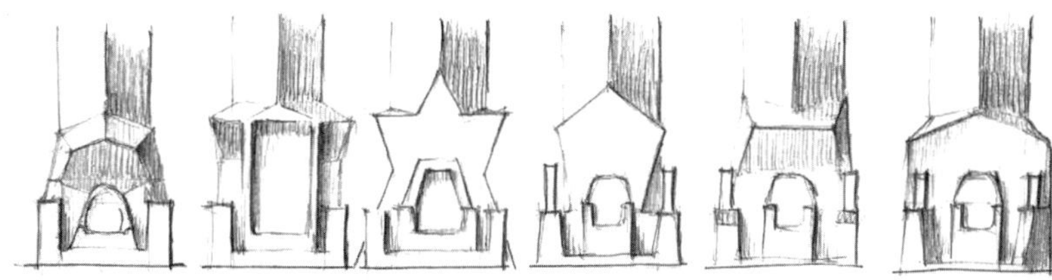

The thrones at the foot of each column may not have been for human beings to sit on but for the spiritual beings painted above which were like the creators and guardians of each column. These beings inspired and guided the particular cultural epochs. The thrones unite with the columns, building their firm foundation out of which the columns rise up. Each one was based on a symmetrical, geometrical

particular composition, protected on either side with short prism-shaped columns like corner stones.

FIRST COLUMN

Standing on either side of the statue of the Representative of Man, the throne on the base of the first column had a protective faceted triangular canopy above the actual seat, which felt to me related to Ahriman's cave in between them. Ahriman is also a highly developed spiritual being, the guardians on either side of his cave acknowledge and accompany this necessary quality for the evolution of man. The seat is based broadly and firmly on the ground, almost filling up the whole width of the base. Its triangular composition is accentuated by the crystalline canopy, culminating in a flat triangular point meeting the edge of the column. Earthbound, reliable and settled, this throne builds a firm foundation for this first column. The two upright pillars on each side of the throne confirm and establish its gravitas. The whole column, throne, capital and architrave was carved in ash wood, a golden-coloured, strong and flexible wood, contrasting and thereby balancing the more protective inward gesture of the throne.

Carrying the observation in the sense Carl Kemper has indicated through all the six capitals of the small dome, I came to the following perception: The capital of the first column has arisen out of the space between the first, the Saturn capital "The It", and the second, the Sun capital "To It" from the great auditorium. This in-between space resounds a calling from an innocent beingness to an awakening. The tender meeting of the two points on the edge of the Saturn capital has transformed itself in the capital of the small domed space into two quiet seed gestures which stand opposite each other as in a conscious supportive and active waiting. The centre of the panel, as an open expectation in the Saturn capital, and awakened to an active involvement with each other in the Sun capital, has transformed in the capital of the small domed space into a mighty convex leading impulse from above downwards. The more crystalline concentrated form on the edge above is able to hold and support this grand swing downwards, balancing it out together with the more seed-like forms from below. I felt this to be a metamorphosis of a special kind: from a transformation in process so to say, from the in between, the 'night between two days' to a completely new formation which is inwardly related and enhanced. It is as if the planetary forces are receiving, and then enlivening the zodiacal forces through their individual rhythms.

Looking at the background on which these new forms of the capital in the small dome appear, one can also imagine that these gestures give rise to the Saturn and Sun capitals in the large cupola, that they are becoming through each other, creating each other as a sounding of the Harmony of the Spheres. Then it is a small step to sense the impulse-giving force of Aries in the seed-like forms on the edge below and the rhythmical contraction and expansion of Libra from above. Together they are able to balance each other in a living symmetry. The space in between is pulsating rhythmically with this mighty giving and receiving. Maybe this is what Rudolf Steiner meant when he said that there is also symmetry in the Zodiac?
And maybe because these two Zodiacal gestures are working together in this capital their very individual and one-sided gestures have already been enhanced towards each other. Could it be that this working together of Aries and Libra is inspiring the formations of the Saturn and Sun capitals in the sense that the 'East is inspiring that, which forms itself in the West'?[1] In this sense one could see it as streams of forces going both ways: from the West to the East and from the East to the West.

The living element of our building (the First Goetheanum) *expresses itself through this, that the one dome has its conscious mirror image in the other dome so to speak, that both domes mirror each other.*

—Carl Kemper, *Der Bau*, p. 100 (translation Gertraud Goodwin)

The impulse from the main motif above the statue of the Representative of Man, reaches far out and down, initiating and impulsating the movement of the architraves, a powerful sculptural gesture reaching downwards right above the first column, giving rise to the motif of the capital. A similarly-shaped sculptural gesture moves on from the architrave in a less vigorous manner, arching above the space between the first and the second column. Above the architraves, the painting in the small cupola depicted the Slavic Man, with the Angel and the Centaur. (See chapter on the Slavic Man in Hilde Raske's book, *The Language of Color*).

1. Rudolf Steiner, *The Foundation Stone Meditation*

CAPITAL

BASE

SECOND COLUMN AUDITORIUM

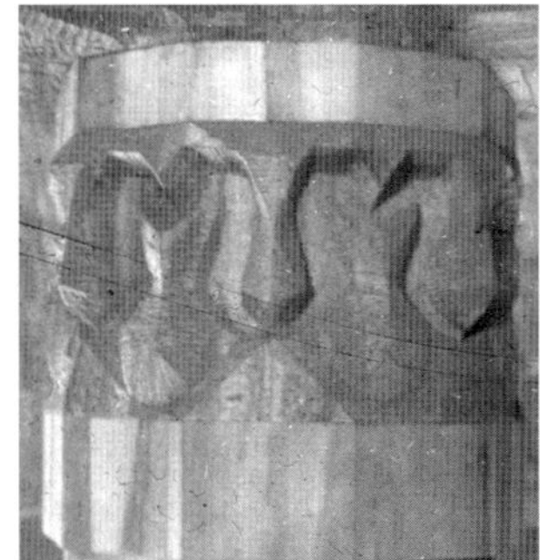

CAPITAL

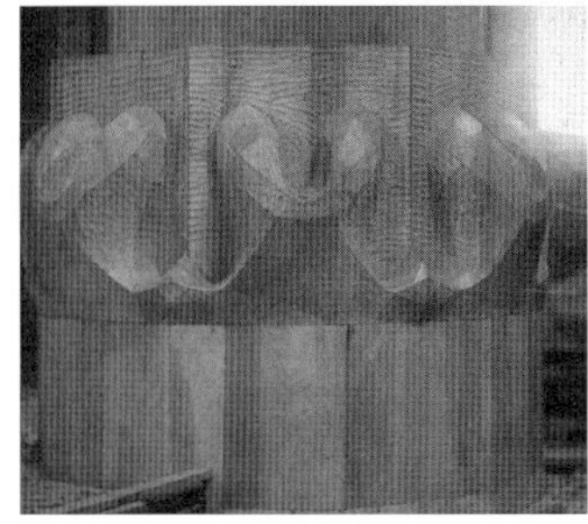

BASE

FIRST COLUMN SMALL DOMED SPACE

ARCHITRAVES ABOVE FIRST, SECOND & THIRD COLUMN

CAPITAL

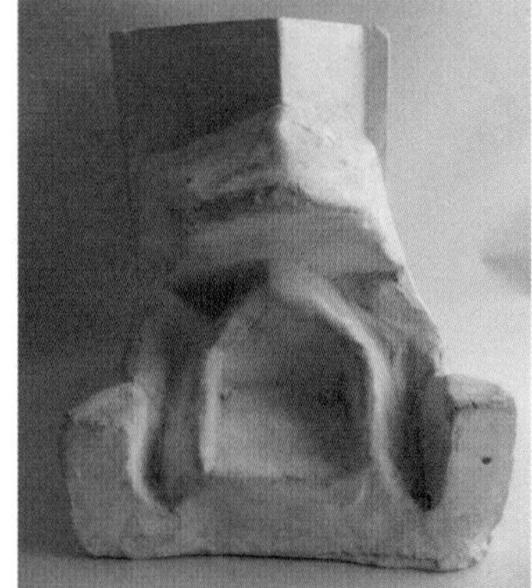

THRONE

SECOND COLUMN

The throne at the base of the second column is marked by two vertical pillars, which create a threefold space: in the centre a more closed space of the seat and on either side open canopied spaces. From the canopied top of the centre space, a horizontal edge marks the base of a triangular slope back towards the column, where the point of the triangle and the edge of the column meet. Two squares above the open chambers below meet the column on either side. The thinner, upright columns on either end of the throne support an open, uplifting, but nevertheless protected gesture.

The whole column was made out of cherry wood, a wood with a variety of hues from olive green to reddish brown to pale beige. The inside of the column was made of ash wood, so both the Sun with the words "To It" and Moon column with the words "Into It" from the great auditorium reverberate their forces into the small domed space. This step from the second to the third capital leads us from an awakening, rhythmical moving and becoming to an internalisation of building a receptive inner space. This leads in the second capital of the small domed space also to a further involvement and internalisation of the formations from above and below to each other. The outer action is occurring along the edge of the capital where a mightily pressing down convex form is being received by a twofold strongly crystalline, earthy form set in itself. In the centre of the panel an upright open space appears. This space stands on the bottom of the edge of the capital, reaches high up in a somewhat flattened convex and has a bridging connection to the next panel. This background negative space is thereby rhythmically structured between a powerful upright and a thinner, but decisively formed connection to its neighbouring panel.

I can see an inner connection to the zodiacal forces of Taurus and Scorpio, already enhanced through their working together, as if liberated from their one-sidedness: a true signature of the Pisces Zodiac, where always the two polar-opposite zodiacal forces are working together, thereby creating a third new element between themselves. Observing in this way, one can perceive the forces of Taurus establishing themselves mightily from above downwards, at the same time creating this grand inner open space and protecting it. The twofold sharpness of the formation on the bottom can be seen as reminiscent of Scorpio's separating, in-between nature, giving space. Another new and alive symmetry is achieved through the working together of both Taurus and Scorpio. Again, I could sense how this formation could inspire the expression from east to west, towards creating the capitals of the second and third column of the great cupola.

The architrave above this capital impulsates it from above with a now stronger wilful convex gesture downwards. It arches up and down over towards the next column, to a new motif which inspires the third capital from above. Between these two a single form appears, rounded and simple in a half-moon shape above, differentiated, threefold towards below – an almost embryonic rendering of the *Hauptmotiv*, like an echo or reminder to carry this impulse onwards.

The painted cupola above the second column showed the Persian-Germanic Initiate with the Child. (See Hilde Raske's book, *The Language of Color*.)

SECOND COLUMN AUDITORIUM

CAPITAL

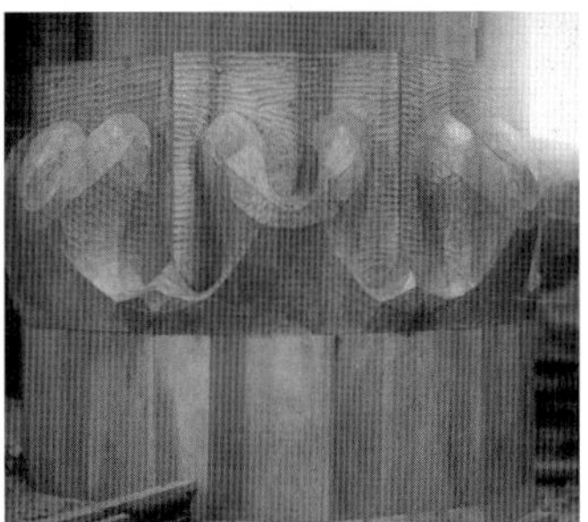

BASE

THIRD COLUMN AUDITORIUM

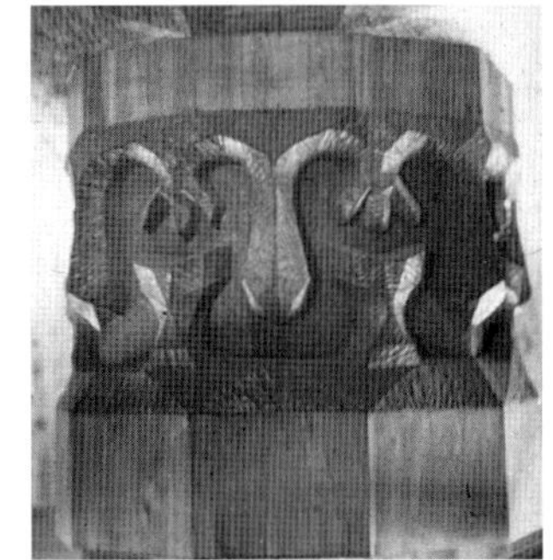

CAPITAL

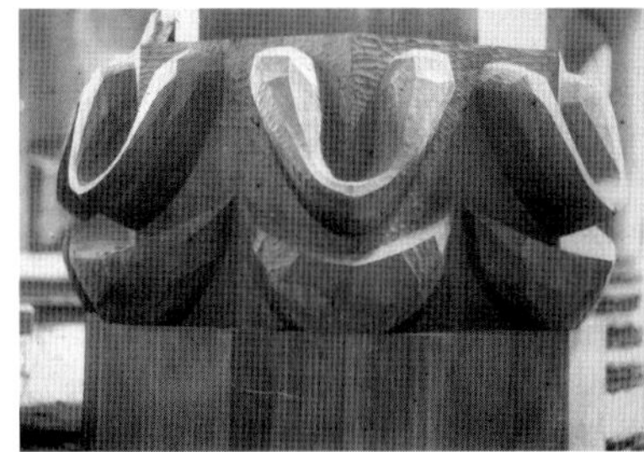

BASE

SECOND COLUMN SMALL DOMED SPACE

ARCHITRAVES ABOVE FIRST, SECOND & THIRD COLUMN

CAPITAL

THRONE

THIRD COLUMN

The third column in the small domed space finds itself related to the space between the third and fourth columns of the great auditorium. The third column with the words "Into It", leads us into an inner space and a gesture of fructification, which in the fourth column with the word "I", becomes a form fulfilled in itself, but isolated in its own space, as in a secluded ripening.

The whole third column was carved outside in oak wood, a durable and strong dark-coloured wood with short fibres, the inside in cherry wood. (The whole of the outside building of the First Goetheanum was carved in oak wood.)

The throne at the foot of this column shows a concentration on the essential: it faces one with a decided strength and clarity. The small prism-shaped columns on either side of the two previous thrones are here the sides of the seat, which continue above and behind, forming a triangular frame with a blunt side on top. Two small steps lead up to the seat on either side. Behind the seat, a plane parallel to the back of the seat rises up to a centre point which meets the edge of the column, and spreads to either side in a triangular star-shape. This large sheer and clearly triangular star-shaped plane pointing upwards gives a powerful authority, strength and a majestic quality to the seat, with its triangular composition pointing downwards. This interpenetration sculpturally expresses: as above – so below.

The third capital in the small domed space seems to reverse the gesture of the Moon and Mars capitals from the large auditorium: they point downwards in their gestures, while here, the sculptural movement is freely holding itself in a strongly convex u-shaped gesture pointing upwards, occupying proudly the space of the panel, holding an inner deep parallel space in itself. A triangular point moves towards this open space from above. It felt to me as if these two forms together created a sound like a wake-up call. A possibility of a Gemini gesture could be seen in the two sides of the lyre-type form, reaching up and also outwards, holding the inner space. The triangular shape from above, focussed towards the open space could be felt as the aim-taking of Sagittarius, with its fiery concentration. Through their sounding together, Gemini's arms receive what Sagittarius can purposefully aim towards – both giving and receiving qualities of each other.

The concentrated triangular point from above downwards in this capital, receives a mighty, warm, giving and open gesture from the architrave, which releases what it had prepared in the two previous gestures above the second and first capitals. At the same time this gesture also receives what the lyre-shaped form of the capital below offers upwards in its dedicated concentration.

Above this sculptural orchestration the theme of the cupola painting was the Egyptian Initiate and his inspirers. (See Hilde Raske's book for details.)

THIRD COLUMN AUDITORIUM

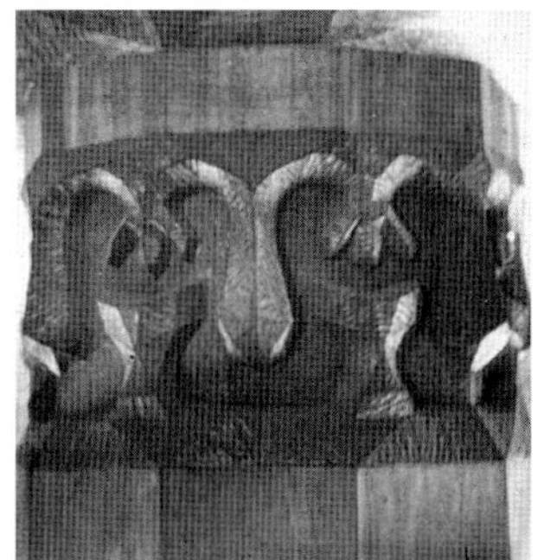

CAPITAL

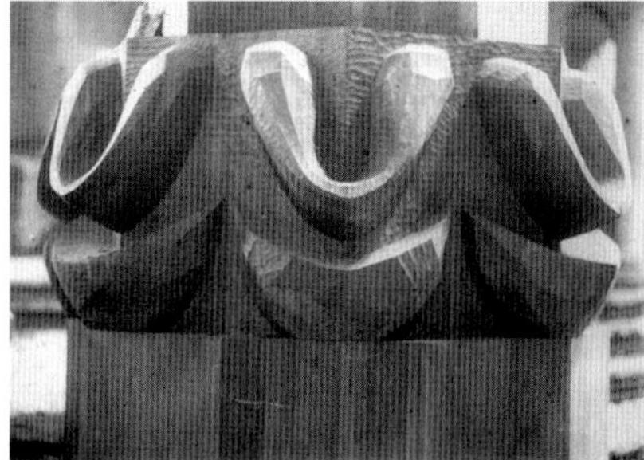

BASE

FOURTH COLUMN AUDITORIUM

CAPITAL

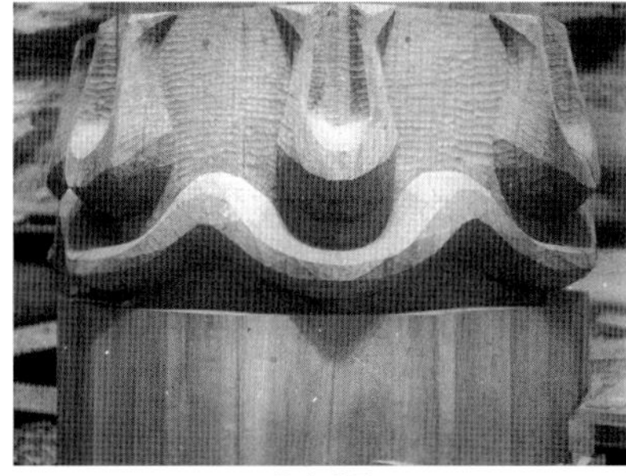

BASE

THIRD COLUMN SMALL DOMED SPACE

ARCHITRAVES ABOVE FIRST, SECOND & THIRD COLUMN

CAPITAL

THRONE

FOURTH COLUMN

The fourth column is inspired by the space between the fourth, the Mars, "I", column and the Mercury, "From the I", column of the large auditorium. In the metamorphic step between, a powerful turning point occurs: what has so far been freely gifted from the spiritual forces above has been intensified, built in, into the Mars stage of evolution and is making its first gesture "From the I" out into the world. In the whole of evolution this is a U-turn and the most important fulcrum of its development!

The whole fourth column of the small domed space was carved in elm wood outside, the Mercury tree wood, which is at the same time dark in colour and has a very lively often difficult grain to carve. It is as if life-forces want to penetrate even the most difficult matter! The inside of the column was made of oak wood.

The throne at the bottom of the column in the small domed space shows this step in a remarkable way: the seat has become much smaller and stays the same in the next two thrones. It stands more isolated within the crystalline composition around it. It is simply shaped with a half-round backrest above which a mighty upward striving pentagonal form rises up, its point meeting the edge of the column, its sides fill in the space towards the two sides of the column which make this pentagonal form a tremendously substantial and powerful gesture. The half-circular backrest of the seat just reaches up into the base of the pentagonal shape, which continues horizontally on either side, giving the sense of an above and a below. But I can also see how an elongated point of the two diagonally upwards striving sides could meet at the bottom and centre of the chair: this observation is supported by the two solid cubic forms on either side of the seat, which echo this upward striving gesture in their conic formation. Thus this throne is connected to the above, right from the bottom, as well as separated from it in a clear horizontal.

As the capital above the space between the fourth capital of the large auditorium arises out of the Mars gesture of "I", and the fifth capital, the Mercury gesture with the words "From the I" a decisive metamorphic development stage had been reached: a particular end in the Mars gesture, and a new beginning in the Mercury gesture. In the invisible step of metamorphosis between the Mars and Mercury column from the large auditorium, this transition from death to a new life is taking place. This resounds in the fourth capital of the small domed space: on the edges of the panels two strongly convex-shaped gestures rise upwards like two guardians, creating a space between each other. From above, a large crystalline seed-like formation makes its way downwards towards the inviting space below. One could sense that the Mars form had metamorphosed, concentrated and detached itself into the seed-like form, becoming an inspiration for the prepared inner space below it: maybe this is a gesture for Cancer. The two guardian-like shapes on either side could be perceived as an expression of a Capricorn mood: creating a space into which the new light of the Christ impulse can be received, held and protected.

I felt that this fourth capital radiated a concentrated simplicity and sincere/stern matter-of-fact deed. Both Cancer and Capricorn stand at turning points in the year from without inwards and from within outwards, both expressing themselves in an inner, soul-spiritual aspect, but finding an outer gesture for it.

The architrave swinging over from the third to the fourth capital shows a seed-like round form open to the above, responding from above with a triangular opening. On either side of this, two small triangular forms, pointing downwards, give this relationship an intimate protection. Further on and directly above the capital, this seed-like gesture seems to be received and handed on downwards towards the capital – where it finds itself concentrated, hovering in space, but embraced and protected from below.

The painting directly above this column shows Athena, Apollo and an angel-being inspiring Apollo. (See Hilde Raske's book for details.)

FOURTH COLUMN AUDITORIUM

CAPITAL

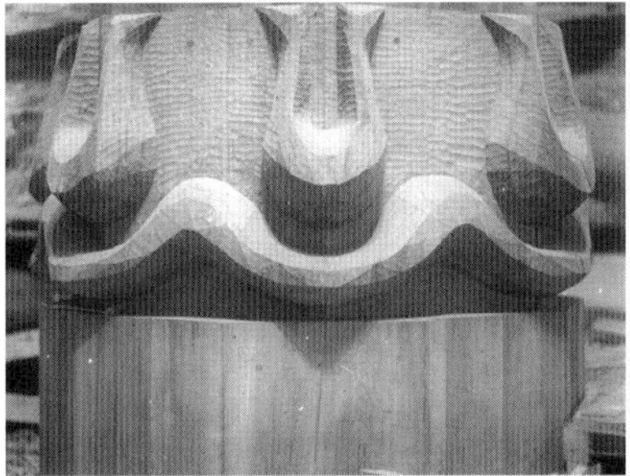

BASE

FIFTH COLUMN AUDITORIUM

MERCURY CAPITAL

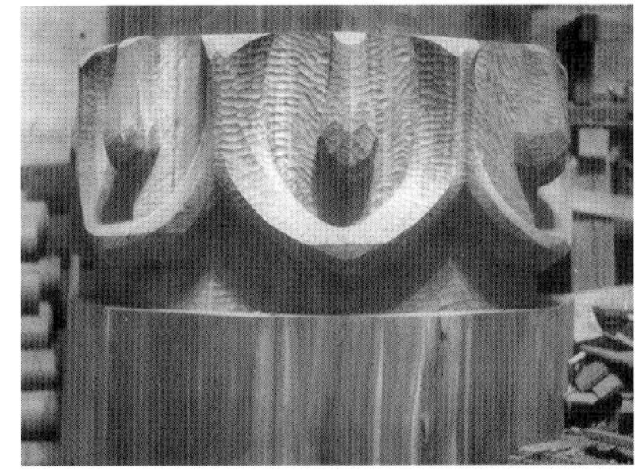

MERCURY BASE

FOURTH COLUMN SMALL DOMED SPACE

ARCHITRAVES ABOVE THIRD, FOURTH, FIFTH & SIXTH COLUMN

CAPITAL

THRONE

FIFTH COLUMN

This column was inspired from the space between the fifth, the Mercury column, "From the I", and the sixth, the Jupiter column, "Out of Myself", in the large auditorium. The whole column was carved in maple wood, a light, durable wood with long fibres. The seat itself, and the step leading up to it, are the same as in the fourth throne. The surrounding geometric composition is very different: the two protective low walls on either side of the seat are quite parallel in width, receding in a slope backwards from the step, then becoming vertical again slightly above the seat. Behind the seat the wall rises up and over the top of it, and comes forward in a protective gesture. At the same time this canopy narrows itself diagonally up from the top end of the walls on either side of the seat, then slopes further upwards to join the actual column in a diagonal angle. This composition creates a gesture of concentrated stability, elevated protection, and a sovereign simplicity.

The metamorphosis from the fifth to the sixth capital of the large auditorium reaches from the newly established ego-consciousness towards sharing this capacity with its neighbours, thereby creating a new space for the forces from above to reach down and inspire again from above. The single upright form in the Mercury capital, which masters the forces around itself, is transformed in the Jupiter capital to a formation which is continuous and connected all around the capital as in a new reaching out to each other, 'holding hands'. The forms swing up into the vertical on the edge of the panel, then touch the ground in a swinging, continuous rhythm.

These new faculties of both capitals come to bear in the fifth capital of the small domed space: an upright gesture stands proudly in the centre of the panel, reaching out horizontally over the edge of the panel to connect with its neighbouring form. Above this a mighty seed-form holds itself on the edge, supported by the horizontal reaching over gesture. Where a global consciousness reaches out towards the other, embracing it, the seed of future possibilities hovers over this gesture.

The upright strength and pride of the central form can remind us of the gesture of Leo. Through the forces of Aquarius, the overall sharing and connecting is made possible, both together enabling the seed for the future to become and unfold itself.

The arch of the architrave from the fourth to the fifth column shows in its upward curve a strongly convex protrusion. I felt this to be the delivery downwards of the prepared seed-formation above the fourth capital. Almost released from the architraves, it makes its way downwards, while immediately above the fifth capital a new open space is left behind, enveloped and protected by fully convex forms as if preparing for a new conception.

The painting above this fifth column depicts Faust, Death, the hovering child facing Faust, and the "Genius". (See Hilde Raske's book for detailed description of the painted motifs.)

FIFTH COLUMN AUDITORIUM

MERCURY CAPITAL

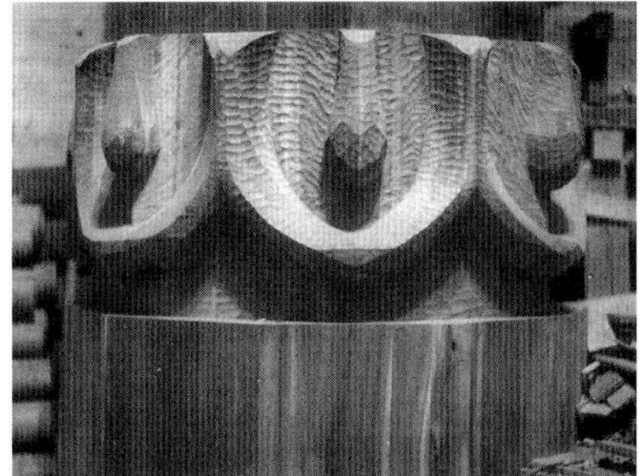

MERCURY BASE

SIXTH COLUMN AUDITORIUM

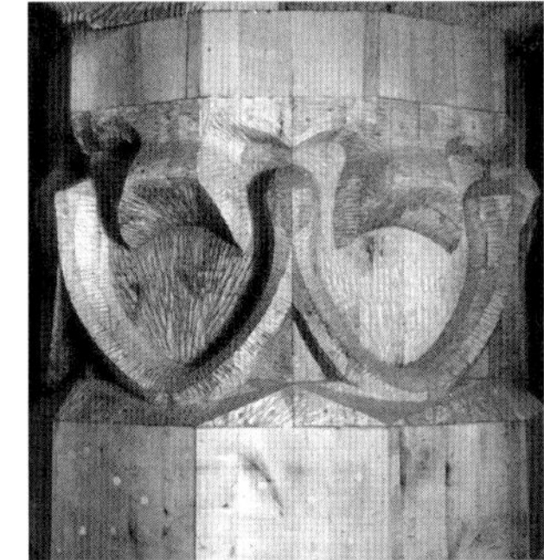

JUPITER CAPITAL

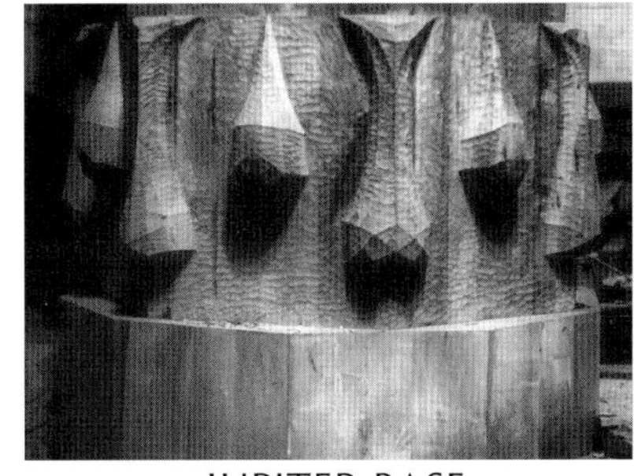

JUPITER BASE

FIFTH COLUMN SMALL DOMED SPACE

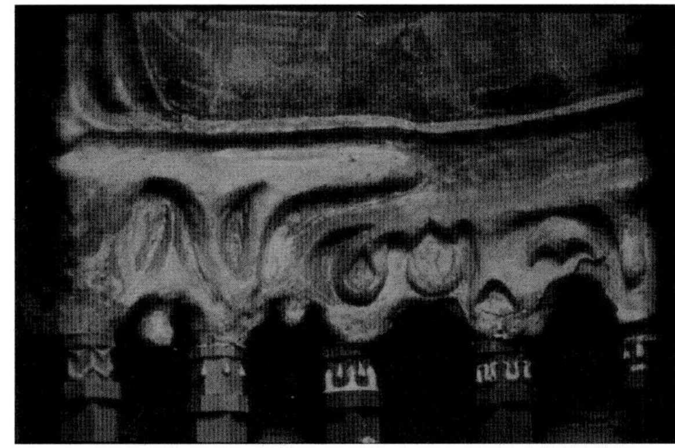

ARCHITRAVES ABOVE THIRD, FOURTH, FIFTH & SIXTH COLUMN

CAPITAL

THRONE

SIXTH COLUMN

The sixth and last column of the small domed space was the nearest to the proscenium arch. It arose out of the in-between space of the sixth and seventh column of the large auditorium. The seventh was also the last one nearest to the proscenium arch on the large auditorium side.

The sixth, the Jupiter column, carries the words "Out of Myself", the last column, the Venus column, carries the words "From the I Into the It". The mood and gesture of these two columns emanates a new openness, a generosity in giving themselves with consciousness, overview and love. This brings a harmonious gesture of inner fulfilment also to the whole of the sixth column of the small domed space.

The actual seat is again unchanged. The whole composition of the throne radiates an open peaceful simplicity. The seat rests against an upright pentagonal plane, its upper point meeting the edge of the column. A quiet, open, grounded and earthy feeling emanates from it, which is strengthened by the slightly diagonal face of this pentagonal shape on either side where it meets the column.

Like the columns in the large auditorium these columns are also tapered, but all six had geometrically a very similar width and height – quite unlike the ones in the large cupola, which grew in height and width considerably from the west to the east. This 'sameness' again underlines the quality of the resting stars, the Zodiac.
The inside of this sixth column was made of maple, the wood for Jupiter. The carvings of the throne, the outside of the column and the capital were all carved in birch wood, a soft, light wood with a silvery shine to it. It is easily perishable, but its bark has a tenacious strength and durability.

The capital above takes up the theme of this peaceful, inner fulfilment in strong and substantial triangular rising and descending zigzag double gestures. The two forces from above and below swing together as in a mighty chord all around the capital in one large breath of a movement. The formation from below rests its downward triangular movement firmly on the ground, making a clear statement from where it originates and belongs. The sister formation from above attaches its upward-pointing movement to the upper rim of the capital. I felt this capital was like a joyful celebration of mutual understanding and support for each other with a character and statement of eternity, as if chiselled in stone.

Making the step towards the last zodiacal pair, Virgo and Pisces, I could sense a deep relationship between their particular individual qualities and the formations of this capital: the forces of Virgo regulate our digestive system with infinite wisdom, rhythmically integrating the food substances we take in, excreting what is not needed. It is an eternally rhythmical peristaltic gesture of in and out, of up and down, brought to an archetypal zigzag formation.

The gesture of Pisces finds its creative expression in the form and function of our feet. We walk on the earth, each step also a step in our destiny. Lifting, carrying and placing our feet we create an up-and-down rhythm touching and connecting with the ground underneath and lifting off the ground to connect to a more vertical, higher reality in this continuous rhythm. Looked at from this zodiacal aspect I can sense a strong relationship between the capitals of the small domed space and the large auditorium. Above this last capital, the architrave quietly takes back its forces and formations, as if to make space for a peaceful breathing out and a conclusion.

The painted motifs in the cupola, the "Genius" above Faust and the Child, project into the area above which is next to the stage opening. (See Hilde Raske's book for detailed description of the painted motifs.)

The proscenium arch rose up immediately from these capitals on either side of the stage. From the large auditorium this last column would not have been fully visible. What would have been fully visible from the auditorium was the main motif, also carved in birch wood: extending itself over the whole proscenium arch, giving itself completely in a gesture of embrace, warmth and love.

SIXTH COLUMN AUDITORIUM

JUPITER CAPITAL

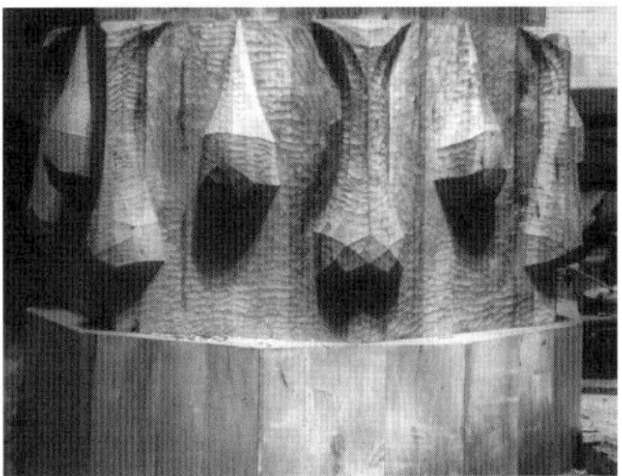

JUPITER BASE

SEVENTH COLUMN AUDITORIUM

VENUS CAPITAL

VENUS BASE

SIXTH COLUMN SMALL DOMED SPACE

ARCHITRAVES ABOVE THIRD, FOURTH, FIFTH & SIXTH COLUMN

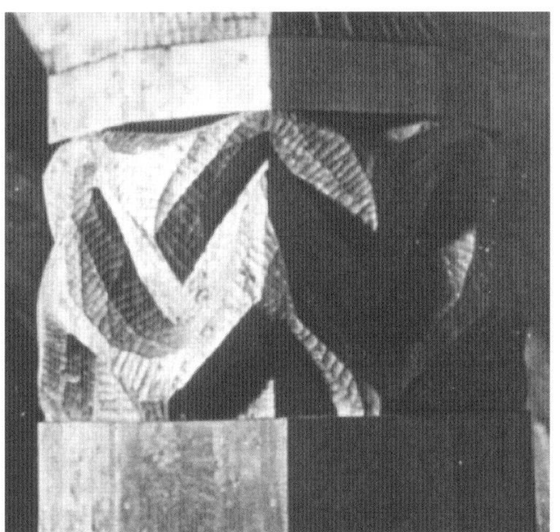

CAPITAL

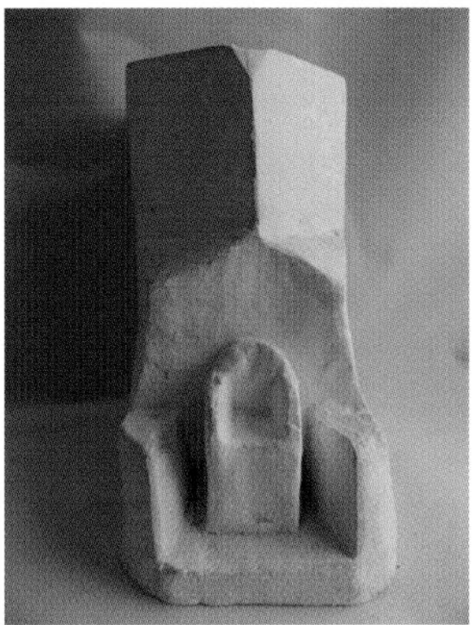

THRONE

REFERENCES – READING LIST

The following reading list / book list, is by no means complete – in fact it is very small compared to what is available.
It is my personal list, so to speak, the books I came across and which helped me further.

Rudolf Steiner,   *Eurythmy as Visible Speech*, Lecture: 7th July 1924, GA279

Human and Cosmic Thought, 4 lectures, Berlin 20 – 23 January 1914, GA151

Man – Hieroglyph of the Universe, Lecture 17th April 1920, GA201

The Riddle of Humanity, Lecture 13th August 1916, GA170

Twelve Moods, GA40

Aïvanhov, Omraam Mikhaël, *The Zodiac, Key to Man and the Universe*, ISBN 0763-2738

Anderson, Isabel, *Die Zwölf Heiligen Nächte*, Ogham Bücherei, ISBN 3-7235-1098-1

Aschenbrenner, M., *Der Tierkreis*, Philosophisch-Anthroposophische Verlag am Goetheanum, Dornach

Barfod, Werner, *Tierkreisgesten und Menschenwesen*, Verlag am Goetheanum

Betti, Mario, *Zwölf Wege die Welt zu verstehen*, Verlag Freies Geisteslaben

Bohm, Werner, *Kosmos, Erde und Mensch*, Vol. 1-IV G

Böttcher, Cordelia, *Das Buch der 12 Heiligen Nächte. Inspirationen für das neue Jahr*, Clavis, ISBN 3-934839-01-0

Davidson, Norman, *Astronomy and the Imagination*, Routledge & Kegan Paul

Falck-Ytter, H, *Kosmos und Apokalypse*, J. Ch, Mellinger Verlag

Gleich, Sigismund von, *Die Wahrheit als Gesamtamfang aller Weltanrichten*, J.Ch. Mellinger Verlag, Stuttgart

Gorrisen, Gisela, *Astrosophie des Tierkreises und der Planeten*, Verlag Urachhaus

Held, Wolfgang, *Im Zeichen des Tierkreises*, Falter im Verlag Freies Geistesleben, ISBN 978-3-7725-2546-9

Horstmann, H., *Der Tierkreis*, Aufsätze und Skizzen aus der anthroposophischen Arbeit. Heft 4, J.Ch. Mellinger Verlag, Stuttgart

Jocelyn, John, *Meditations on the Signs of the Zodiac*

Julius, Fritz, *The Imagery of the Zodiac*, Floris Books, ISBN 0-86315-177-9

Kemper, Carl, *Der Bau*

Lin, Jean-Claude (Herausgeber), *Die Tugenden im Jahreslauf*, Verlag Freies Geistesleben

Poeppig, Fred, *Menschenbegegnung, Sternenordnung*, Im Selbstverlag – Vergriffen

Prokofieff, Sergei O., *The Twelve Holy Nights and the Spiritual Hierarchies*

Raske, Hilde, *The Language of Color in the First Goetheanum*

Soesman, A, *Our Twelve Senses: How Healthy Senses Refresh the Soul*

Wegmann, Ita, *Die Signatur der Tierkreis und Planetenkräfte in der menschlichen Organisation als Ausdruck des Weltenwortes*, Natura Heft III, 9/10, März/April 1929

FURTHER READING REFERENCES

There are a number of artists who have worked with the Zodiac and researched the forces of the Zodiac artistically and have published their work themselves. I will list their publications here as far as I know of it:

Rösler, Margot, *"Aus der Sprache des Tierkreises" nach Hinweisen von Rudolf Steiner.*
Band I: Das Sonnen-Tierkreis Erlebnis, J.Ch. Mellinger Verlag
Band II: Die Planeten-Tierkreis Erlebnisse und ihre Farben, Das Erden-Tierkreis Erlebnis, J.Ch. Mellinger Verlag
Anthroposophischer Kalender im Jahre 1966 nach des Ich Geburt aufgreifend das Anliegen des Kalenders 1912/13, von Rudolf Steiner, mit Zeichnungen von Imme von Eckardstein, mit erneuerten Tierkreisbildern in Bezug auf Sonne und Mond, gezeichnet von Christine Cologna.
Zu beziehen: "Förderkreis des Kalenderimpulses Rufold Steiners". p.A. Rudolf Steiner Bau, A-5026 Salzburg, Friedrich Inhauserstrasse 27.
Raske, Hilde, *Farbstudien zu den zwölf Stimmungen von Rudolf Steiner*, ISBN 3-85636-143-X, Pforte Verlag
Wagner, Gerard, *"Eurythmische Lautbilder"*, Tierkreis Kalender, der an Ostern beginnt.

In English
Anderson, Adrian Ph.d., *The Lost Zodiac of Rudolf Steiner*, ISBN 978-0-9941602-5-6, Threshold Publishing

BIOGRAPHIES

AUREL MOTHES
Member of the BBK ("Bund Bildender Künstler", the German union of fine artists)

Aurel Mothes was already in his childhood trained in painting by his father, Peter Andreas Mothes. At the age of eighteen he had his first public exhibition. He continued to create holistic and pleasing work and living spaces through artistic concepts in communal spaces such as kindergartens, factories, restaurants, institutions and doctors' surgeries. Currently, Aurel Mothes is creating his wall designs and exhibiting in multiple European countries while also making works in oil and acrylic in his studio. Large format acrylic and sand paintings can currently be seen at the design hotel "Steinernes Schweinchen" in Kassel, Germany. He looks forward to contributing several large format paintings to the Museum of Contemporary Art in Beijing in May 2019.
Aurel Mothes lives and works in Kassel, Germany.

www.mothes-farbraum.de

MARIJE ROWLING

I studied Art and Education in the Netherlands, followed by Art at Emerson College and Tobias school of Art. For many years I taught at Canterbury Steiner School. My subjects were Art, History of Art and G.C.S.E. exam Art. This was followed by teaching at Emerson College and Tobias. Whilst life was very busy I kept painting and have had regular exhibitions of my work. These included joint and solo ones. Themes I explored were usually painted as series such as Nature Moods, Seasonal Impressions and the Zodiac, and more recently the Elements. This latest project on the Zodiac started as an artistic study and developed into a freer interpretation. It has been a wonderful inspiration and I intend to take it further into larger paintings.

EDWIN BOECK

Born in Bruchsal, Baden, Germany, 14 August 1956. Three year apprenticeship as interior decorator. Ceramic workshop in Sentheim, Alsace, France. Training in sculpture and art with Reimar von Bonin in Switzerland. Then College of Art in Freiburg Munzingen, now called Edith Marion Schule, from 1982 to 1986. Sculpture teacher at the above school from 1986 until 1990. Since 1990 living in Kalmar in South Sweden, working as a freelance artist: public commissions, exhibitions, art performance, sculptures in snow, ice and sand.

www.edwinboeck.se

DOROTHEA KUTH

After my attendance at Waldorf School, I became a nurse, married, had five children and have long been a passionate mother. Later, I attended a part-time Waldorf teacher training and taught during the next fifteen years in Waldorf Schools in Germany, England, Australia, New Zealand and South Korea. In 2012, I became physically ill and had to give up my teaching work. I went to Hoathly Hill Sculpture Studio for sculpture therapy and after one and a half years, began a training in sculpture and drawing, which led to a diploma. I also completed an art therapy training course for schools in Munich. I discovered my love of art during therapy – for which I am deeply grateful, because it has led me through my own healing process to link me back to my profession of nursing, healing and teaching. Now, I teach in Hoathly Hill Sculpture Studio and work with children and adults in groups or one-to-one.

MANNING GOODWIN

Engaged in his own sculpture at Hoathly Hill Sculpture Studios, West Hoathly, Sussex (1992 – 1999). The Zodiac forms were created in 1995.
Sculpture Training at Alanus – Hochschule, Bonn, Germany (1975 – 78).
St. Albans Art Therapy training at Hertfordshire College of Art & Design (Postgraduate Diploma & Certificate 1983).
Sculpture Therapy practice at Oeschelbronn Klinik (1984 – 85) and in England with private clients.
His sculptures have been exhibited locally, in London, and in Italy near Pietrasanta.

PHILIP NELSON

Philip Nelson was born 1950 in Washington D.C., USA and grew up there and in Arizona. After he finished school he studied history and media sciences, and worked as an architectural draftsman. For several years he worked as a teacher in Washington and Detroit. He travelled extensively through USA and Europe. In 1981 he started his training as a painter. Since his diploma in 1986 he lives and works as a freelance artist near Basel, Switzerland.

STEPHAN KRAUCH

Born 1957, married with three children.Certified educational sociologist, curative educationalist, cabinetmaker and artist. Stephan works at the early development centre »Haus des Kindes« [»House of the Child«] as well as in adult education (»der hof« [»the farm«], Niederursel, Frankfurt am Main). For me, painting is a moment of reflection and stillness. In working with young people, I have tried to characterise them in abstract pictures, using colour and form, so as to acquire a clearer picture of their nature. The death of a woman who was a colleague of mine had a significant impact on my painting. As a result, the question of the activity and closeness of the other side has become a motif in many of my pictures. My engagement with the twelve virtues is a continuation of my attempts to present the moods, powers and qualities of the soul in visible form and to enrich them through working with them artistically. The pictures do not constitute a representation of the virtue for each month, but are momentary snapshots taken from my engagement with these virtues.

CLAUDIA GRAH

Claudia Grah-Wittich, born 1957, married with three children. Studied History of Art, MA in Philosophy, certified social worker. Works in the early development centre »Haus des Kindes« [»House of the Child«] as well as in adult education (»der hof« [»the farm«], Niederursel, Frankfurt am Main). The twelve exercises were created as a result of my collaboration with Stephan Krauch teaching courses in adult education. They have been cast in this new form for the calendar, and a commentary has been added to make clear their relationship to the twelve virtues.

ROLF JANSSEN

1954   Born in Oss, Netherlands
1973–79   Study of visual arts at the Academie voor Beeldende Vorming in Tilburg, NL
1984   Study of Art Therapy at Academie De Werfel in Driebergen, NL
1986   Move to Germany and work as Art therapist and care for the elderly in Stuttgart, Germany
1987   Training as a Waldorf teacher
1988–2004 Art and Crafts teacher in various Waldorf Schools
Since 2004 Freelance artist and musician

DORIS HARPERS

Doris Harpers, painter and painting teacher, was born in Germany and has lived in Italy for more then thirty years. Her artistic studies are based on Rudolf Steiner's indications for a new artistic approach. She studied this method for three years at the Alanus Accademy in Germany with Wilfried Ogilvie and for a further two years at the school for art therapy "De Wervel" with Eva Mees in the Netherlands. Since this time she has been seeking for the relationship between the arts and often paints inspired by poems or music. Her exhibitions are often accompanied by concert musicians and recitations. Doris Harpers has exhibited and given painting workshops in various European countries (as well as in Mexico and Egypt). She has often collaborated in international conferences organised by the Art Section of the Goetheanum (Dornach, Switzerland) or by IDRIART (Institute for the Development of Intercultural Relations through the Arts). She teaches painting and drawing at the Free Accademy "Aldo Bargero" in Oriago (Venice) in its Pedagogical Seminar and in the Painting School "Tiziano", of which she is the founder. She has developed a special study method for her painting students. Her ex-students are now teaching in various parts of Italy and Croatia, where she also had a painting school for seven years.

GERARD WAGNER 1906-1999

Gerard Wagner was born in Wiesbaden, Germany in 1906, and from 1912 grew up in England. In 1924 he became a pupil of the Post-Impressionist painter John Anthony Park at the St Ives Art Colony in Cornwall, and a year later entered the RCA in London. He came to Dornach, Switzerland in the summer of 1926. There he met the artistic work of Rudolf Steiner, and has since made it his life-task to develop Steiner's indications. Starting from Rudolf Steiner's call to learn painting "out of the colour" – to immerse oneself in the inner life of colour, in order to find the creative will of the colour itself – Wagner sought an approach to the sketches which Steiner had made for his pupils as a path of training. If there is an inherently law-governed relationship between colour and form, it would be discoverable here – and thereupon began a decades-long path of practice and experimentation devoted to the selfless study of the inner quality of colours.

JOHN SALTER 1921-2018

John Salter was born in Harrow, NW London on 23rd May 1921. He served in the artillery (1939 – 1946) in the 2nd World War. He subsequently worked in the oil business until 1973, during which time he part-time studies colour and form, particularly in relation to the First Goetheanum in the context of the art of the first part of the 20th century.
From 1973 he worked full time, principally in sculpture (wood, stone, clay). He exhibited his work in the Rye Art Gallery, Sussex in 1980. In 1991 he completed the 7 piece metamorphic sculptural sequence in concrete at Kibbutz Harduf, Israel. He held a Studio Exhibition in Ashurstwood, Sussex in 2002.

REIMER VON BONIN 1930 – 1997

Reimar von Bonin spent his childhood in Finland. He moved to Garmisch-Partenkirchen after the war (1946) where he did an apprenticeship in woodcarving at the Woodcarving College, in Garmisch (1948-1951). From 1955 – 1959 he did a sculpture training with Raoul Ratnowsky in Dornach, Switzerland. He founded a family and opened his own studio for commercial art, exhibitions and from 1977 he taught regularly at the Alanus High-school for Visual Arts, as well as teaching private students. He founded the Free Artschool Munzinge in 1982 as a four-year sculpture training. He took commissions and also taught at various art colleges.

TORSTEN STEEN

1962 Born in Dortmund, Germany.
1969-1982 Rudolf Steiner School in Bochum-Langendreer, then Civil Service.
1984-1989 Art training with Gerard Wagner and teacher training at the Goetheanum,
Switzerland.
1989-2002 Teaching Art, Art history and biology in Silkeborg, Denmark, in Winterthur and Ins, Switzerland..
Since then at the Rudolf Steiner School in Ittingen, Bern.
Various publications in anthroposophical magazines on the subject of Rudolf Steiner's impulse on art.
I live with my wife in Worb near Bern, Switzerland.

WOLFGANG HELD

Born in 1964, father to three daughters.
He studied in written mathematics for the paedagogy for Waldorf education. He worked for many years in the Mathemetical-Astronomical section of the Goetheanum. He is now the main editor of the magazine *The Goetheanum*. Held is the publisher of the star calendar and regularly writes on topics related to Anthroposophical subjects. He also guides study travels to Egypt, Greece and the Polar Lights.

GERTRAUD GOODWIN

Gertraud was born in 1951 in Germany. Her first career was in nursing. She worked as an operating theatre nurse at the Royal Infirmary in Edinburgh. Her sculpture training at the Alanus-Kunsthochschule near Bonn, 1976 – 1979, was followed by a two-year training for sculpture therapy. Gertraud moved to England in 1982 where she taught at the Tobias School of Art in East Grinstead and at Emerson College, Forest Row, as well as working graphically. In 1987 she started to work and teach sculpture and graphics in her own studio, www.sculpturestudioshoathlyhill.com. Gertraud has exhibited in galleries in London, Brighton, Italy, Germany and Switzerland.